Royal Cookbook

FAVORITE COURT RECIPES FROM THE WORLD'S ROYAL FAMILIES

Royal Cookbook

Antiquity **Nada Saporiti**	Russia and Poland **Theresa K. Soulsby** **Jean Karsavina**
England **Sheila Hutchins**	Greece **James Delihas**
France **Robert Jay Misch**	Middle East and Asia **Elisabeth Lambert Ortiz**
Italy **José Moreno-Lacalle** **Anna Gosetti della Salda**	Japan **Daniel Joseph Meloy**
Spain and Portugal **Manuel Martínez Llopis**	China **Lucille Davis**
Middle Europe **Alan N. Stone**	Africa **George Weeks**
Scandanavia and the Low Countries **Shirley Sarvis**	Pacific Islands **Richard F. MacMillan**

Translations **Mario A. Pei**

Research Director **Celia G. Segal**

Food Consultant **Eileen Gaden**

Parents' Magazine Press • New York

**Parents' Magazine Press
A Division of
Parents' Magazine Enterprises, Inc.**

International Standard Book Number 0-8193-0436-0
Library of Congress Catalog Card Number 70-124709

The *Royal Cookbook* was created, produced, and made ready
for publishing by Stravon Educational Press, New York, N.Y.

Editorial Staff

Coordinating Editor	Robert H. Doherty
Copy Editor	Elvin Abeles
Art Director	Morton Garchik
Index	Betty W. Brinkerhoff
Special Research	Barbara Goddard
Recipe and Photo Research	Margaret Chang
	Dee Dickson
	Michael M. Halpin
	Kerrie Lafontaine
	Fern Lifton
	Nancy Merwan
	Robert M. Segal
	Patricia Wen
Editorial Assistants	Louis Bressan
	Martha De Vita
	Diane Pearson
Art and Production	Nicholas Amorosi
	George Geygan
	Albert E. Nolan
Cover and book design by	Morton Garchik

Contents

Covered sauce tureen from a service of Elizabeth II

Porcelain compote, cup and saucer

Early Italian knives and forks

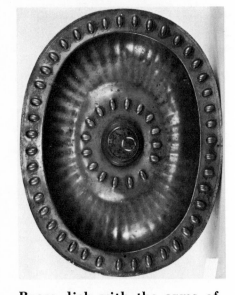

Brass dish with the arms of Charles I

Moussaka (Beef and Eggplant Casserole)

Monk's cap jug, Hsüan-te ware

NADA SAPORITI, author of the chapter on Antiquity, is a member of the staff of the Metropolitan Museum of Art. She has contributed articles on Greek and Roman art to the *McGraw-Hill Dictionary of Art* and is presently working toward a Ph.D. degree in archaeology. Mrs. Saporiti has traveled extensively throughout Europe and has lived in Morocco, England, German, and Greece, always taking every opportunity to learn something new about her special hobbies: ancient and Arabic cookery.

SHEILA HUTCHINS, author of the chapter on England, is the cookery writer for the London *Daily Express.* She also writes a daily column on cooking and gastronomy that appears in other British newspapers. Miss Hutchins, who speaks French, German, and Hungarian, owns a large collection of cookery books in six languages, including more than two hundred valuable English books dating to the 16th century. She was first taught to cook at a convent school in Switzerland. "All the rest," she says, "is the result of an inquiring mind and a healthy appetite."

ROBERT JAY MISCH, author of the chapter on France, is a member of the Chevaliers du Tastevin and of the Wine Committee for the United States Department of State. He holds the French Medaille Agricole des Vins de France and is a Commander in the Bontemps de Barsac-Sauternes. A Dartmouth College alumnus, Misch writes a widely syndicated newspaper column, "Eat, Drink and Be Merry," and is the author of three books: *Quick Guide to Wine, Foreign Dining Directory, and Quick Guide to the World's Most Famous Recipes.*

JOSÉ MORENO-LACALLE, coauthor of the chapter on Italy (he wrote on the period that preceded the House of Savoy), writes a wine column for a New York magazine and is presently at work on a cookbook about wine and food. An alumnus of Drew University, he has, as he says, "a passion for wine and Italian food."

ANNA GOSETTI DELLA SALDA, coauthor of the chapter on Italy (she wrote on the House of Savoy), is the director, since 1952, of the magazine *La Cucina Italiana,* the most important periodical of gastronomy in Italy and one of the oldest in Europe. She is author of *Le ricette regionali italiana* ("The Regional Recipe of Italy"), published in Italy and scheduled to appear in the United States in an English translation.

MANUEL MARTÍNEZ LLOPIS, author of the chapter on Spain and Portugal, practices medicine in Madrid, specializing in nutrition, and is a professor of gastronomy and of gastronomic history at the Superior School of Hostelry in Madrid. Dr. Martínez Llopis has

written several books on nutrition and is a regular contributor to various magazines on gastronomy.

ALAN N. STONE, author of the chapter on Middle Europe, is an instructor in Medieval Art at Rutgers University. A graduate of Haverford College, he spent several years in Europe, traveling through Germany, Austria, and Italy, and teaching in London. There he met his wife, an Austrian who has a passion for cooking in her mother's tradition. The Stones now share a hobby of cooking and perfecting a variety of Middle European dishes.

SHIRLEY SARVIS, author of the chapter on Scandinavia and the Low Countries, has five cookbooks to her credit, including the coauthorship of *Cooking Scandinavian.* Her articles on food, wine, and travel appear regularly in *Gourmet, Better Homes and Gardens, American Home, Farm Journal,* and other magazines. She is a graduate of Kansas State University.

THERESA SOULSBY, coauthor of the chapter on Russia and Poland (she wrote on Russia), has a particular interest in things Russian, especially foods, through her position as Consultant Dietitian to the Tolstoi Foundation. Mrs. Soulsby, a graduate of New York University, took advanced courses in food and nutrition at several other universities. She has been employed as a nutritionist by the New York City Department of Health and has worked at recipe testing and development for the United States Department of Agriculture. Her European travels have increased her knowledge of the food preferences of many peoples. Of her assignment for the *Royal Cookbook,* she says, "All the recorded history of Russian cookery concerns the Russian nobility. What was good either originated in their kitchens or was soon borrowed, adopted, and Russified."

JEAN KARSAVINA, coauthor of the chapter on Russia and Poland (she wrote on Poland), says about herself, "I was born in Warsaw but am American by adoption. My background is bilingual as well as bicultural. I learned to cook from my mother in self-defense, because there wasn't a single good Polish restaurant in New York City. Since I am a writer and editor by profession, it was a natural matter for me to start doing cookbooks. I wrote *Polish Cookery* and the section on Polish cooking in the *Woman's Day Encyclopedia of Cooking.*

JAMES DELIHAS, author of the chapter on Greece, is an American of Greek parentage. He recalls growing up eating baklava instead of peanut butter, and speaking Greek before learning English at the age of five. He is a free-lance writer and a member of the staff of the Museum of Modern Art. His interest in foods developed when he helped his wife start a personal catering business in New York City. Of this enterprise he says, "The more successful the business venture became, the less fun it was, so we dropped it and catered to our own interest in the foods of foreign lands." He has lived and traveled widely in Greece, studying its ancient art and savoring its culinary treasures.

Daniel Joseph Meloy, author of the chapter on Japan, is deputy director of the Japan Society, and his career made it inevitable that he should develop an interest in Japanese gastronomy. From 1949 to 1962 he served as a United States Foreign Service officer in Japan, and he speaks Japanese fluently. In 1958 and 1959, as Official American Observer, he accompanied the Third Japanese Antarctic Expedition, for which service he was awarded the United States Antarctic Medal.

Elisabeth Lambert Ortiz, author of the chapter on Asia and the Middle East, has lived and worked as a journalist all over the world, including several years in the Far East, where she was based in Bangkok, Thailand. She was principal consultant on two books in the *Time-Life Foods of the World* series, and she contributes articles on food and travel to *House and Garden, Gourmet,* and *Venture* in the United States and to *Wine and Food* magazine in London. She is the author of the *Complete Book of Mexican Cooking,* which won the R. T. French Tastemaker Award of 1967.

George Weeks, author of the chapter on Africa, is a diplomatic correspondent for United Press International. He has had many opportunities to sample the cooking of Africa first-hand, and he has both interviewed and dined with the rulers of African nations. Although his interest in African cookery is that of an objective reporter, he maintains an active interest in African affairs as a free-lance writer, and he was a contributing author to *Handbook of African Affairs.*

Lucille Davis (Su Chung), author of the chapter on China, is an American citizen of Japanese ancestry. She was married to the second grandson of the great Chinese scholar and poet Cheng Hsiao-Hsu, who had been in turn a tutor, a minister, and a relative by marriage of the former emperor of China, Hsüan T'ung (last of the Ch'ing Dynasty and later, as Henry Pu-yi, ruler of Manchukuo). At the time of this marriage she took the name Su Chung. She writes, "By this marriage I became a sister-in-law of the Chinese Emperor, as Cheng's first grandson, my brother-in-law, married the Emperor's younger sister, Princess Jun Ho. Through Princess Jun Ho, I was introduced to Princess Aichingioro, who had married Prince P'u Chieh, younger brother of Hsüan T'ung. Princess

Aichingioro had compiled material for a cookbook on the court dishes of China but was not able to complete her work. She turned over to me her collection of menus, recipes, and other data, saying, 'I hope that you will complete this material, for I'm sure the world would like to know the real story behind Peking cooking as it was developed by the imperial families of China.' I used this material in the preparation of my book *Court Dishes of China: The Cuisine of the Ch'ing Dynasty.*"

Richard F. MacMillan, author of the chapter on the Pacific Islands, is director of public relations of the Hawaii Visitors Bureau, and a free-lance writer on Pacific subjects. His assignment for the *Royal Cookbook* came at a most propitious time, when he had just completed a tour of Micronesia, Nauru, Fiji, and Australia to gather material for varied publications. He makes regular visits to Tahiti, Samoa, Fiji, and New Zealand as part of his publicity assignments.

Mario A. Pei, translator of the section on the House of Savoy in the chapter on Italy, is professor of philology at Columbia University and one of the world's foremost linguists. Among his books are *The World's Chief Languages, The Italian Language,* and *The Story of Languages.* Cookery, one of his favorite hobbies, has led to a study of its history and to occasional writing on the subject. He wrote the historical introduction to *The Talisman Italian Cook Book,* considered by many culinary experts to be the most authentic Italian cookery book. Dr. Pei acted as both adviser and *amicus curiae* to the *Royal Cookbook:* his special help is gratefully acknowledged.

Celia Green Segal, research director for the *Royal Cookbook,* has in recent years made cookery research her specialty. She conducted the research for *National Treasury of Cookery, First Ladies Cook Book,* and *Come Into the Kitchen Cook Book.* Her research has involved interviewing master chefs, menu planners, archivists, librarians, or staff members of famous restaurants and royal palaces in countries around the world, including England, Sweden, Monaco, Denmark, Iran, Thailand, and Japan, and of historic homes in the United States, including the White House in Washington, D.C. Mrs. Segal holds a B.S. degree from Hunter College and an M.A. from The City College of New York.

Eileen Gaden, who is responsible for the recipe testing and the food photography in the *Royal Cookbook,* conducts a food consulting firm, a service to manufacturers and advertising agencies. Her food photographs are well known in newspapers and magazines throughout the United States. She has also been an associate editor of a leading food magazine and has coauthored several cookbooks.

Notes to Research

DESPITE A RESEARCH team of 25 persons, including the 16 authors of the *Royal Cookbook,* who were also involved in the work, the task of compiling royal recipes from antiquity to about the 14th century proved much more formidable than anticipated. Not that the literature of the past is barren of references to royal repasts, banquets, and feasts. Quite the contrary, the references are abundant, on Babylonian tablets; on tombstones of Egyptian Pharaohs; in the writings of Homer, Aristotle, Plato, Horace, Petronius, Juvenal, Suetonius, and Clement, to mention just a few. Sadly however, recipes listing the ingredients and describing the preparation of particular royal or imperial foods or dishes are not.

Nevertheless, there are some wonderfully gratifying exceptions—for example, the first-century Roman gourmand Apicius, to whom is attributed the first cookbook of antiquity to come down to modern times. Because Apicius lived during the time of the Roman Emperors Augustus and Tiberius, we chose to assume that many of his recipes were indeed of imperial origin, and so we included dishes from Apicius in the *Royal Cookbook* without specifically attributing them to Augustus or Tiberius. (A facsimile from a 16th-century edition of Apicius' work appears on page 20.) Another example is Athenaeus, the Greek scholar who in his *Deipnosophists* describes a number of dishes that he attributes to ancient kings. The term *recipe* can be applied only loosely to these descriptions, because quantities are absent and some of the ingredients specified are either unknown or unavailable. For the *Royal Cookbook,* of course, the recipes have been modernized with ingredients that are available at any grocery store.

The period historians call the Dark Ages—variously dated as between the breakup of the Roman Empire and the 12th or 13th century—proved equally dark to our researchers. The renaissance for cookery did not occur until the 14th century, coinciding almost exactly with the social, political, economic, and artistic Renaissance that occurred in most of Europe during the 14th, 15th, and 16th centuries. Whether, in fact, the historical Renaissance brought about a rebirth of cookery, or whether it was mere coincidence, the fact remains that in the 14th century two extraordinary cookbooks were written by master chefs having the most prestigious royal credentials. The first is the French *Le Viandier* by Taillevent, who was cook to Philippe de Valois and to Charles V. The second is the English *The Forme of Cury,* written by the Master Cook of Richard II and containing recipes from the royal kitchen. Here, at last, are recipes of unquestioned royal origin.

Subsequent to this period, a profusion of recipes became available, but a new problem arose: that of achieving a cross section of recipes from countries around the world. Cookery literature, royal archives, and old histories produced a plethora of recipes for some countries but few for others. The literature of the regions noted for their exotic cuisine, such as Middle Europe, Asia, and the Middle East, contained few recipes that could be directly traced or attributed to a particular royal household. Of course, there were old records, menus, diaries, biographies, and histories with references to favorite foods and dishes, but, as in antiquity, no explicit royal recipes. There seemed but one logical recourse: to find authen-

Emperor Tai Tsung

tic regional recipes in old cookbooks of the time in question and to use these on the assumption that they are similar to those that might have been served in the royal house of that particular country. On the other hand, research disclosed that royal favorites, particularly of recent centuries, were not necessarily indigenous to the monarch's country. Occasionally a favorite might be foreign, French being a popular choice. Accordingly, the reader should not conclude that the editors have misplaced some recipes if, for example, Swedish Meat Balls is found in the English chapter or Cotelettes de Veau à la Provençale in the Russian chapter.

And on the subject of recipes, it will be noted that several inconsistencies in style for recipe titles appear in the book. For example, some titles are given both in the foreign language and in transliteration, whereas others carry but one title. This procedure was followed for the user's convenience, to avoid carrying part of a recipe to the following page. In these cases, if the foreign title was widely known, the English title was dropped, but if the foreign title was relatively unknown, only the English was retained. In the chapter on Antiquity, the Latin titles are given in lower-case type, to conform to the original style. Latin recipe titles are freely translated to make them fit the ingredients in the modernized version.

The research for the 20th century included correspondence with all the world's reigning royal households, their embassies in Washington, D.C., and members or heirs of present or past reigning families. From these sources, interesting favorite recipes were obtained. For example, from the household of Prince Rainier III of Monaco came the recipe for Pissaladière, appearing on page 82, accompanied by a note that it is the "favorite of Princess Grace." The recipe for Bhutuwa, on page 176, was sent by the Royal Nepalese Embassy, with a note that it is a favorite of Princess Princep. From the household of King Hassan II of Morocco came recipes for Couscous and Kaab el Ghzal, on pages 198 and 200 respectively. The recipes for Moussaka, Fenikia, Kourabiedes, and Karidopeta, on pages 162 and 163, favorites of King Constantine II and Queen Anne-Marie of Greece, were sent us by the Royal Greek Embassy in Washington. The sources of other recipes are given in the *Acknowledgments*.　　C.G.S.

Plate from the Coronation service of George IV

Notes to Recipes

MOST OF THE ingredients called for in the *Royal Cookbook* are available in neighborhood stores, but obtaining some exotic herbs and spices may present a challenge—a pleasant one, I hope. A resourceful chef should be able to buy asafoetida, liquamen, hazlewort, cumin, and lovage at a drug store. Oriental, Middle Eastern, or African ingredients may require the cooperation of the grocer in ordering the needed items from his wholesale supplier.

With few exceptions, the recipes in the *Royal Cookbook* were modified to meet present-day standards and to make use of today's kitchen facilities. Rarely did an old recipe specify quantities, and frequently important ingredients were omitted (as soon became evident to the recipe tester). The disappearance from the market of certain ingredients made substitutions necessary. Despite this necessary tampering, however, the look, taste, and flavor of the foods made from the modified recipes should, in my judgment, closely resemble the original.　　E.G.

Acknowledgments

THE PUBLISHER WISHES to thank the following individuals and organizations for their help in the preparation of this book.

Andre Deutsch Ltd., publisher, and John Farquharson Ltd., agent, for permission to reprint the ten recipes from *Court Favourites; Recipes from Royal Kitchens* by Elizabeth Craig, copyright 1953 by Elizabeth Craig.

The Charles E. Tuttle Co., Inc., for permission to reprint the nine recipes from *Court Dishes of China; The Cuisine of the Ch'ing Dynasty* by Su Chung (Lucille Davis), copyright 1965 by the Charles E. Tuttle Co. Inc.

Simon & Schuster, Inc., for permission to reprint the five recipes from *To Set Before a Queen; Royal Recipes and Reminiscences* by Alma McKee, copyright 1963 and 1964 by Alma McKee.

The museums, private collectors, picture sources, and photographers who generously made available the photos of royal portraits and artifacts are gratefully acknowledged here and are identified in the Illustrations on page 211.

Breakfast Room of the Imperial Palace, Vienna

Many people not directly associated with this book considerately gave information, advice, and clues to specific material. The following individuals were particularly helpful: Mr. Stanley Mays of the *London Daily Express,* Mr. George Kelly of Cookbooks Only, Mrs. Eleanor Lowenstein of the Corner Bookshop, Mrs. Elisabeth Woodburn of Booknoll Farm, and the staff of the special collections at the New York Public Library. A special note of thanks is due to Mrs. Grace Chu, Mrs. Maruja Hatheway, and Mr. Ted Morello, who took time away from other duties to apply their special knowledge in the research of authentic recipes.

Following is a combined short bibliography and source list for the recipes named. Complete publication data for most of these old cookery books will be found in the *Gastronomic Bibliography* by Katherine Golden Bitting or in the *Bibliographie Gastronomique* by Georges Vicaire. Where an author's name is given without a book title, the recipes listed are adapted from incunabula, manuscripts, or notes available to the author.

Juan Altamiras, *Nuevo Arte de Cocina:* Partridge in Spiced Sauce.

Apicius, *De Re Coquinaria:* Ova spongia ex lacte (Honey Omelet), Patina de asparagis (Asparagus Soufflé), Isicia de scillis vel de cammaris amplis (Crab Rissolés), Patina Zomore (Fish Stew), Vitellina fricta (Veal in Wine and Herb Sauce), Porros in baca (Leeks and Olives), Rapas sive napos (Turnips), Cardui (Artichokes), Caroetas elixatas (Carrot Salad), Apothermum sic facies (Hominy Grits Dessert), Patina de piris (Poached Pears), Dulcia domestica (Custard Sauce).

Athenaeus, *The Deipnosophistae:* Broth with Groats, Pickled Horaeum (Baked Fish with Herb Sauce), Brains Fragrant with Roses (Brain Cutlets).

A. Beauvilliers, *L'Art du cuisinier:* Potage à la Condé (Kidney Bean Soup), Brioche au Fromage, Lemon Biscuits, Puff Pastry.

Franz Beutel, *Die Moderne Kalte Küche:* Edam Cheese Tart.

Antonin Carême, *Le Patissier royal parisien:* Omelette Soufflé, Ballotine of Pheasant.

S. Chamberlain, *Italian Bouquet:* Umberto's Salad.

Grace Chu: Tsui-Chi (Drunk Chicken).

Charles Cooper, *The English Table in History and Literature:* Sausage Meat.

Elizabeth Craig, *Court Favourites:* "The Only Soup Ever Eaten by Queen Victoria," Hotch Potch, Fillet of Sole in Claret, Patties à la Reine, Scotch Beef and Onion Collops, Cinnamon Peas, Victorian Salad, Duke of Windsor's Gingerbread, Queen Cakes, Queen Mary Pudding.

Lucille Davis, *Court Dishes of China:* San Hsien T'ang (Chicken, Shrimp, and Vegetable Soup), Ch'ing Ch'ao Hsia Jen (Fried Shrimp), Wa Kuai Yü (Fried River Fish), Cha Pa Kuai (Fried Chicken with Peppercorns), Fu Yung Chi Szu (Fried Chicken with Egg White), Liu Jou P'ien (Sliced Pork Fried and Simmered in Cornstarch Dressing), Wu Hsiang Chu Kan (Pork Liver Cooked with Five Spices), Shrimp and Bean Curd Salad, Niu Yu Ch'ao Mien (Flour Fried with Butter).

Charles Francatelli, *The Modern Cook:* Quenelles of Polenta, White Stock, Pheasants à la Dauphinoise, Allemande Sauce, Italian Sauce.

Ferdinand Grandi, *Cuisine Italienne:* Cavour Lemonade (Wine Punch).

Christian Guy, *An Illustrated History of French Cuisine:* Oeufs en Meurette, Shrimp with Sauce, Fillets de Sole Pompadour, Chicken in the Pot, Potatoes à la Choiseul.

Friedrich Hampel, *Lucullus, Ein Handbuch der Wiener Kochkunst:* Kaiser Gugelhupf (Raisin Cake), Wiener Eiskaffee (Coffee Parfait).

Maruja Hatheway, *Authentic Spanish Cooking:* Royal Eggs.

Maruja Hatheway: Cocido (Meat and Chick-pea Stew), Salsa de Tomate, Pheasant Alcantara Style, Chuletas de Cordero à la Farnesio (Lamb Chops and Dumplings), Ensalada de la Reina (The Queen's Salad), Ensalada del Rey Martín (King Martin's Salad), Monte Blanco (Puréed Chestnut Whip Cream).

W. Carew Hazlitt, *Old Cookery Books and Ancient Cuisine:* Florendine of Veal, Fricasy of Double Tripe (Tripe in Wine), Potato-Lemon Cheesecakes, New College Pudding.

Jean Karsavina: Borju Paprikas (Veal Paprika), Barszcz (Beet Soup), Bitki w Smietanie (Meat Balls), Bigos (Hunter's Stew), Chrust chyli Faworki (Cookies).

Patrick Lamb, *Royal Cookery:* Soup Lorrain, Matelotte of Fish, Farced Mushrooms, Beef à la Mode, Rhenish Wine Cream.

La Varenne, *Le Cuisinier François:* Almond Macaroons.

Alma McKee, *To Set Before a Queen:* Swedish Meat Balls, Peppers with Risotto Filling, Cumberland Sauce, Prince Charles' Summer Pudding, Chocolate Cake Made with Orange Marmalade.

François Marin, *Les Dons de Comus:* Trout in Wine.

Manuel Martínez Llopis: Pa de Carneiro (Shoulder of Mutton or Lamb in Wine), Peito de Vitela Entolado (Rolled Breast of Veal), Almond Honey Turnovers, Honey Nut Bread, Nut Filling.

Juan de la Mata, *Arte de Reposteria:* Eggs Portuguese.

Christofaro Messisbugo, *Libro novo:* Tortellini.

Carlo Molina, *Messaggero della Cucina:* Soft-Cooked Eggs Humbert I Style (Eggs on Puréed Artichoke with Sauce Suprême).

Monaco Information Center: Pissaladière (Anchovy Tomato Pie).

Francisco Martinez Montiño, *Arte de cocina:* Wild Fowl Montino.

Ted Morello: Alecha (Chicken with Sweet Sauce), Zigne Watte (Spiced Meat Sauce), Niter Kebbeh (Garlic-Spiced Butter), Injera (Ethiopian Bread).

Ruberto de Nola, *Libro de cozina:* Mutton Soup.

Elisabeth Lambert Ortiz: Baba Ghannuj (Eggplant Appetizer), Tabouleh (Burghul, Tomato, Parsley Appetizer), Cinnamon Wine Soup, Namprik (Shrimp Hot Pepper Sauce), Alo-Balo Polo (Chicken and Cherries with Rice), Mughlai Biryani (Spiced Lamb), Kibbi Nayya (Uncooked Wheat and Meat), Kebab, Chelo (Buttered Rice), Imam Bayaldi (Stuffed Eggplant), Raita (Cold Spiced Tomato and Yoghurt), Pooris (Fried Unleavened Bread), Chapatis (Griddle-Fried Bread), Naan (North Indian White Bread), Dessert Raita (Fruit Yoghurt).

Samuel Pegge, *The Forme of Cury:* Oysters in Gravy, Jellied Fish, Egurdouce of Fysshe (Sweet and Sour Fish), Pork Tartlet, Comadore (Fruit and Nut Tarts).

Jerome Pichon and Georges Vicaire, *Le Viandier de Guillaume Tirel dit Taillevent:* Hen Hotch Potch.

Amedeo Pettini, *La Cucina Italiana,* Dec. 1929: Stracciatella (Rag Soup).

Domenico Romoli, *La Singolare Dottrina:* Stuffed Omelette, Lingue Arroste Peverone (Roast Tongue with Pepper Sauce).

Royal Greek Embassy: Moussaka (Beef and Eggplant Casserole), Dolmadakia Yialandji (Stuffed Grape Leaves), Kourabiedes (Shortbread), Fenikia (Honey-Dipped Cookies) with Syrup, Karidopeta (Nut Cake) with Syrup.

Royal Moroccan Embassy: Couscous (Lamb Stew with Semolina), Kaab el Ghzal (Gazelle Horns).

Royal Nepalese Embassy: Bhutuwa (Fried Mutton).

Anna della Salda: Aragosta (Creamed Lobster), Rice Salad, Peaches Marengo with Apricot Sauce.

Shirley Sarvis: Norwegian Paprika Chicken, Aebleskiver (Danish Raised Pancakes).

Louis Ude, *The French Cook:* Court-Bouillon with White Wine, Court-Bouillon with Red Wine, Saumon à la Genevoise, Grand Espagnole Sauce, Brown Stock, Merlans Entiers au Gratin (Whole Whiting with Bread Crumbs), Pike à la Polonaise, Trout in Court-Bouillon, Fricassée of Chicken, Boudin à la Reine (Chicken Croquettes), Béchamel Sauce, Wings of Fowls à la St. Laurent, Maréchale Sauce, Roast Duckling, Compotte de Perdrix à Blanc (Partridge in White Sauce), Soufflé of Chicken à la Crême, Gigot de Sept Heures (Leg of Mutton Braised), Le Rognon de Boeuf au Vin de Champagne (Beef Kidneys in Champagne Sauce), Jambon au Vin d'Espagne (Ham with Espagnole Sauce), Les Escalopes de Foie de Veau (Scalloped Calf's Liver), Haricots Verds à la Poulette (Green Beans with Chicken Sauce), Choux-fleurs au Parmesan (Cauliflower with Parmesan Sauce), Crême au Thé.

A. Viard, *Le Cuisinier Impérial:* Oeufs à la Neige (Snow Eggs), Meringue.

Preface

DOES IT SEEM an anomaly to publish a book of royal recipes in an age of proliferating republics? Gone are the Tsars of Russia, the Kings of France, the Kaisers of Germany, and the Emperors of China. No longer do kings reign in Italy, Austria, Hungary, Rumania, Egypt, or Libya, to name just a few of the countries that have been removed from the list of monarchies in the 20th century. On the other hand, it is interesting that, despite this attrition, more than 20 monarchies remain as active reigning political institutions. (Surprised at the number?) Here is the list, in random order: Great Britain, Norway, Sweden, Denmark, The Netherlands, Belgium, Iran, Morocco, Jordan, Japan, Thailand, Nepal, Ethiopia, Lesotho, Swaziland, Laos, Kuwait, Saudi Arabia, Bhutan, Greece, Monaco, Luxembourg, and —nominally—Spain.

Thus, although it is quite true that kings and queens comprise a dwindling profession and the cry "The King is dead, long live the King" is heard with diminishing frequency in the world, it is just as true that "fit for a king" retains its rank as an aphorism defining the ultimate in excellence—especially culinary. Certainly this was the case when royalty was in full flower and the best of all worldly goods, including cookery, found their way into the royal household. The best chefs were trained in the royal kitchens. The first French and English cookbooks were the works of royal chefs. Only in the royal kitchen, with its unlimited resources, could a cook develop his culinary talents unhindered by budgetary considerations. Nothing was too good for the king, and generally no expense was spared to please him. Perhaps royal chefs no longer set pies stuffed with 24 live blackbirds before their king, as in the nursery rhyme (and such displays were actually exhibited at special royal banquets), and royal households no longer have unlimited resources, as the world recently learned when it was announced that the British Royal Family was experiencing difficulty in meeting household expenses. Despite these changing times and fortunes for royalty, however, an interest in their gastronomy persists. The elegance and pomp are gone, but the recipes remain. One need not possess the riches of an American industrial tycoon, a Greek shipping magnate, or the ruler of a Middle East oil-rich sheikdom to enjoy the dishes favored by past and present monarchs. Most are surprisingly simple and relatively easy to duplicate. The favored ones are here in the *Royal Cookbook* for anyone to try and to savor—so *"Bon appetit!"*

ANTIQUITY

Amenhotep and his mother, from an Egyptian wall painting

HE PREPARATION OF elaborate types of foods, one of the prerequisites of most complex societies, first appeared in the classical Greek period and developed further during Hellenistic and Roman times.

The kings of Sumer, Akkad, and Babylon at their banquets would be served an ox, a camel, and a horse, roasted whole in ovens. The Assyrian kings, because of the mild climate of their country, used to hold their feasts in the palace gardens. The hanging gardens of Babylon and the garden of the Assyrian king Merodachbaladan (8th century B.C.) were quite famous; the latter used to keep fowl in his garden and liked to cultivate aromatic plants such as mint, thyme, coriander, basil, saffron, and asafoetida. Both the king and queen were present at the feasts; the Assyrian king Ashurbanipal (7th century B.C.) would recline on a couch while his queen sat beside him on a chair. The vessels used by the Babylonian and Assyrian kings were made of stone, clay, bronze, gold, or silver.

At the royal feasts, food was served on tripods. It included unleavened bread and a variety of meats, such as mutton, beef, goat's meat, camel's meat, and ox, as well as fowl, geese, and ducks. The kings of Babylon and Assyria were heavy drinkers, favoring beer made of barley and different kinds of wine, including a sweet wine from palm trees. Wine was served in attractive gold or silver *rhytons* (drinking horns). The drinking usually started after dinner, accompanied by music, singing, and dancing. For dessert they would be served fruit and sweets. The Assyrian sweets were renowned in antiquity and were sold all over the ancient world: sesame cakes made with sesame and honey and fried in oil; or cakes made from barley or wheat flour, sesame oil, butter from goat's milk, rose water, and sweetened with honey or sugar from the palm trees.

The Persian kings of the 6th century B.C. used to give sumptuous royal feasts on their birthdays, serving as many as 100 courses. The king used to eat by himself in one room, while in an adjoining room, separated by curtains, the guests would sit.

The Egyptian kings seem to have been more restrained in their banquets; their feasts were less sumptuous than those of the Babylonian and Assyrian kings. The royal family used to eat together, including the children, and the king and queen would sit beside each other on a large chair. They ate from separate portable round tables piled high with food, meat, game, vegetables, and fruit. Their dinnerware was made of alabaster, and they used silver and gold cups. Although forks and knives were known to the Egyptians, it is most likely that they ate with their fingers. Servants would carry washbasins in which the guests could wash their hands between courses. Both men and women participated at the banquets, but they sat on opposite sides of the room. Servants offered the guests flowers and perfumes. On the guests' heads were placed conical ornaments containing a sweet-smelling pomade that gradually melted and ran down their clothes and perfumed their bodies.

Before the meal the Egyptians would eat boiled cabbage as a precaution against intoxication. Such delicacies as spleen and the liver of an ox were brought in first; although fish was not included in the diet of the royal household, the dry roe of the mullet (a caviar-like delicacy) was also included with the hors d'oeuvres. The main course comprised a variety of breads, also a stew made of meat and vegetables; the fillet of an African ox, fowl (geese, ducks, quails, pigeons); and small pieces of different kinds of meat—lamb, beef, and goat's meat—all grilled on a spit over a low stove. Cakes and fruits were served for dessert. After the meal, both male and female musicians and dancers would entertain the guests.

The national drink of the Egyptians was beer made of barley or wheat; it was manufactured by lightly baking thick loaves of wheat or barley, then allowing them to ferment in vats of water. Wine, both red and white, was served at the royal banquets. A local sweet wine from Buto and the Nile delta was particularly famous, as well as wine spiced with honey. Imported wines were brought to Egypt from Syria and Palestine.

The Egyptian kings were fond of good food. Their cuisine seems to have comprised a large variety of vegetables such as onions, leeks, beans, garlic, lentils, chick-peas, turnips, radishes, carrots, and lettuce; also a number of palatable dishes prepared by special cooks, and as many as 40 kinds of bread.

The ancient Jews were profoundly religious and considered their evening meal the "gift of God"; as a result they uttered prayers and sanctified themselves before eating. In early biblical times, the kings of Israel, who lived in tents, sacrificed a domestic animal before the evening meal, and its flesh would be served with the meal. The king or priest who performed the sacrifice would eat the breast of the animal. King Solomon with the elders and priests of Israel, after a sacrifice of sheep and oxen, held a feast that lasted 14 days. The kings of Israel always sat with their backs to the wall facing the entrance to the tent, to guard against a surprise enemy attack. This custom was maintained in later times, and in the royal palaces the king always occupied the center of the table, with his guest of honor at his right hand and the other guests at a distance from the king according to rank. The arriving guests would be greeted with a kiss by the master of the house, and servants would wash their feet in brass basins.

Jews once sat on chairs at a large table (*shulhan'aruk*) on which were spread out a variety of dishes, such as various kinds of fish, vegetables, honey, fruits, and cakes. In later times, influenced by the Greeks and Romans, they would recline on couches, and food would be served on separate tables brought in by slaves.

The Jews ate and drank in moderation, always governed by dietary laws that became more complex with the passage of time. They abstained from eating pork and from serving dairy products along with meat.

Dinner consisted of various courses, mainly a variety of fish roasted on the fire; roasted meat such as lamb, goat's meat, and calf; vegetables, fruits, figs, dates, grapes, nuts, honey, and cakes, and finally wheat bread, both leavened and unleavened, served in baskets. Only unleavened bread was served during Passover. The women had complete charge of the preparation of food in the household. Rebekah and Tamar, according to the Old Testament, prepared and dressed meals. The Jews seasoned their food with a variety of spices such as cinnamon and myrtle.

The Jews ate with their fingers. Soup was eaten by dipping bread into it. Wine was served freely at meals; it was poured from bottles by cupbearers into goblets of silver and gold that were passed to the guests before the meal itself began. It is likely that the Jews drank their wine unmixed. The wine served with dessert was mixed with aromatic herbs.

The early kings of Israel, like the kings of neighboring Persia, Babylon, and Assyria, used to give sumptuous feasts in the gardens of the royal palaces. Something is known from the Old Testament about the festive customs of these contemporaries of the Jewish kings. King Ahasuerus (Xerxes) of Persia (about 520 B.C.) held a feast in the court of the garden of his palace at Shushan, to which he invited the noblemen of Persia and Media. This court was decorated with white, green, and blue curtains fastened with cords of fine linen, and contained couches of gold and silver.

The king on most occasions ate separately from his wives. While Ahasuerus was entertaining his guests, Queen Vashti held her own feast for the women in the royal palace. At times, however, the king would invite the women of his household to partake with him in the feast. King Belshazzar of Babylon (6th century B.C.), when he held a feast for 1,000 of his courtiers, served wine in the gold and silver vessels inherited from his father, Nebuchadnezzar, and he invited his wives and concubines to drink with him.

The Jewish kings of the early period always had music with their dinner. King David himself was "a cunning player on the harp." In later periods, influenced by the Romans, they introduced female dancers, and when King Herod (A.D.31) held a feast for his birthday, he invited female dancers to the banquet.

The earliest Greek kings, those of the late 2d millennium, were little more than tribal chieftains, but they were depicted larger than life by the poet Homer, who wrote his *Iliad* and *Odyssey* many centuries after the period he portrayed. It is not easy to know whether the way of life, including the eating customs, attributed to the heroic kings of the Trojan War period—Agamemnon, Achilles, and the rest—were not to some extent those of Homer's contemporaries, or their more recent ancestors.

The diet of the Homeric kings consisted mainly of unleavened bread, goat's-milk cheese, honey, and roasted meat such as mutton, beef, pork, and goat's meat. Meat, according to Homer, made men vigorous in body and mind. Both fresh- and saltwater fish were probably favored by the kings, although they are not specifically mentioned by Homer.

Banquets of the heroic era were organized by the men; they themselves cooked the food for their guests, for the women of the house were never present at the feasts. Food was probably cooked by means of earthenware pots on hearths

that occupied the center of a large room. Such hearths were found in the great palaces of Mycenae and Pylos.

At the feasts of the Homeric kings, men from all walks of life participated—i.e., princes, bards, beggars, and swineherds. The seats of honor and the choicest pieces of meat were reserved for the most distinguished guests. The diners sat at their feasts; they did not recline on couches, as did the later Athenians and Romans. Small tables that also served as plates were placed beside the guests. No individual plates or eating utensils were used; the Greeks in Homer's time and until the late Hellenistic period ate with their fingers.

Before each meal, water was poured upon the guests' hands by young slave girls. Then an apéritif was served, a form of punch made of Pramnian wine (a muscatel type from Lesbos) mixed with grated goat's-milk cheese and sprinkled on top with white barleymeal. When King Nestor entertained his guests, a slave woman prepared the punch of Pramnian wine and placed before

A page from the 1541 edition of Apicius' cookery book

LIBER IX. 283

tuminibus, figillatim indes , tudiculáq; aut cochleari cir= cunquaq; reftringes in rotundum redigens . Coloratiora ubi effe cœperint, coɗa ſcito, tenella intus ſint neceſſe eſt. Coqui difficilius hæc quàm quæ ſuprà conſueuerunt.

Aliter: Oua integra in carbones ardentes conijcito, ac calida donec frangantur, fuſte percutito. Coɗa & ex= empta, petroſelino & aceto ſuffundito . Hoc non faceret Pomponius noſter , qui temerè adeo amiſis duobus ouis, unde alia emeret præ inopia non haberet.

Oua friɗa.

Caſeum pinguem & tritum , parum mentæ ac petro= ſelini conciſi, uuæ paſſæ minimum, modicum piperis tunſi, duo uitella ouorum cruda ſimul miſcebis . Mixta in oua more Florentino friɗa, ut inde per tenue foramen uitellũ exemeris, indito, ac iterum frigito, donec farcimen coqua= tur. Conuoluenda ſæpius ſunt: & coɗa, agreſta aut ſucco malarancij cum gingiberi ſuffundenda ſunt.

Oua in paſtilli morem.

Farinam ſubaɗam, tenuem admodum facies, extenſæ ta bulam, oua recentia diſtinɗa ſpatijs addes, inſpergendo ſemper unicuiq; parum ſaccari, aromatũ, minimum ſalis. Inuoluta deinde ut paſtillos ſolemus, aut elixabis, aut fri= ges, friɗa tamen laudabiliora ſunt . Dura fiant caueto. Oua enim dura mali alimenti, ac difficilimæ concoɗionis habentur.

De Boletis & Fungis.

Manduntur & Boleti, multis exemplis in crimen ad= duɗi. Hac opportunitate illeɗa Agrippina , Claudium principem boletis admixto ueneno necauit . Frigidæ & humidæ naturæ boleti habentur, & ob hanc rem uene= ni uim obtinent. Rimoſa terrà à fimo aſperſa naſcuntur,
quam

each guest the drink and an appetizer consisting of onions, pale honey, and ground barleymeal. The main course consisted of unleavened bread of ground wheat or barley, served in bronze baskets, and meat roasted on spits over the fire. When the Greek hero-kings Odysseus, Phoenix, and Ajax, serving as Agamemnon's emissaries, visited Achilles in his tent, they were entertained by Achilles and his friend Patroclus. Patroclus set a meatblock by the fire and on it he put a shoulder of mutton, the shoulder of a goat, and the chine of a fine fat hog. Achilles then cut the meat into small pieces and put it on bronze spits. Once the coal fire was ready, Patroclus placed the spits on the fire and sprinkled the meat with salt. As soon as the meat was roasted, it was removed from the spits and was placed in platters. Patroclus handed the guests the baskets of bread and Achilles served the meat. After supper, libations of unmixed wine were made to the gods, and paeans were sung.

The Homeric heroes drank in moderation. One part of wine was diluted with three parts of water, a proportion that persisted throughout the Greek and Roman period. The best wines in Homer's time were the Thracian and the Lemnian. Aged wine, preserved inside sealed clay jars, was greatly appreciated, and King Nestor would bring out his 11-year-old wine for his guests, who drank from separate golden beakers or goblets, since silver was very rare at that time. As is customary today in Greece, the heroes would salute one another's health before drinking.

The preparation of simple, unsavory types of food probably continued in Greece until the end of the 6th century B.C., by which time it became customary in Athens to summon professional cooks to prepare the menu and cater the whole banquet. Only men were invited to the Greek banquet, which took place after sunset. Before the banquet the guests would wash their hands with water—soap (*smema*) was introduced during the Hellenistic period. The guests reclined on couches around a central table, and other auxiliary tables were brought in and placed next to the guests.

At an Athenian banquet the dinner began with hors d'oeuvres, such as onions roasted in ashes and dressed with cheese, honey, sesame oil, and vinegar; radishes dressed with vinegar and mustard; olives, herbs, fresh cucumbers, and cabbage. A broth was also served, made of poultry, kid, or lamb. Since spoons were unknown to the Athenians of the classical period, soup was eaten by scooping the bowl with pieces of bread. Various kinds of bread both leavened and unleavened, made of wheat flour, groats, or rye, were brought in with the appetizers. The Athenians were great eaters of fish, and the second course consisted mostly of different kinds of fish: shellfish, such as oysters, crabs, and mussels; squid, eels, and salt-water fish such as swordfish, tunny, conger; fried Phaleron anchovies, roasted shark dressed with sauce and vinegar, or roasted lamprey. The fish was always seasoned with sauce. The main course consisted of several dishes: hare roasted on a spit, served with a sauce of cheese and oil; kid dressed in asafoetida; boiled pork, poultry, and black pudding.

At an Attic banquet given by a certain Xenocles (described by Plutarch) the following dishes were served: hors d'oeuvres (greens, onions, and herbs), oysters, and anchovies; a main course of royal sturgeons, lampreys, turbot, and red mullet; then sweetmeats, cheesecakes, and fresh and dried fruit. The servants would crown the guests with fresh-flower garlands and the drinking would start, followed by the game of *cottabus*. The young Athenians at a banquet would throw the dregs of wine left in their cups at a target, usually a disc set up on a stand; at the same time they would invoke the name of their beloved.

The Athenians drank wine from a common cup (*kylix*), passing it round from left to right. Wine was kept cool in a wine-cooler (*psykter*), a special type of vessel that stood inside a large *krater*, packed with snow from Mount Parnes. Famous Greek wines were the well-seasoned Thasian, the Lemnian, the rosy sparkling Lesbian, and the sweet and delicate Mendaean.

In contrast to the Athenians, the Spartans were known to be very frugal in their eating habits. At a simple banquet held by King Cleomenes I of Sparta (early 5th century B.C.) food was served on a common table, with just enough for everyone. The famous black broth of the Spartans was served before the meal, followed by barley cakes, boiled pork, olives, cheese, and figs. Wine was served only to those who asked for it.

The Thracians were known to give sumptuous but rather barbaric banquets. At the banquet of Prince Seuthes (about 400 B.C.), described by Xenophon in his *Anabasis*, the guests were seated in a circle. Then tripods were brought in for the whole company, filled with cut meat and loaves of leavened bread fastened with skewers to the pieces of meat. The Thracians' custom was to break the bread and meat into small pieces and throw the pieces to whomever they pleased. Wine was served in horns.

The Macedonians, on the other hand, were famous for their rich, elaborate banquets. At a wedding feast given by Caranus the Macedonian in the beginning of the 4th century B.C., 20 guests were invited. For the first course they were served poultry, ducks, pigeons, and geese. Then a second platter was brought in with hares, kids, partridges, doves. As a second course they were served a whole roast boar in a large silver platter, stuffed with roasted thrushes, paunches, figpeckers, yolks of eggs, oysters, and periwinkles; this was followed by a glass goblet two cubits in diameter filled with roast fishes of every imaginable sort. For bread they were served Cappadocian loaves in silver baskets.

The Macedonians were renowned for their heavy drinking, and wine was usually served with the first course. Both King Philip (359–336 B.C.) and Alexander the Great (336–323 B.C.) could drink until dawn, and the same habit was continued by the Ptolemaic kings of Egypt. It is said that King Philip drank out of his own personal golden cup, which weighed 50 drachmas. He never parted with it, and even took it to bed with him. Furniture was made of silver, and when Alexander the Great gave a feast, he made his guests sit upon silver chairs and covered them with purple covers. Unlike the Athenians, the Macedonians used to sit in chairs at their banquets.

In Hellenistic Egypt, King Ptolemy VII (2d century B.C.) used to raise pheasants in his palace at Alexandria, to be served at his banquets, cooked and elaborately dressed. Food was served on silver dishes that would be placed on golden tripods in front of the guests. Silverware was abundant in the palaces of the Ptolemaic kings—gifts of silverware were even offered to the guests. At the banquet given by Cleopatra (late 1st century B.C.) for Mark Antony and his friends, the golden dishes were inlaid with precious stones; after the banquet Cleopatra presented Antony and his friends with all the gold and silver that was in the room.

The Romans of the republican period were frugal in their meals. A feast given by Cato (2d century B.C.) would consist of dried pork, ham some fresh meat, eggs, wild asparagus, and fruit. The ancient culinary art reached its highest degree of sophistication with the Romans of the empire, when the expansion of their territory enabled them to enrich their menus with imported foods and all kinds of delicacies. The roasted pea-

cock, for instance, was introduced about the middle of the first century B.C. by the orator Hortensius, who imported it from Spain. The liver of goose (foie gras) was a delicacy first discovered by the Romans, and its recipe was attributed to Scipio Metellus (1st century B.C.): The liver of the fattened bird was removed, and then soaked in milk and sweetened with honey.

Augustus (27 B.C.–A.D. 14), the first emperor, used to give simple banquets at which he would serve a dinner consisting of three courses. He introduced musicians, actors, and story-tellers at these dinners. He liked plain food, coarse bread, small fishes, home-made fresh cheese, green figs, and grapes, and he drank his favorite Raetian wine in moderation. As an appetizer before dinner he would have a bit of bread soaked in cold water, a slice of cucumber, and a sprig of fresh lettuce.

Augustus' successors, however, became notorious for their sumptuous feasts. Emperor Claudius (A.D. 41–54) used to give frequent and grand dinner parties, to which he would invite as many as 600 people at a time. Emperor Vitellius (A.D. 69) was a heavy eater. He made a banquet even out of breakfast, which had been a very light meal consisting of bread dipped in wine, grapes, olives, cheese, milk, and eggs. Vitellius used to prepare his own enormous platter, called "The Shield of Minerva." In this platter, the emperor mingled the liver of pike, the brains of pheasants and peacocks, the tongues of flamingoes, and the mill of lampreys. All these delicacies were imported specially for Vitellius from the remotest parts of the empire.

Before a Roman banquet, the guests were bathed; then young maids would wash the guests' feet and hands. They used a perfumed soap mixed with the oily juice of lilies. Then towels of finest linen were handed to the guests. The Romans ate from individual tables set in front of them. The Romans used silver or iron knives and spoons made of bone or bronze or silver. Food was served in silver plates, or in bronze plates imported from Corinth. The Romans wore while eating a large linen napkin over their clothes. For toothpicks they used silver quills. Bread was served in a silver chafing-dish.

The Roman dinner consisted of three courses:

1) The hors d'oeuvres (*gustatio*, or *promulsis*) comprised eggs, raw and cooked vegetables such as mushrooms and asparagus, delicious Roman salads made of rue, lettuce, cress, mallows, and sorrel; also mussels, snails, shellfish, and light

Apothermum sic facies (Hominy Grits Dessert)

kinds of salt fish. *Mulsum,* wine mixed with honey —the proportions being four parts of wine to one of honey—was served with this course. The *mulsum* prepared the stomach for the heavier meal to follow.

2) The main course (*mensae primae*) comprised several dishes: game such as partridges, quails, pheasants, peacocks, ducks; roast hare; roast boar stuffed with thrushes; large pig seasoned with pepper and cumin and stuffed with sausages and black pudding; also pieces of tripe, sow's bellies in deep sauce, goose liver, thrushes stuffed with raisins and nuts; a cold tart with Spanish wine poured over warm honey; and cheese mellowed in young wine with snails all round it. The Romans had a rich variety of wines, the best of this time being the Falernian, which came in two varieties, a dry yellow wine and a sweet wine of darker color; the sweet and dry Alban; the Sorrentine wine. Wine was preserved in glass jars fastened with gypsum, and could be aged for as long as 100 years. The Roman ladies were present at banquets, but were not allowed to drink grape wine—they drank instead *passum,* a sweet wine made of raisins.

3) Dessert (*mensae secundae*) consisted of dry and fresh fruits such as grapes, apples, pears, quinces, plums, cherries, and figs, all served in transparent glass vases; also a variety of sweetmeats such as cheesecakes, or the famous Roman *catillus ornatus,* biscuits made with must. With the *mensae secundae* the servants washed the guests' hands, then crowned them with wreaths of real flowers. Heavy drinking usually started after the meal. Liqueurs would also be served after dinner. The Romans had about 50 kinds of liqueurs made of herbs and flowers such as roses, violets, aniseed, thyme, myrtle.

The Romans used a great variety of sauces with their meat and fish. One particular sauce, *garum* or *liquamen,* which strengthened the particular flavor of the meat or fish, was prepared in factories; a factory of Umbricus found in Pompeii was known in antiquity for its best strained *garum.* Most of the cooking was done on small iron tripods and gridirons over burning charcoal. Boars and other animals were roasted on spits over a wood fire.

Royal Recipes

Ova spongia ex lacte (Honey Omelet)

4 egg yolks	4 egg whites
5 drops tincture of hazlewort or ½ teaspoon vanilla	¼ teaspoon salt
	1 tablespoon butter
	¼ cup honey

Beat the egg yolks with hazlewort or vanilla until light and lemon colored. Beat the egg whites with salt until stiff, and fold into egg yolks. Melt the butter in an 8-inch skillet. When the butter is warm and foamy, turn in beaten eggs and cook over low heat until lightly browned around the edges. Place in a 350°F oven for about 15 minutes or until the center is set. Loosen omelet, make a crease down the center with a spatula, fold over and turn out on a warm plate. Pour the honey over the top. Makes 4 servings.

Patina de asparagis (Asparagus Soufflé)

1 pound asparagus	¼ teaspoon coriander
3 tablespoons butter or margarine	¼ teaspoon ground lovage
2 tablespoons minced onions	¾ cup milk
3 tablespoons flour	¼ cup white wine that has been reduced by half
1 teaspoon salt	
⅛ teaspoon freshly ground pepper	6 eggs, separated

Wash and clean asparagus. Finely mince tips and tender part of the stalks of the uncooked asparagus to make 1 cup. Melt butter, add onion, and sauté 3 minutes. Blend flour and seasoning and gradually stir in milk and wine. Cook over low heat, stirring constantly until thickened. Stir in minced asparagus and cool. Beat egg whites until stiff and yolks until thick and lemon colored. Stir yolks into first mixture. Fold in whites. Pour into a 2-quart casserole. Bake in a 350°F preheated oven for about 30 to 40 minutes or until the tip of a knife inserted in the center comes out clean. Serve immediately. Makes 6 servings.

Broth with Groats

2 to 3 pounds lamb, chicken, or veal bones	10 peppercorns
	2 bay leaves
3 quarts water	1½ teaspoons salt
2 celery stalks	2 tablespoons clarified butter or margarine
1 whole carrot	2 cups groats
1 whole medium onion	

Put the bones and the next 7 ingredients in a large kettle. Bring to a boil, skimming the surface when necessary. In a small pan brown the groats in the butter until quite dark and toasted. Add to the liquid in the kettle. Partially cover and cook for 2½ hours. Discard the vegetables. Correct the seasoning. If more than 6 cups, reduce the broth. Yields 1½ quarts.

Pickled Horaeum (Baked Fish with Herb Sauce)

1½ cups finely chopped lettuce	¼ teaspoon salt
roe and liver of fish	⅛ teaspoon freshly ground pepper
3 slices bread, crusts removed and crumbed	1 cup beef broth
olive oil	1 cup white wine
½ teaspoon thyme	1 2- to 3-pound bass or other white fish
¼ teaspoon cumin seed	3 to 5 drops asafoetida (optional)
1 teaspoon sesame seed	

Combine lettuce, roe, liver, crumbs, 1 tablespoon olive oil, and seasoning. Mix broth and wine together and add just enough to moisten the crumb mixture. This may be used to stuff the fish or may be placed under the fish in the roasting pan. Rub fish well with olive oil and oil the bottom of the pan. Pour over ½ cup of the wine-broth liquid and bake in a preheated 375°F oven. Bake for 30 to 45 minutes, depending on size of the fish. Remove fish to a warm platter. If dressing has been cooked under the fish, make a bread sauce with the pan juices, and the remaining wine-broth liquid if necessary. Correct the seasoning and add asafoetida. Pour sauce over the fish. Makes 4 to 6 servings.

Note: Recipes of antiquity often called for pepper, which could be many herbs mixed together or if a dessert type recipe could mean many mixed nuts.

The reference to cheese in recipes did not necessarily mean a dairy product. It consisted of lettuce mixed with wine, oil, and wheat flour or poppy and sesame seeds mixed with many different kinds of nuts and boiled with honey and herbs.

Isicia de scillis vel de cammaris amplis (Crab Rissolés)

3 tablespoons butter
3 tablespoons flour
1 cup milk
¼ teaspoon cumin
1 teaspoon salt
⅛ teaspoon pepper
2 teaspoons liquamen (optional)

3 drops asafoetida (optional)
1 pound fresh or canned crab, lobster, or shrimp
2 eggs, beaten
1¼ cups dry bread crumbs
cooking oil

Make a thick cream sauce with butter, flour, and milk. Add the seasoning and mix in the shellfish, which has been flaked and finely chopped. Refrigerate for several hours. Shape into 8 cakes or about 40 little balls for appetizers. Dip in beaten egg and roll in bread crumbs. Fry in deep fat (375°) until golden.

Vitellina fricta (Veal in Wine and Herb Sauce)

Patina Zomore (Fish Stew)

¼ cup butter or margarine
2 large onions, sliced
3 teaspoons salt
¼ teaspoon pepper
1 teaspoon lovage
1 teaspoon oregano
3 teaspoons liquamen (optional)
4 drops asafoetida (optional)

2 pounds cod, haddock, or any firm white fish
2 cups dry white wine that has been reduced by half
3 cups water
1 pound cleaned prawns
3 cups light cream
2 egg yolks (optional)

In a large casserole sauté the onions until transparent. Stir in the seasoning and add the fish cut into 1½-inch squares. Pour in the wine and water. Cover and bake in a preheated 375°F oven for 1 hour. Remove from the oven and drop in the prawns; cook for 10 minutes more. Stir in heated cream. Thicken with egg yolks if desired. Makes about 3½ quarts.

Vitellina fricta
(Veal in Wine and Herb Sauce)

4 tablespoons olive oil
1 veal cutlet, weighing
about 2 pounds

In a skillet sauté the cutlet in the oil until well browned on both sides and tender. Remove cutlet from skillet and keep warm while making sauce.

Wine and Herb Sauce

1 cup dry white wine	2 teaspoons dried
2 tablespoons butter	onion flakes
or margarine	2 teaspoons honey
2 tablespoons minced	3 tablespoons golden
shallots	seedless raisins
½ teaspoon ground	1½ cups beef gravy or
lovage	Espagnole sauce
¼ teaspoon celery seed	salt
¼ teaspoon cumin	pepper
¼ teaspoon oregano	

Drain off any remaining fat in the skillet and add the wine. Let it heat slowly while stirring in any natural brown glaze from the skillet. Sauté in butter the shallots. Add the next 7 ingredients and simmer until reduced to half. Stir in gravy and salt and pepper to taste. Return the cutlet to the skillet, cover, and cook gently for 10 minutes or until well heated and the veal has absorbed some of the sauce. Makes 4 servings.

Brains Fragrant with Roses
(Brain Cutlets)

Inner petals from	2 teaspoons sweet
2 roses	cucumber pickle
1 pair calf's brains	juice
1 quart ice water	1 tablespoon white wine
3¼ teaspoons salt	½ teaspoon rose petal
1 tablespoon wine	powder
vinegar or lemon	⅛ teaspoon freshly
juice	ground pepper
4 egg yolks, slightly	olive oil
beaten	

Pick the petals from the roses and spread on a piece of foil. Place in a preheated 250°F oven for 1 hour. Crumble with a mortar and pestle until as fine as powder. Soak brains in ice water with 2 tea-spoons salt for 30 minutes. Drain and remove all membranes with a sharp knife. Place brains in a saucepan with enough water to cover and add 1 teaspoon salt and the wine vinegar. Simmer gently for 15 minutes. Remove brains with a slotted spoon and pat dry with paper towel. Chop brains with a sharp knife and then work with a fork to make a paste. Add egg yolks, the remaining salt, and the pickle juice, wine, and rose petal powder and pepper. Mix and divide into fourths. Coat skillet with oil and add the brain mixture. Shape slightly with a fork while cooking to form cutlets. Cook until golden on one side, turn and cook the other side. Makes 2 to 3 servings.

Porros in baca
(Leeks and Olives)

10 leeks	¼ teaspoon caraway
12 large olives or ½	seed
cup stuffed olives	⅛ teaspoon freshly
¾ cup white wine	ground pepper
3 tablespoons olive oil	¼ teaspoon liquamen
¼ teaspoon cumin	(optional)
¼ teaspoon coriander	

Clean leeks, cut off 3-inch pieces from the root end, and cut into ¼-inch slices. Wash brine off the olives and chop coarsely. Pour wine in a saucepan, add oil and seasoning. Simmer until leeks are fork tender. Cool and refrigerate until ready to serve. Makes 2 to 4 servings.

Rapas sive napos (Turnips)

1 pound turnips, cut	1 teaspoon vinegar
into small cubes	1 teaspoon salt
½ cup dry white wine	¼ teaspoon cumin
that has been	⅛ teaspoon ground
reduced by half	rue
3 teaspoons liquamen	1 teaspoon honey
(optional)	3 tablespoons butter or
2 drops tincture of	margarine
asafoetida	
(optional)	

Cook turnips until fork tender. Drain, add wine and the remaining ingredients. Cook 1 to 2 minutes more until turnips are coated with sauce. Makes 4 servings.

Cardui (Artichokes)

⅛ teaspoon rue	½ cup white wine
⅛ teaspoon fennel	that has been
½ teaspoon coriander	reduced by half
⅛ teaspoon fresh or	¼ cup water
dried mint	1½ pounds artichoke
½ teaspoon lovage	hearts
1½ teaspoons salt	4 tablespoons butter
½ teaspoon honey	or margarine

Mix seasoning, honey, wine, and water together in a saucepan. Bring to a boil and drop in the artichokes. Cover and simmer until fork tender. Add butter and toss together. Makes 6 to 8 servings.

Caroetas elixatas (Carrot Salad)

5 tablespoons white	½ teaspoon coriander
wine that has	½ teaspoon salt
been reduced by	⅛ teaspoon pepper
half	4 cups diced cooked
¼ cup olive oil	carrots
½ teaspoon cumin	¾ cup chopped onions
powder	

Beat wine, oil, and seasoning together thoroughly. Toss carrots and onions with the dressing and chill. Makes 6 to 8 servings.

Apothermum sic facies (Hominy Grits Dessert)

2 cups boiling water	½ cup quick-cooking
½ teaspoon salt	white hominy
3 tablespoons honey	grits
⅓ cup pignolia nuts	1 tablespoon sweet
2 tablespoons golden	sherry
seedless raisins	¼ cup toasted almonds
1½ teaspoons grated	dates
lemon peel	

To rapidly boiling water add all ingredients except the last three. Cook for about 8 minutes over direct heat, stirring occasionally. Remove from heat and add sherry. Turn into a warm serving dish. Sprinkle with almonds and arrange some pitted dates on top. Makes 4 to 6 servings.

Patina de piris (Poached Pears)

Patina de piris (Poached Pears)

8 very firm pears	10 drops tincture of
2 cups sweet white	hazlewort or ¼
wine	teaspoon ground
2 tablespoons honey	lovage
¼ teaspoon cumin	Custard Sauce

Peel pears, leaving the stems on. Place in a large skillet. Mix wine, honey, cumin, and hazlewort together and pour over the pears. Cover and poach about 10 minutes or until tender, basting often. Drain liquid and reserve for Custard Sauce. Chill pears. When ready to serve, arrange pears in a dish and pour over the Custard Sauce, which may be served hot or cold.

Dulcia domestica (Custard Sauce)

1 cup heavy cream	3 tablespoons honey
1 cup reduced wine	⅛ teaspoon salt
from the pears	3 eggs

Scald the cream in a double boiler. Add wine, honey, and salt. Beat the eggs with a fork and very gradually stir into the eggs some of the hot liquid. Return to double boiler. Add remaining liquid and cook, stirring constantly, until mixture thickens. Makes 8 servings.

ENGLAND

Queen Elizabeth

LTHOUGH THERE HAVE been plenty of cookery books, there have been virtually no serious histories of food in royal palaces or anywhere else. Now, the average Briton knows nothing and cares less about all those kings before 1066. For example, during the Danish invasion of England, Alfred the Great (871–899), King of Wessex, is supposed to have taken refuge in a peasant's hut near Athelnay. The woman who lived in the hut, not recognizing the king, asked him to watch some cakes cooking on hot stones before the fire. The king, preoccupied with strategy or tactics, let them burn, and she slapped his face for it. Historians say that this tale is not true But bakestones similar to those of Alfred's time are still used in remote parts of Wales, Ireland, and Scotland to make bannocks, drop scones, and crempogs.

Life in the Middle Ages must have been extremely boring. The rather dreary food was served on great occasions fancifully garnished and elaborately arranged—a trick still practiced in restaurants and the food trade when the basic material is a bit tasteless. Peacocks in panoply and roast swans with flaming camphor in their beaks may look marvelous, but their taste is not a great gastronomic experience. Most diets were dull and monotonous, and details of some court banquets have come down to us precisely because they were so unusual that someone felt an account of them should be preserved for posterity.

Good cooking, as opposed to a good blowout, really started with the introduction of forks in the 17th century. Before this, food had to be prepared so that it could be scooped out of a basin with a spoon, hacked off a carcass with a knife, or munched in the fingers. It was probably remarkable enough, in those days, not to be actually hungry, and few had the luxury to fuss about what they were eating.

In Saxon and Norman England one good meal a day was served in Hall. The food was set on a high table and on side tables. The diners sat with their backs to the walls, facing the center space, which was reserved for serving and for entertainment. The loaves of salt were crushed and put in heavy silver "cellars" on the high table, with smaller ones on the side tables. People sat at table in decreasing order of rank, and those far down the table were described as "below the salt."

Before eating, people washed their hands with perfumed water, served in ewers by pages, who also provided napkins. The old English name for a page was *haunsman* (because he stood at his lord's haunch or side), more often written *henchman* or *henxman*. A nobleman usually had several henchmen, classing them with his wards and next to his own sons. Since almost everything was eaten in the fingers, hand washing was repeated at intervals throughout the meal. The custom was observed on solemn days in the colleges of the older universities long after it had died out elsewhere.

Dishes, particularly in royal courts, were often "tasted" to make sure that they were not poisoned. The wine was often passed round from one diner to another in the same cup for people to drink in turn. Each diner brought his own set of spoons and knives and spike contained in elaborate and often very valuable cases.

After the Norman Conquest of 1066, the king and court had French cooks, and persons of any standing spoke French. Animals were called sheep or swine, calves or oxen when alive and tended by the Saxon serfs; but they became *le mouton* or mutton, *le porc* or pork, *le veau* or veal, *le boeuf* or beef when they came to table. Since cattle were not grazed in winter, and only a few were kept for breeding, the rest were slaughtered in autumn and eaten, or salted down or made into sausages. The Feast of Sausages and Gut Puddings at Martinmas (November 11) was celebrated all over Europe throughout the Middle Ages.

But it was not all feasting. Gluttony was one of the Seven Deadly Sins. No meat was eaten on Fridays or other fast days or in Lent. The religious houses had "stew ponds" where they bred fish for the monks' Friday dinners; and during the reign of Henry III (1216–72) there were extensive stew ponds near Westminster Palace. In one order for the purchase of 600 luces, or pike, it was specified that 100 of them were to be put into the king's ponds at Westminster.

Mackerel are mentioned in 1247 as allowed to certain religious on the third day of Rogation. Red herrings and fresh herrings by the "last" (10,000) were sent from Hull to London in the time of Edward I (1272–1307) for consumption on Fridays and during Lent. In the tariff for fish prices fixed in the same reign, the best soles cost threepence a dozen, the best turbot sixpence, the best mackerel in Lent one penny each, fresh oysters twopence a gallon, the best pickled herrings twenty for a penny, and the best eels twenty-five for twopence.

Whales were salted down for food even in Anglo-Saxon times, but by Act 17 of Edward II (1307–27) whales and great sturgeons taken in the sea were reserved for the king except in certain privileged places.

The royal family was particularly fond of lampreys, considered a delicacy at the English Court for centuries. King John (1199–1216) levied a fine of 40 marks on the city of Gloucester for failing to "pay him sufficient respect in the matter of his lamperns" (lampreys). Until 1836 the city of Gloucester sent a lamprey pie to the sovereign every year, but the custom was discontinued, except on the occasion of coronations, because of the cost. The fish is something like an eel and has a soft, delicate, very rich, and indigestible flesh. Henry I (1100–35), the youngest son of William the Conqueror, died of a surfeit of lampreys. Still popular in France, lampreys are eaten at banquets all along the river Loire, and in Bordeaux, where *lamproies à la bordelaise* (cooked in red wine

Mary, Queen of Scots (after Nicholas Hilliard)

with leeks and garnished with croutons) are one of the gastronomic specialties. "Of this kind of fish there are two different sorts in general use for the table," Queen Victoria's chef Francatelli wrote in 1886, "one being the sea or marine lamprey, which is abundant at Gloucester and Worcester, where it is dressed and preserved for the purpose of being given as presents. The other sort, the lampern, is much smaller. This is to be found in the Thames and may easily be obtained at any London fishmonger from the month of October till March, at which period they are in season. The lamprey is considered to be in best condition during the month of April and May when it ascends the Severn from the sea for the purpose of depositing its spawn." But lampreys are no longer found in the Thames or in English fishmongers' shops; the liking for them seems to have died out.

King Richard II (1377–99) was a man of extravagant tastes and great worldly elegance. He was devoted to exotic food, as indicated by a manuscript on cookery in the British Museum compiled in the 1390's by Richard II's master cooks, a long parchment roll called *The Forme of Cury*. (The word *cury* means "cooking.") The

manuscript mentions olive oil rather than butter, Lombard mustard, mace, ginger, saffron, and even spikenard as ingredients of the cuisine. There are recipes for fish cooked with sliced almonds, chopped dates, and raisins. It discourses on birds and fish in "little coffyns," or piecrusts, and there is a recipe for oysters done in Greek wine, several dishes "in gravy" (the broth in which the meat was boiled), flavored with ground almonds, powdered ginger, and sugar. The main course was often a sort of huge pâté. Meat does not seem to have been served at the royal table, but there is mention of *mawmenee*—basically, minced pheasant in cinnamon, cloves, ginger, Greek wine, and sugar. *The Forme of Cury* was first printed as a book in 1780 by Dr. Samuel Pegge, who edited it for the Society of Antiquaries and added "other congruous matters including some Rolls of Provisions with the Princes Dishes etc. during the reign of Henry VIII."

The 196 recipes in this book and those in other medieval works remind one of modern Oriental and Arab dishes, and may have been brought to Europe by the Crusaders, for the manuscript includes a recipe for "Saracen Sauce."

Henry VIII of England by Hans Holbein the Younger

Queen Jane Seymour, Third Wife of Henry VIII by Hans Holbein the Younger

Spices were much used, as they had been by the Romans, though they were rare, costly, and exotic. The "mincemeat" traditional in Britain at Christmas, to fill "mince pies," nowadays a mixture of sugar, spices, suet, dried fruit, and sometimes brandy, originally contained meat; minced beef and minced tongue were included until the end of the 19th century. Large spiced pies still made in Cumberland contain not only dried fruits and spices but also meat, and are similar to dishes that were fashionable in the Middle Ages.

At the coronation of Henry V in 1413 there was a great banquet at which were served antelopes as well as swans and eagles, "each with the holy scriptures written on her bylle." There were only three courses, two of mixed dishes and the middle one consisting of what, in France, was called an *entremets* (Spanish, *entremes;* Italian, *tramesso, intromesso*), meaning the middle course of a banquet. In old French it meant literally "between dishes"—the ensemble of dishes that followed the roast, not only sweets but vegetables too. Later it came to mean the ornaments that diversified a banquet—the decorative cakes and pies or roasted meats. By the 14th century it also meant any kind of entertainment in the middle of a meal, provided by buffoons or troubadours. A special table decoration, such as a fancy fortress, made not by the royal cooks but by special craftsmen, might be wheeled into the hall to amuse the guests. Sometimes such decorations bore wooden figures, sometimes heavily disguised and masked people. At intervals during the banquet, fresh *entremets* were introduced containing people who danced or sang or acted in mime.

In England the word *subtilty* or *soteltie* was used for such elaborately dressed dishes or table decorations. At the coronation of Henry V appeared "a pelican sitting on her nest with her young" and "an image of Saint Catherine holding a book and disputing with the doctors." Another *soteltie* was the cockatrice, "an ancient conceit"— a fantastic animal, half chicken and half rabbit, made up with a carved head, golden beak, four legs, and a golden egg between its paws.

An enormous pie, out of which flew a flock of living birds, was a variety of *soteltie* that appeared at some medieval banquets and was still popular in Stuart England. One example is immortalized in the nursery rhyme about "four-and-twenty blackbirds baked in a pie," which relates how

Edward VI as a Child by **Hans Holbein the Younger**

> When the pie was opened,
> The birds began to sing.
> Wasn't that a dainty dish
> To set before a King?

On one occasion a dwarf underwent such an incrustation: About the year 1630, when Charles I and Queen Henrietta Maria were entertained by the Duke and Duchess of Buckingham at Burleigh, Jeffrey Hudson, a dwarf, was served up in a cold pie.

Robert May's *Accomplish'd Cook*, published in 1660, gives a recipe for live frogs in a pie. When the pie was opened, he wrote, the frogs would leap up "and cause the ladies to squeak and hop about."

At medieval feasts there were always many peacocks in full panoply. In 1466, at the enthronement of Archbishop Nevil, no fewer than 104 peacocks were brought in to a fanfare of trumpets, with all the gorgeous tail feathers fully displayed. For such presentations, the bird was first skinned and the feathered tail, head, and neck were laid on a table and sprinkled with cumin. The body was then roasted, glazed with raw egg yolk, cooled, sewn back into the skin, and served as the last course.

In the 15th century the whale was also a great delicacy, found on the royal table and on that of the Lord Mayor of London. The cook

Willam III (after Peter Lely)

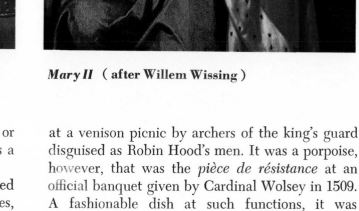

Mary II (after Willem Wissing)

either roasted part of it and served it on a spit, or boiled it and sent it up with peas. The tail was a favorite part.

Whole suckling pigs and calves were roasted on a spit or broach. Sometimes the roasted calves, game birds, and elaborate pastries were covered with gold leaf.

The grampus or seawolf was much liked, too, as were more conventional fish, including salmon and sometimes sturgeon from the Thames. Roasted swans were served at banquets for centuries. They were often brought to table with a piece of blazing camphor in their beaks.

Not all the feasting was at the palace. On Midsummer Eve there used to be singing and dancing and rough games in the streets, and the well-to-do citizens of London set out tables with wine and bread and biscuits and invited all passers-by to drink with them.

Henry VIII (1509–47) used to keep the popular folk custom of going out into the woods on May Day with his knights and squires and returning every man "with a grene bough in his cappe." In 1515 the royal party were entertained at a venison picnic by archers of the king's guard disguised as Robin Hood's men. It was a porpoise, however, that was the *pièce de résistance* at an official banquet given by Cardinal Wolsey in 1509. A fashionable dish at such functions, it was brought into the hall whole, carved, and eaten with mustard. On this occasion it probably was followed by strawberries and cream, a dish which the cardinal made fashionable.

Wolsey gave sumptuous receptions in his palace at Whitehall, "set forth with masques and mummeries in so gorgeous a sort and costly a manner that it was heaven to behold," wrote Sir George Cavendish.

In the intervals of the masque, dinner was brought to the accompaniment of twelve trumpets and two kettledrums that made the hall ring for half an hour together, and the Yeomen of the Guard, bareheaded and clothed in scarlet with a golden rose on their backs, brought in a course of twenty-four dishes, served mostly on gold plates.

Then "the dishes of the banquet were clean taken up and the tables spread after with new and sweet perfumed cloths. Then in came a new banquet of a hundred dishes and more and the whole night was passed in banqueting, dancing, and other triumphant devices."

"About the fifteenth [year] of Henry VIII['s reign]," another authority tells us, "it happened that diverse things were newly brought into England, whereupon the rhyme was made:

Turkies, Carps, Hoppes, Picarell and Beere
Came into England all in one year."

It seems very probable that, as the peacock with its tail feathers spread out was in such demand for feasting, when the turkey was first introduced into England it was used as a kind of "economy peacock," with its tail feathers sticking up handsomely at the rear of some gold-plated serving dish.

The food eaten at Court in Tudor England is well known from such sources as the writings of Bartolommeo de' Sacchi, also known as Platina, the librarian at the Vatican, after 1475, and author of the first printed cookery book, published in about 1474. The first cookery book printed in English was *The Boke of Cokery,* published in 1500 and intended for "A Princys Household or Any Other Estates." The *Boke of Kervynge* (carving) appeared in 1508. The *Earl of Northumberland's Household Book,* begun in 1512, gives a fair picture of domestic life at Court. It describes the household life of Henry Algernon Percy, 5th Earl of Northumberland (who died in 1527) at his castles in Yorkshire.

Bishop Percy, its 18th-century editor, points out that it describes "the great magnificence of our old nobility." All the officers in the household were gentlemen both by birth and office, such as the comptroller, "clark of the kitchen," chamberlain, etc. There were also a "yoman cook for the mouth" and a "grome cook for the mouth" (titles also used in the royal household), who saw to the roasting of the meat. They attended hourly in the kitchen at the *haisty,* or fireplace, presided over by the *haister* just as the butler presided over the buttery and the pantler over the pantry.

The *Northumberland Household Book* contains bills for "Beefis and Muttuns, for Gascoin Wine, Rede Herynge, Salmon, Salt Sturgeon, Hopps for Brewing, Waxe, Oile, Bay Salte, Parishe Candell and Brasse Pottis." The "Orders for Braikfasts" allowed daily in Lent were as follows: "for my Lorde and My Ladye, Furst a Loif of Brede in Trenchers, ij [2] Manchets, a Quart of Wyne,

ij Percys of Saltfish, vj [6] Baconn'd Herryng, iiij [4] white Herryng or a Dysche of Sproits . . . for the Nurcy for my Lady Margaret and Maister Ingeram Percy—Item a Manchet, a Quarte of Bere, a Dysche of Butter, a Pece of Saltfisch, a Dische of Sproits, or iiij White Herryng."

Queen Elizabeth I (1558–1603) was very fond of sweetmeats and often received gifts of marchpane (marzipan), sometimes molded into fantastic shapes. Marchpane castles, mermaids, dolphins, eagles, and camels appeared on great occasions. One winter loyal subjects gave her a marchpane model of Old Saint Paul's, a marchpane chessboard, and many other sweets as a New Year gift.

The Michaelmas goose, fattened on corn stubble and the gleanings of barley left by the reapers, was eaten on September 29, the Feast of Saint Michael and All Angels, by generations of patriotic Englishmen. They were celebrating not only the bringing home of the harvest but the

James I by Daniel Mytens

***Charles I Hunting* by Sir Anthony van Dyck**

English victory over the Spanish Armada in 1588. According to the story, Queen Elizabeth, who adored good food, was already at table sinking her teeth into a bit of roast stubble goose when the news of the sea triumph was brought to her. To mark the occasion, she decreed that roast goose should be eaten on that day every year thereafter.

According to Gervase Markham, writing in 1615, sauce for a stubble goose was "diverse according to men's minds, for some will take the pap of rosted apples, and mixing it with vinegar boyll them together on the fire with some of the gravy of the Goose and a few Barberies and breadcrums, and when it is boyled to a good thicknesse, season it with sugar and a little cinnamon, and so serve it up. Some will add a little Mustard and onyons unto it, and some will not rost the apples but pare and slice them, and that is the neerer way but not the better. Others will fill the belly of the Goose full of onyons shred, and oat-meal-groats, and being rosted enough, mix it with the gravy of the Goose and sweet hearbs well boyled together, and seasoned with a litle Verjuyce." A dish called Poor Man's Goose, made from minced pig's liver and various herbs, is still remembered in country places all over England, although Michaelmas goose is forgotten.

The Elizabethans put sage, cinnamon, nutmeg, and mace in their butter, perhaps as a prototype of our cinnamon toast, or to garnish the meat like the *maître d'hôtel* butter of today. Although spices were less in demand than formerly, they were still extremely valuable. Sailors went on voyages of exploration in search of spices. Sir Francis Drake reached the Spice Islands toward the end of the 16th century, and tried to bring back to England six tons of cloves. Catherine of Aragon, who had gone to live in Bedfordshire after her divorce from Henry VIII, relieved her boredom by teaching the villagers to make lace and to grow saffron crocuses. (The growers were called "crokers.") This part of England became famous for its saffron, a spice made by drying the yellow stamens of the saffron crocus. The town of Saffron Walden in nearby Essex took its name from the once flourishing local industry.

Until about the mid-19th century, Kattern (Catherine) cakes were made in some Bedfordshire villages every year on December 6, Catherine of Aragon's birthday, and in many places a bellman went round crying:

> Rise, maids, rise!
> Bake your kattern pies,
> Bake enough and bake no waste
> And let the bellman have a taste.

In Elizabeth's day, people dined at ten o'clock in the morning at the universities but somewhat later in London. Supper was at five or six o'clock, according to one's profession. But there were also rear (late) suppers in Tudor England. Richard Greene, the playwright, was the victim of a surfeit of pickled herring and Rhenish wine taken with friends at a rear supper.

At the end of a feast the scraps and above all the gravy-soaked trenchers (slices of bread used as plates) were collected and distributed to the poor at the castle gates. But Raphael Holinshed says in his *Chronicles* that the laboring man was seldom able to taste any other than the poor bread sometimes made from rye or barley but more usually of beans peason or oats mixed with acorns. In Holinshed's day—he died about 1580—there was manchet, cheat, or other wheaten bread, and another inferior wheaten bread called "raveled and brown" bread, which was "drie and brickle," but better when mixed with rye flour. Bran bread was "for slaves and servants and the inferior kind of people to feed on."

The first book of diet and health cooking, Andrewe Boorde's *Compendyous Regyment or a Dyetary of Health*, was published in 1562. "Pygges, specially some pygges, is nutrytyve, so be it the pygge be fleed, the skyn taken off and then stewed with restoratives, as a cocke is stewed to make a gelye."

The *Queen's Delight*, in the edition of 1696, gives a recipe for "A Cordial Water of Sir Walter Rawleigh's": "Take a gallon of Strawberries and

Queen Anne, **attributed to Michael Dahl**

put them into a pint of Aqua Vitae, let them stand four or five days, strain them gently out, and sweeten the water as you please with fine Sugar; or else with Perfume."

It also gives "Queen Elizabeth's Perfume": "Take eight spoonfuls of Compound water, the weight of two-pence in fine powder of Sugar and boyl it on hot Embers and Coals softly, add half and once of sweet Marjoram dried in the sun, the

weight of two-pence of the powder of Benjamin. This Perfume is very sweet, and good for the time."

James VI of Scotland and I of England (1603–25), the son of Mary Queen of Scots and poor Henry Stewart, Lord Darnley, was known variously as "God's silly vassal" and "the wisest fool in Christendom." According to his physician, Sir Theodore Turquet de Mayence, he had "a very steadfast brain, which was never disturbed by the sea, by drinking wine, or by travelling in a coach. As regards food," his doctor went on, "there is nothing wrong except that he eats no bread. . . . He eats fruit at all hours of the day and night. . . . In drink he errs as to quality, quantity, frequency, time, and order. He drinks beer, ale, Spanish wine, sweet French wine . . . and sometimes Alicante wines."

The banquet and entertainment given by James I to the Constable of Castile at Whitehall Palace on August 18, 1604, was served by gentlemen of high rank and followed by music and dancing in which Prince Henry, his son, performed a galliard "with much sprightliness and modesty."

Thomas Coryate, the son of a parson who wrote Latin verse for the nobility, was a buffoon at court in Prince Henry's household. He became famous after traveling through France to Venice, mostly on foot, and coming back through Switzerland, Germany, and Holland. In his *Crudities,* an account of his travels published in 1611, he revealed the appearance of a new gadget for eating, the fork. The oft-quoted passage from Coryate's book is cited in full in the chapter on Italy.

Gervase Markham's cookery book, *The English Hous-Wife,* containing "The Inward and Outward Virtues which ought to be in a compleat Woman," appeared in 1615. It was the most influential of early English cookbooks and was reprinted until 1683. Its success is the more remarkable when one reflects that even highly born and wealthy women were not always taught to read. There are remedies in it for palsy and for the "falling-sicknesse," and preservatives against the plague as well as ordinary cooking recipes. It tells what to do in childbirth and teaches about wine, brewing beer, and making cider and perry.

A slim little book entitled *A Queen's Delight: or the Art of Preserving, Conserving and Candying* is inscribed: "A right knowledge of making Perfumes and Distilling the most Excellent Waters. Never before published. Printed for Nathanil Brook at the Angel in Cornhill, 1656." It is really part of another larger work called *The Queen's Closet Opened,* a popular 17th-century cookery book, which contains "Incomparable Secrets in Physick Chirurgery Preserving Candying and Cookery; As they were presented to the Queen by the most Experienced Persons of our times many whereof were honoured with her own practice, when she pleased to descend to these more private Recreations . . ." The books refer to recipes used by Queen Henrietta Maria, the French wife of Charles I, and the dishes may well have been prepared at Greenwich Palace, which Inigo Jones built for her. They were "transcribed from the true Copies of her Majesties own recipt-books by W.M., one of her late servants. *Vivit post funera virtus* 1656."

One recipe in *A Queen's Delight* tells how "To make a Cake the way of the Royal Princess." (This was the Lady Elizabeth, daughter of Charles I; she died a prisoner in Carisbrooke Castle at the age of fifteen in 1650.) To make her cake: "Take half a peck of flower, half a pint of Rose-water, a pint of Ale yeast, a pint of Cream, boyl it, a pound and an half of butter, six Eggs (leave out the white), four pound of Currans, one half pound of Sugar, one Nutmeg, and a little Salt, work it very well, and let it stand half an hour by the fire, and then work it again, and then make it up, and let it stand an hour and a half in the Oven; let not your Oven be too hot."

The Puritans, under Oliver Cromwell, tried to introduce to England austerity and a diet consisting largely, people said, of pickled herrings. This was very unpopular in some quarters. One clandestine Royalist toast during the rule of Protector Cromwell involved filling the mouth with bread, then gulping some wine, and saying: "God send this crumb well [Cromwell] down!"

After the restoration of the monarchy in 1660, Charles II and his friends, having spent some time as exiles at the French court, returned to England with a love of French cooking. In elegant households there was now at least one French cook, often a Huguenot refugee. Dela Hay Street, in the City of Westminster (downtown London), was named for Peter de la Haye, Charles II's French pastry cook.

The Restoration period was noted for its rich and amoral living, and in "good King Charles's golden days" the Court was the scene, not only of much license and scandal, but also of fashion and freedom for the arts.

A recipe for "King Charles II's Surfeit Water," probably a hangover cure, appeared in Eliza Smith's *The Compleat Housewife,* a work of uncertain date but perhaps contemporary with the Merry Monarch:

"Take a gallon of the best aqua-vitae, a quart of brandy, a quart of aniseed-water, a pint of poppy-water, and a pint of damask rose-water, put these in a large glass jar, adding to it a pound of fine powder'd sugar, a pound and a half of raisins stoned, a quarter of a pound of dates stoned and sliced, one ounce of cinnamon bruised, cloves one ounce, four nutmegs bruised, one stick of liquorice scrap'd and sliced; let all there stand nine days close cover'd stirring it three or four times a day; then add to it three pounds of fresh poppies, or three handfulls of dry'd poppies, a sprig of angelica, two or three of balm; so let it stand a week longer, then strain it out and bottle it."

The gastronomic genius of the day was Patrick Lamb, master cook at St. James's Palace, Hampton Court, and Windsor for nearly fifty years. He cooked for Charles II, James II, William and Mary, and Anne, and his *Royal Cookery* was published in 1710, shortly after his death.

George I

He maintained that the sumptuous English court banquets were then the envy of all Europe: "Our credit and esteem with foreign ministers has in great measure been built and supported on this foundation. For those whose shortness of parts or perhaps residence among us, would not qualify 'em to embark upon the nicer parts of our constitutions, have yet gone away with such relish of our magnificence as to lament their own barrenness, whenever they reflect on the fleshpots they left behind them."

The food he prepared must have been very good, whether it was "boil'd Pullets with Oysters and Bacon, the Patty of Mushrooms, the Almond Tart, Spinage with Eggs, or Pupton of Pigeons." It has the simple elegance of much of the furniture and architecture of the period, but he had an obscure way of writing that makes the recipes difficult to follow. Often he seems to omit ingredients, as if, like most professional cooks, he were reluctant to reveal quite all his kitchen secrets to everybody.

Born about 1650, Lamb was appointed "child of the Queen's kitchen" in 1672, then "groom of the mouthe," and was sworn as master cook in the Queen's kitchen in 1677, at the then huge salary of £80 a year.

Fresh produce was plentiful in Restoration London. Fish used to be sent up from Lyme Regis by relays of fast-trotting horses. The dairymen of Hackney had a great name for butter, which was so good that, in 1654, they were able to charge tenpence a pound for it, although ordinary butter cost only sixpence a pound. There were several old established markets—Billingsgate for fish, Leadenhall for poultry, Smithfield for meat; and Charles II gave a charter to Spitalfield Market for fruit and vegetables. There were numerous market gardens all around 17th-century London, growing pot herbs and green vegetables; some seedmen's and nurserymen's trade cards have been preserved. A market garden at Whitechapel specialized in rare and choice fruit, especially nectarines and peaches, and also the dwarf plums and cherries then fashionable. Battersea was famous for asparagus. Mulberries, figs, and cherries all did well in London soil, but strawberries grew best of all. Prices varied according to season. In 1589, for instance, they went from one shilling a pint on May 23 to threepence on June 7. John Rose, gardener to Charles II, was the first in Britain to grow pineapples successfully on hotbeds.

William III (1689–1702) was asthmatic, very

Queen Charlotte **by Thomas Gainsborough**

foreign, and rather unpopular. People complained that the glories of court life had grown dim and that "like most Dutchmen he never failed to attend the tea table every evening." It was he who introduced the habit of tea drinking to the British. Patrick Lamb, in William's service, introduced Dutch methods to English cooking. Still available are his recipes for "Haddock and Scate or Thornback the Dutch way" and "Dutch [dried] Beef." In his delicious recipe for "Pike Cabilow the Dutch Way," he writes: "In Holland the sawce is only oil'd Butter, melted gently over the Fire, and stirred about with a Ladle, and so pour'd over, for their Butter is as thick oil'd as ours is drawn up. But for the Queen we draw our Butter Up. A Pound of Butter with a Spoonful of Water, drawn up, is as thick as Cream; Squeeze a Lemon and so serve it hot."

These are the dishes he prepared for the King's Dinner on May 20, 1700:

"Pottage 2 Ducklings, Hamb and Chickings, Carps Stewed, Patty of Squabs, Pearches, 2 Geese, Bisque of Pigeons, Veal Royalé, Chicken Fricacy, Pulpatoons, Olio terreyn, Rabbits forst, Pudding, Beans & Bacon, Beef alá Royalé, flounders, Mackril, Hasht Loavs, Pottage of Pullets, Shoulder of Mutton in blood and stakes. Souced Salmon, Sallad, Crabbs butterd and broyled, 4 Rabbets, 6 Chickens, Artichocks, Morrells, Cream Puffs, Sweetbreads, Machroons, Tarts, Cold Lamb & Chickens, Cheescakes, Dutch Beef, Cherry Tarts, Lamb Stones, Ramkins, Mushrooms, Pease."

The age of Queen Anne (1703–14) was the prelude to a long era of content. There were good harvests and cheap food, and, according to Daniel Defoe, England was the most flourishing and opulent country in the world.

***George III*, from the studio of Allan Ramsay**

Some people said that Anne was an alcoholic, others that "her only hobby was eating." But according to the epicure Anthelme Brillat-Savarin, the art of cooking flourished at her court: "Queen Anne was a dedicated gourmet; she did not disdain to discuss matters personally with her cook and English cookery books contain many preparations bearing the designation 'After Queen Anne's Fashion.'"

Anne, on her accession, issued various warrants to increase the household expenses:

"Whereas our Master Cookes, in their respective waitings, furnish all sorts of Herbs in their several seasons for all the Pottages served daily at our Tables, and do besides provide at their own charge Morellas, Trouffles, Champignons and many other things . . . we grant them an additional allowance, four shillings a day for the Plates by them daily served . . ." The Queen's personal physician, Martin Lister, was the editor of the English edition of Apicius published in London in 1705. It is fully annotated, and Dr. Lister must have been a not inconsiderable gourmet himself.

Several members of Patrick Lamb's family worked in the royal kitchens; his father was evidently Yeoman of His Majesty's Pastry. Patrick Lamb himself was associated with the Court from the cradle to the grave (he died in 1709). The following dinner was prepared by Lamb for the Queen in 1704:

"Turkie en fillé, Calves head hasht, Hare Pie, Pigeons Comport, Lamb alá Royalé, Olio, Cheyn of Mutton & Veal Collops, Pottage 2 Pullets, Hamb & Chickens. Ducklings, Partridges, Pigeons, 2 Capons, Teals Chickens, Woodcocks. Asparagrass, Coxcombs, Oyster Loavs, Butterd Chickens, Morrells, Jeillys, Blamange, Lupins, Smelts ala Cream, Pulpatoon, Shampinions, Lampor Eell."

Lamb, like his father before him, had a warrant to sell "Wyne Strong Waters, Ale Beer and All other Liquors and Tobacco within and about our Palaces of White hall, Windsor and in whatever other Palace our Court shall reside."

The Queen's Royal Cookery, by T. Hall, "Free Cook of London," published in 1710, contains a delightful picture of Queen Anne and pictures of some kitchens (presumably the royal ones). Free cooks were those engaged on a temporary basis, perhaps for a big dinner or a party, and Hall seems to have cooked at Court over a long period. His book was printed at Pye Corner, Cheapside, and perhaps he sold pies in one of the famous cooked-meat shops there when not cooking for royalty. His recipes for pies are excellent. There are also recipes for "Clouted Cream, Almond Custards, A Gooseberry Tart Baked green and clear as Crystal, Scotch Collups of Mutton, Rabbets roasted, Lobsters Fried, and Pickled Oysters." One recipe, described as "The Queen's Preserving Woman's fine white Jelly of Quinces," reads:

"Take Quinces newly from the Tree, wipe them clean, and boil them whole in a large Quantity of Water, the more the better till the Quinces crack and are soft; then press out their juice hard, but so, that only the Liquor run out, but none of the Pap; take three pound of this strained liquor, being settled, and one pound of fine Sugar, and boil them up to a jelly, with a moderate fire; they may require near an hour's boiling to come to a jelly, the Tryal of that is to take a thin plate and wet it with fair Water, and drop a little of it upon the wet Plate, if it stick to the plate it is not enough, but if it falls off (when you stop the Plate) without sticking at all to it, then it is enough; then put it into flat, shallow Tin Forms, first melted with cold water, and let it stand in them four or five hours; then reverse the Plates that it may shale and fall out, and so put the Parcels up in Boxes."

George I (1714–27), the Elector of Hanover, was an elderly German who spoke no English. Newly arrived from Hanover, he is said to have been so excited by the English puddings that people nicknamed him Pudding George. The Nursery Rhyme about Georgie Porgie Pudding and Pie is thought to be about him. George III (1760–1820), "Farmer George," was often lampooned for his stodgy domesticity and cheese-paring habits. A contemporary cartoon shows the royal household in two compartments, with King George toasting muffins for his breakfast and Queen

A Music Party, 1733, showing Frederick, Prince of Wales, and his sisters, by Philippe Mercier

Charlotte in a very commonplace unfashionable dress (but with money falling out of her pocket) cooking sprats for his supper. In 1791 he bought Buckingham House, which had been built by the Duke of Buckingham on the site of James I's mulberry orchard. Later his son, the prince regent, had it altered by John Nash, and the great Antonin Carême, king of cooks and cook to kings, designed the kitchens for him.

Carême was with the prince regent for two years, but he left London because "the fog depressed him." When the prince regent, as George IV (1820–30), offered Carême the then enormous salary of £1,000 a year to return, he refused, saying that in London "all was sombre" and that he was cut off from his friends and deprived of "that most alluring French conversation."

Half the crowned heads of Europe tried to get Carême to work for them. He cooked for the tsars, the Rothschilds, and for Prince Talleyrand, and he is said to have left the Duke of Wellington because the Iron Duke, who was frequently late for meals, took no interest in the dishes set before him.

A chef of the romantic school of cookery, Carême devised recipes far too elaborate for modern domestic use. People used to say that they would wish Carême to prepare the sauce were they under the necessity of eating an elephant or their own grandmother. It was rumored that, while he worked at Carlton House, immense prices were paid by aldermen for what remained of pâtés after they had appeared at the prince regent's table.

"Carême," the prince regent used to complain, "you will kill me with a surfeit of food. I have a fancy for everything you put before me. The temptation is really too great." "My great concern," the chef would reply, "is to stimulate Your Highness' appetite by the variety of my dishes. It is no concern of mine to curb it."

The English version of *The Royal Parisian Pastrycook and Confectioner,* from the original of M. A. Carême of Paris, edited by John Porter, formerly cook to the Marquis of Camden, etc. etc., published in 1834, was a 19th-century classic, and Carême's work was much copied in the great English kitchens. In it are recipes for "Hot Snipe Pie with Truffles, Croustades of Quails au Gratin, Ramequins, Forcemeat Balls of Soft Roes of Carp, Cold Duck Pie, and Large Sturgeon Pie with Truffles." Part V is devoted to *pièces montées,* with instructions for preparing:

"A French Helmet: the horse hair on the top

of the helmet is made of gold-coloured spun sugar and the feather of white spun sugar . . . after you have fastened the helmet on its pedestal lightly mark it with a very clear apricot marmalade."

There are "A Grotto Ornamented with Moss, A Cascade with Palm-Trees, An Ancient Fountain on an Island, A Chinese Summer House, A Venetian Pavillion on a Bridge, the Ruins of Palmyra," and many similar edifices. They must be the direct descendants of the fantastic dishes and *sotelties* that were prepared for Richard II and at other medieval banquets.

Two brothers of King George IV had famous French chefs. The Duke of Cambridge was cooked for briefly by both Philippe Soyer and his famous brother Alexis, who later followed Florence Nightingale to the Crimea and invented the field kitchen. The very unpopular Duke of York for years had Louis Eustache Ude as chef. Ude had been cook to Madame Mère, Napoleon's mother, but left her and went to England after a row about the household accounts. It was Ude who introduced the light sandwich supper, during the Regency, at routs and fashionable soirées. For this he was much criticized by rivals, who said he was starving the nation to death. Ude gave himself great airs and insisted that he and his colleagues be known not as chefs but as artists. On hearing of the death of his former patron, the Duke of York ("one of Queen Victoria's wicked uncles"), he was silent at first. "Oh milord!," he muttered, shaking his head, "how much you will miss my cooking in the place you are going to!"

Charles Elme Francatelli, who was for a time chief cook in ordinary to Queen Victoria (1837–1901), is said to have added a new dimension to British cooking. He may well have added a new dimension to Queen Victoria, too, for some of the dinners he cooked for her in 1851 were enormous.

The menu for Her Majesty's dinner on September 21 lists the following: Potages; À la Purée de Volaille, À la Brunoise. Poissons; Le Saumon sauce au persil, Les Harengs sauce Moutarde, Le St. Pierre sauce Homard, Les Eperlans frits. Relevés; Le Rond de Veau à l'Anglaise, Le Jambon glacé aux haricots verts. Flancs; Les Petits Poulets au gros sel, Les Filets de Mouton à la Jardinière. Entrées; Les Poitrines d'Agneau à la purée de pommes de terre, Les Perdreaux à la Périgueux, Les Kromeskys de Volaille à la Russe, L'Emincé de Boeuf à la Polonaise, Les Ris de Veau à la Financière, Les Petites Quenelles de Volaille, Les Amourettes frites sauce Tomates, Les Petits Vol-

au-Vent aux huîtres. Rôtis; Les Poulardes, Les Perdreaux. Relevés; Les Omelettes soufflées à la fleur d'Orange, Le Pudding Bavaroix. Entremêts; Les Epinards au jus, Les Pommes de Terre frites, La Gelée de Pieds de Veau au Vin, Les Fenchonettes à l'Abricôt, La Charlotte à la Parisienne, Le Gâteau de Compiègne, Les Homards au gratin, La Salade de Volaille, La Crème au Caramel, Les Nougats de Pommes au Citron, La Gelée de

Queen Victoria by George Hayter

Fruits, La Grosse Meringue à la Chantilly, Les Corbeilles garnies de Noix. Side Board; Roast Beef, Roast Mutton, Haunch of Venison, Riz au Consommé, Hashed Venison.

The modern customs of having servants to wait at table, introduced to the Prussian Court by

Urbain-Dubois, chef to William I (1861–88), had become fashionable in England, too. At first this was called *service à la Russe*. Instead of two or at most three vast courses with dozens of dishes, sweet and savory, placed on the dining table for diners to look at and help themselves, hot food was now brought straight from the kitchen dish by dish and passed around by footmen to the seated guests before being placed on the sideboard. The vast display of ornamental dishes and grandiose set pieces in sugar or aspic, which had been customary at banquets since the Middle Ages, was no longer necessary. It was the age of the huge ornamental silver or gold epergne and of elaborate and often hideous floral decorations. The food was now hot, however, and it was not hacked to pieces by guests who could not carve.

Of Italian extraction, Francatelli was born in London in 1805, was educated in France, and was a pupil of the great Carême. His contemporaries described him as a charming, cultured, and sensitive man. He was also a very successful author, and his *The Modern Cook*, which contains several recipes dedicated to members of the royal family, reached twelve editions. Its elaborate recipes require stupendous quantities of food in the high Victorian manner. In a recipe for "Hunting Beef," he suggests putting a whole round of beef, weighing about 30 pounds, in a highly spiced pickle for about three weeks, then boiling it in home-brewed ale. He had the grace, however, to apologize for the "apparent extravagance" of the recipe by suggesting that "the broth could be given to the poor of the surrounding parishes."

Although his specialty was banquets, Francatelli could also do simple things well, and his *Cook's Guide and Housekeeper's and Butler's Assistant*, published in 1861, is not only full of good things but eminently practical. "I could feed a thousand people every day," he used to say, "on food that is wasted in London." Here one finds the dishes that the royal family obviously preferred to eat when they were not undergoing the tedium of a state banquet: Prince of Wales sauce, Victoria biscuits, Albert biscuits, marrow toast, and Queen Victoria's favorite soup. It also includes the recipe for a "Royal Posset for a Cold," made with white wine, cloves, honey, and Robinson's Patent Groats, "to drink quite hot just before going to bed"—which may well have been the very concoction that the Prince Consort was taking before he died of pneumonia.

"For Victoria Soup: Wash and scald ½ pound Frankfort pearl barley and put this into a stewpan with 3 pints of good white veal stock, and simmer it very gently over a slow fire for an hour and a half, by which time the barley will be nearly dissolved. Remove a third of it into a small soup pot, rub the remainder through a tammy or sieve. Pour it to the whole barley. Add half a pint of cream. Season with a little salt. Stir it over the fire until hot, and serve. This soup may be prepared with rice."

"They are or at least were," Francatelli writes, "the only soups eaten by the Queen when I had the honour of waiting on Her Majesty."

The Daughters of Edward VII

Beef marrow bones, served hot in a napkin, were much liked in Georgian and Victorian England, and are still served at City dinners. The marrow was eaten with the aid of a special silver spoon, narrow enough to go inside the bone. In the 19th century, however, ladies usually took their beef marrow on toast as being more delicate. It "used to be eaten every day at dinner by the Queen," Francatelli reports, describing the procedure:

"Procure a small marrow-bone, or get the butcher to break the bone for you, as this is rather an awkward affair for ladies. Cut the marrow into small pieces the size of a filbert and just parboil them in boiling water with a little salt for one minute; it must then be instantly drained upon a sieve, seasoned with a little chopped parsley, pepper and salt, lemon juice, and a mere suspicion of shallot; toss lightly altogether, spread it out upon squares of crisp dry toast and serve immediately."

Francatelli lost his appointment at the Palace, contemporaries say, as the result of kitchen intrigue. He later succeeded Louis Eustache Ude as *maître d'hôtel* at Crockford's Club, also ran the Coventry House Club, was seven years *chef de cuisine* at the Reform Club, and afterwards managed the St. James's Hotel in Berkeley Street, and finally the Freemasons' Tavern, until shortly before his death in 1873.

If there was a striking improvement in aristocratic morals in the last part of the 19th century, this was due, according to Frank Harris, not so much to the good example of Victoria, then almost a recluse, but to the Prince of Wales— later King Edward VII—who was leader of the Smart Set:

"Fortunately for England, he preferred the Continental habit of coffee after dinner, black coffee enjoyed with a cigarette. No one who smokes can taste the bouquet of a fine claret, and so the cigarette and coffee banished the habit of drinking heavily after dinner. The Prince, too, preferred champagne to claret and so . . . in the course of a single decade it became the habit in London to join the ladies after having drunk a glass or two of pure champagne during dinner and a cup of coffee afterwards, while smoking a cigarette. . . . The cigarette introduced by the Prince of Wales made London society sober."

Toward the end of Victoria's reign, M. Ménager, a tall Frenchman with a bushy gray moustache, was chef. He was paid £400 a year with a living allowance of £100 a year, which enabled him to live extremely well and to maintain a London house. To assist M. Ménager there were 18 master cooks in white toques, assisted by 2 pastry cooks, 2 roast cooks, bakers, confectioners' chefs, and 2 larder cooks. Under them were 2 assistant chefs, 8 kitchen maids, 6 scullery maids, 6 scourers, and 4 apprentices. Apprentices in the royal kitchens received £15 a year and their keep, but had to buy their own clothes and white overalls (clean every day), and to pay for their own laundry.

In those days there was a permanent indoor staff of more than 300, many of whom were declared redundant and pensioned off on Queen Victoria's death. They included the Queen's four pages, the Scottish servants who rode in full regalia on the box of her carriage, and her Indian servants.

Whenever Emperor William I of Germany visited Queen Victoria, his favorite pie was served. It contained a whole turkey stuffed with a chicken, the chicken stuffed with a pheasant, the pheasant with a woodcock. The mutton pies that Queen Victoria liked are still served at Buckingham Palace. The lamb was brought from Wales, as the Queen considered it to be the tenderest lamb available and would have no other served in the royal household.

Meat was eaten in enormous quantities. Huge coal ranges roared away at either end of the Buckingham Palace kitchens, with six spits in front of each, large enough to take 35 chickens at once. Often up to 350 pounds of meat would be roasted in a day. A great amount of venison was also served, and chefs thought nothing of using 200 pheasants at a meal. The 140-pound barons of beef served at banquets, or at Christmas, were always roasted before these open coal ranges in the kitchens, as was all the food served at breakfast each day for the royal family and household, when the spits were packed with chops, steaks, bloaters, sausages, chicken, and woodcock, which the roast chefs piled onto huge platters. Usually Queen Victoria had just a boiled egg for

The Royal Family of George V, by John Lavery

***Conversation Piece at the Royal Lodge, Windsor,* showing George VI, the Queen Mother, Elizabeth II, and Princess Margaret Rose, by Herbert James Gunn**

breakfast, served in a gold egg cup with a gold spoon, while two of her Indian servants in their showy scarlet and gold uniforms stood behind her chair in case she wanted anything. The Indian cooks and servants, because of their religion, could not use the meat that came into the kitchens, so they killed all their own sheep and poultry for the royal curries. Nor would they use even the best imported curry powder, but worked Indian-style, grinding their own spices between two large round stones and preparing all their own flavorings. The curry was served every day at luncheon, whether it was eaten or not. Leftovers were given to charitable organizations and the poor. After any large function at Buckingham Palace, queues of people came with baskets to collect the broken food from the royal table.

When Edward VII (1901–10) came to the throne, he got rid of his mother's curry-makers, and engaged an Egyptian to serve Turkish coffee in the dining room in full regalia after dinner.

King Edward and Queen Alexandra took a more active interest in good food than Queen Victoria. Edward liked plain food, "good English cooking." Although, of course, there were elaborate French dishes at banquets and he enjoyed such dishes as ortolans sautés in brandy, he was just as fond of boiled beef and carrots. It was Edward who introduced the custom of serving roast beef with Yorkshire pudding and horseradish sauce at Buckingham Palace every Sunday night.

There were lunches and hampers for Ascot, the Derby, and Goodwood each year, and cold suppers to be served in a private room at the Royal Opera House, Covent Garden. Food was taken there in hampers, and the guests dined in the interval from 8:30 to 9:30 in a room at the back of the royal box. Six footmen and a chef went down in the afternoon with hampers of gold plate. Sometimes there were ten or twelve courses, all cold. The meal always began with cold consommé, followed by lobster mayonnaise, plovers' eggs, lamb cutlets, mixed sandwiches, and fruit, and ending with patisserie. At Balmoral in October, 1906, the picnic lunch for the stag shooting party led by Edward VII consisted of Scotch broth and mulligatawny soup, hashed venison, stewed mutton, game pies, and Irish stew, with plum pudding and apple fard.

George V (1910–36) had very simple tastes and was really interested in almost no food except curry and Bombay duck. Queen Mary had a great feeling for royal traditions and was a connoisseur

Dining room at the Royal Pavilion, Brighton

of good food, but when the royal family dined at home, there was a good deal of Irish stew, cottage pie, and cutlets with mashed potatoes—fare that the king had become used to in the Navy. With the outbreak of war in 1914 George ordered strict food rationing; at the royal table meals were cut to three courses, meat was served only three times a week, and no wine was served. M. Henri Cedard, the royal chef, could hardly believe his instructions and sent up a note asking what was to be served. The answer came back in Queen Mary's handwriting: "Serve boiled water with a little sugar in the dining room." Centuries of rich living were now at an end.

Elizabeth II likes simple, nonfattening foods, and some years ago canceled the weekly order for her favorite chocolate-coated violet creams. Prince Philip is a "hearty, unfussy eater" who likes "good red meat." No oysters have been served at the Palace since the reign of Edward VIII (later the Duke of Windsor), who was very fond of them. The Queen enjoys barbecues at Balmoral, at the picnic parties that follow royal shooting expeditions. In the past, queues of servants used to lay out quantities of food on checked tablecloths; now, however, Queen Elizabeth likes to cook at the barbecue, and serves her guests with her own hands. One wonders what her ancestors would have said!

Royal Recipes

Quenelles of Polenta

1 cup water	2 whole eggs
¾ cup butter or margarine	2 egg yolks
1 teaspoon salt	2 ounces grated Parmesan cheese
1 cup yellow corn meal	

In a saucepan heat water, butter, and salt. When it comes to a rapid boil add the corn meal. With a wooden spoon stir the corn meal until it becomes a compact paste. Remove from heat and stir in one by one the whole eggs, egg yolks, and Parmesan cheese. Shape the mixture into quenelles with two dessert spoons, the bowls of the spoons measuring about 3 inches long. Push the quenelles from the spoon with a rubber spatula into simmering water. Cook about 5 minutes on each side, turning with a slotted spoon. Drain on a paper towel. Makes 12 quenelles.

Soup Lorrain

¼ pound blanched and finely ground almonds	1 sliced hard roll
	1 egg yolk
2 cups minced cooked chicken	3 tablespoons butter or margarine
1½ quarts veal or chicken stock	¼ teaspoon mace salt and pepper
	1 loaf French bread

Put almonds, chicken, stock, and the sliced hard roll in a saucepan and boil for 5 minutes. Remove from heat. Beat egg yolk slightly and stir in about 1 cup of hot stock, blending well; return to saucepan. Pour through a fine strainer. To the almond-chicken mixture add butter, mace, and salt and pepper to taste. Cut the top off the French bread and lay top aside. Scoop out the soft inside of the bottom, leaving the crust intact. Fill the shell with the mixture and replace the top. Put the filled loaf in a tureen or deep platter and pour over the soup. Makes 6 servings.

Kitchen at the Royal Pavilion

The Great Kitchen at the Royal Pavilion, from the John Nash print

Spit mechanism in the kitchen of the Royal Pavilion

"The Only Soup Ever Eaten by Queen Victoria"

¼ cup barley
1 cup water
1½ quarts white stock
1 cup heavy cream
salt

Rinse barley and put into a deep saucepan with 1 cup water. Scald and drain. Add stock to the barley, cover, and simmer over low heat for 1 hour. Remove a third of the soup to another saucepan. Rub remainder through a hair sieve or put into a blender. Pour into the unsieved soup. Add 1 cup heavy cream gradually, stirring constantly. Salt to taste. Makes 6 servings.

White Stock

1½ pounds veal or
 chicken bones or
 both
4½ quarts cold water
1 tablespoon salt
1 small carrot
2 turnips
2 leeks
1 onion stuck with 2
 whole cloves
bouquet garni

Parboil bones just long enough for scum to rise to the top. Skim thoroughly and drain. Cover the bones again with 4½ quarts cold water, and remaining ingredients. Bring to boil and cook slowly for 2 hours. Strain and cool. Remove any fat that has risen to the top and refrigerate. Makes about 1½ quarts.

Hotch Potch

2 pounds neck of
 mutton or lamb
3 quarts water
6 small carrots,
 chopped
6 small turnips,
 chopped
6 small onions,
 chopped
2 cups peas
1 small cabbage,
 chopped
1 small cauliflower,
 broken into florets
salt and pepper
2 tablespoons chopped
 parsley

Trim away any fat and cut meat into pieces. Place meat in a large deep kettle and add water. Bring slowly to a boil and carefully remove scum. Cover and simmer for 1 hour. Add carrots, turnips, onions, and peas and cook for 15 minutes. Drop in cabbage and cauliflower and cook until all vegetables are done. Salt and pepper to taste. Ladle into a soup tureen and sprinkle with parsley. Makes 6 to 8 servings.

Oysters in Gravy

1 quart oysters
1 cup dry white wine
¼ teaspoon mace
¼ teaspoon ground
    ginger
2 tablespoons butter
    or margarine

3 tablespoons flour
salt and pepper to
    taste
½ cup blanched and
    finely ground
    almonds

Pick over the oysters, removing any small pieces of shell. Put the oyster liquor (about ¾ cup) into a saucepan and add the wine, oysters, mace, and ginger. Cook gently until the edges of the oysters begin to curl. Remove the oysters and strain the liquid through a dampened piece of cheesecloth. Melt the butter, add flour, salt, and pepper, and let cook 1 minute. Pour in the liquid and cook while stirring until thickened. Add the almonds and oysters. Adjust the seasoning and serve with toast points if desired. Makes 6 to 8 servings.

Matelotte of Fish

1½ pounds halibut, cod,
    or other firm
    white fish
    salt and pepper
4 ounces fresh mush-
    rooms, sliced
2 truffles (optional),
    sliced
2 tablespoons chopped
    chives or green
    onions
2 sprigs parsley

1 bay leaf
1 onion stuck with a
    clove
1 cup white wine
    (not too dry)
1 cup fish stock or
    water
beurre manié (3
    tablespoons flour
    rubbed into 2
    tablespoons
    butter)

Cut fish into serving pieces and sprinkle lightly with salt and pepper on both sides. Put in a shallow baking dish and surround with mushrooms, truffles, and the next 6 ingredients. Cover with foil and bake in a preheated 375° F oven about 45 minutes or until fish flakes easily. Remove dish from oven and take out the onion, parsley, and bay leaf. Pour the liquid into a saucepan and keep the fish warm. Reduce the liquid to 1½ cups, whisk in small pieces of *beurre manié* at a time and cook until thickened. Adjust the seasoning. Spoon the mushrooms and truffles on top of the fish and pour over the sauce. Serve from the baking dish. Makes 4 servings.

John I of Portugal Entertains John of Gaunt, from a manuscript of the *Chronique d'Angleterre*

Jellied Fish

1 whole fish, about 4
    pounds, carp,
    haddock, or other
    white fish
1 large onion, cut in
    quarters
1 bay leaf

1 whole carrot
2 teaspoons salt
2 cups white wine
2 cups water
    lemon slices
    parsley
    mayonnaise

Clean fish and remove head and tail. Put the head and tail in a kettle and add the next 6 ingredients. Cover and simmer 1½ hours. Strain stock through a damp cloth and return to kettle. Cut fish into pieces and cook in the stock for about 15 minutes. Remove fish, discard skin and bones, and flake coarsely. Return stock to heat and reduce to 1½ cups and cool. Put fish in serving dish and completely cover with chilled stock. Refrigerate until jellied. Garnish with lemon slices, parsley, and mayonnaise. Makes 6 servings.

Fillet of Sole in Claret

4 fillets of sole
4 tablespoons butter
    or margarine

2 teaspoons anchovy
    paste
½ cup claret
    lemon or orange
    slices

Place the fillets in a greased baking dish. Melt butter in a saucepan and stir in anchovy paste. Add the claret and heat. Pour over the fish and cover with foil. Place in a 375° F oven and cook for about 20 to 30 minutes. Baste the fish twice during the cooking time, but do not turn. Remove the fillets to a warm platter and pour over the sauce. Garnish with slices of lemon or orange. Makes 4 servings.

Egurdouce of Fysshe
(Sweet and Sour Fish)

1½ pounds flounder, cod, or other white fish	2 tablespoons vinegar
	1 tablespoon sugar
salt and pepper	1 small onion, sliced
2 to 3 tablespoons flour	2 teaspoons raisins
¼ cup cooking oil	2 teaspoons currants
¾ cup white wine (not too dry)	1 whole clove
	1 bay leaf

Cut fish into serving size pieces. Lightly salt, pepper, and dust with flour on each side. Fry fish in the oil until golden, and drain on paper towel. Boil together wine, vinegar, sugar, onion, raisins, currants, and seasoning. Cook until onion is transparent and just fork tender. Arrange the fish on a warm platter. Spoon the onion on top and pour over the sauce. Makes 4 servings.

Pheasants à la Dauphinoise

2 pheasants	2 cups white stock (chicken or veal)
2 carrots, diced	¼ teaspoon thyme
2 onions, diced	1 bay leaf
2 stalks celery, diced	salt and pepper
3 tablespoons butter or margarine	Allemande sauce
2 slices bacon, chopped	1 cup fine bread crumbs
2 tablespoons Madeira	2 ounces grated Parmesan cheese
2 cups white wine	butter or margarine

Clean and truss the pheasants. In a large kettle cook carrots, onions, and celery in butter with bacon for about 5 minutes. Add Madeira and cook 2 minutes more. Place pheasants in kettle and add wine, stock, thyme, and bay leaf. Cover and simmer 1½ hours. Remove the pheasants to a low casserole, cool, and cut away the string. Reduce the stock to 1½ cups, salt and pepper to taste, strain and reserve for Allemande sauce. Spoon cooled Allemande sauce entirely over the pheasants and sprinkle with the combined crumbs and cheese. Dot with butter. Place in a 375° F oven and bake unil golden. Serve the pheasants on a large platter and garnish with a border of quenelles of polenta. Pour Italian sauce around them. Makes 10 to 12 servings.

Allemande Sauce

5 tablespoons butter	2 teaspoons lemon juice
4 medium mushrooms, chopped	¼ teaspoon nutmeg
5 tablespoons flour	2 egg yolks
1½ cups pheasant or chicken stock	4 tablespoons heavy cream

Sauté mushrooms in butter for 2 to 3 minutes. Stir in flour and blend well. Add chicken stock, lemon juice, and nutmeg. Cook, stirring, until mixture is smooth. Mix together in a bowl the egg yolks and cream. Beat in very gradually ½ cup of the hot sauce. Pour yolk mixture back in the saucepan, beating all the time. Reheat without boiling. Strain and discard the mushrooms. Yields 1½ cups.

Italian Sauce

6 shallots, minced	3 cups Espagnole sauce or brown gravy
¼ cup butter or margarine	
½ cup chopped mushrooms	salt and pepper
¾ cup white wine	2 tablespoons chopped parsley

Mince shallots and simmer in butter until soft but not colored. Stir in mushrooms and cook 3 minutes more. Add wine and reduce to ½ cup. Add Espagnole sauce or gravy and cook for 10 to 15 minutes. Salt and pepper to taste and sprinkle with parsley.

Farced Mushrooms

2 cups cooked finely minced chicken	¼ teaspoon nutmeg
	16 to 20 large mushrooms
⅓ cup fine bread crumbs	¼ cup melted butter
3 tablespoons light cream	½ cup hot water
2 egg yolks	2 teaspoons lemon juice
½ teaspoon salt	
⅛ teaspoon pepper	beef gravy (optional)

Mix together chicken, bread crumbs, cream, and egg yolks. Add salt, pepper, and nutmeg, and blend thoroughly to form a smooth paste. Wipe the mushrooms with a damp paper towel and remove the stems. Fill the mushrooms with the chicken mixture, mounding it up over the tops.

Place in a shallow baking pan. Pour in the melted butter, water, and lemon juice. Cover with foil and bake in a preheated 350° F oven for about 20 minutes. Baste twice during the cooking with the liquid in the pan. Serve on a warm platter surrounded by gravy if desired. Makes 4 to 6 servings.

Patties à la Reine

½ pound mushrooms, sliced
¼ cup butter or margarine
¼ cup flour
1 teaspoon salt
⅛ teaspoon pepper
1 cup chicken stock
2 egg yolks
¾ cup medium cream
1 cup cooked diced chicken
¾ cup cooked diced tongue
6 patty shells

Sauté mushrooms in butter. Blend in flour, salt, and pepper. Add stock and cream and cook, stirring constantly, until thickened. Add beaten egg yolks and cook 1 minute more. Fold in chicken and tongue and cook until heated. Fill patty shells. Makes 6 servings.

Florendine of Veal

2 veal kidneys
2 tablespoons butter
3 tablespoons flour
1 cup white stock
½ cup dry white wine
2 teaspoons orange flower water
¾ teaspoon salt
½ teaspoon mace
1/16 teaspoon cayenne pepper
peel of ½ lemon, grated
2 tablespoons currants
1 medium apple, chopped
puff pastry

Wash kidneys thoroughly in cold water. Pat dry with a paper towel. Cut kidneys into 1-inch pieces. Sauté in butter for 3 or 4 minutes. Stir in flour, add stock, wine, and flower water. Cook until thickened. Mix in the seasoning, lemon peel, currants, and apple. Pour into a 4-cup casserole and cover with puff pastry. Bake in a preheated 425° F oven for 30 minutes or until golden. Makes 4 to 6 servings.

Patties à la Reine

Pork Tartlet

⅛ teaspoon saffron	½ teaspoon thyme
2 eggs, slightly beaten	peel of 1 lemon cut
2 pounds ground pork	in slivers
½ cup bread crumbs	2 tablespoons currants
¾ teaspoon salt	pastry for 1 pie
⅛ teaspoon pepper	crust

Stir saffron into beaten egg and add to pork with the remaining ingredients except pastry. Shape mixture into an oval loaf about 8 inches long and 4 inches wide. Roll out pastry in an oval shape about 3/16 inch thick and place loaf, top side down, on the dough. Bring the long sides of the dough up and over to just lap, moisten the edges with water and press to seal. Shape and trim the dough at each end, fold up and seal. Place on a clean cloth slightly longer than the loaf. Roll it tightly and tie both ends with string. Place a small rack or pan in a kettle so that the loaf does not touch the bottom. Fill with salted water just to cover the loaf. Bring to a boil and boil gently for 1½ hours. Remove from kettle and unwrap. Place on a warm platter and garnish with parsley. This resembles a meat loaf wrapped in dumpling dough. If a sauce is desired, add 1 cup of the liquid to 1 cup of thickened chicken broth. Makes 6 to 8 servings.

Dining room at Osborne House, Isle of Wight, the favorite country residence of Victoria

Swedish Meat Ball

½ pound uncooked chicken	4 cups well-seasoned chicken or veal stock
½ pound uncooked veal	3 tablespoons flour
⅓ cup soft bread crumbs	1 tablespoon lemon juice
1¼ cups light cream	1½ teaspoons sugar
1 egg, unbeaten	1 egg yolk
1¼ teaspoons salt	
½ teaspoon white pepper	

Put meat through grinder three times. Soften crumbs with ¼ cup cream and mix into the meat. Mix in the egg, salt, and pepper and form into balls. Heat the stock in a large skillet and simmer the meat balls for about 15 minutes. Turn them several times during the cooking. Remove with a slotted spoon and keep warm until all are cooked. Reduce the stock to 2 cups, mix the flour with a little water to make a thin paste, and add to the stock. Cook until slightly thickened. Stir in the remaining cream, lemon juice, and sugar. Beat ½ cup of the hot sauce into the egg yolk and return to the sauce. Do not let boil after adding the yolk. Arrange meatballs on a warm platter and pour over the sauce. Makes 4 to 6 servings.

Beef à la Mode

4 pounds top round	1 bay leaf
10 to 12 strips larding pork	4 peppercorns
brandy	2 shallots, chopped
1 tablespoon finely chopped parsley	1 large clove garlic, crushed
salt	2 tablespoons bacon drippings
pepper	1 cup beef stock
nutmeg	2 calf's feet, blanched
2 cups white wine	(optional)
¼ teaspoon basil	12 small white onions
¼ teaspoon thyme	12 small carrots,
2 whole cloves	scraped

Lard meat with strips of pork that have been dipped in brandy and sprinkled with parsley. Rub the meat with salt, pepper, and a grating of nutmeg. Place meat in a bowl and add the next 8 ingredients. Marinate for several hours or overnight in the refrigerator, turning the meat from time to time. Remove meat and pat dry with a paper towel. In a large kettle, brown meat on all sides in bacon drippings. Add marinade, beef stock, and calf's feet. Cover and simmer slowly about 3 hours or until tender. Add the onions and carrots the last half hour of cooking. Adjust the seasoning. Remove the meat and vegetables to a warm platter. Spoon over some of the strained liquid and serve the remainder in a sauce boat. Makes 8 servings.

Victorian Salad

Scotch Beef and Onion Collops

2 tablespoons butter
  or margarine
1 pound ground round
  steak
1 onion, chopped
1 cup water
2 tablespoons oatmeal
1 teaspoon salt
½ teaspoon pepper
4 slices toast, crust
  removed, cut in
  half and deep-
  fried

Melt butter in a skillet and add meat. Stir until the meat browns. Add onion, water, oatmeal, salt and pepper. Cover and simmer for 40 minutes, stirring occasionally. Remove to a heated meat platter and garnish with deep-fried croutons. This may be served with poached eggs on top, allowing 1 to each person. Makes 4 servings.

Sausage Meat

2 pounds ground
  pork (put through
  grinder twice)
2 tablespoons finely
  minced onion
2½ teaspoons sage
½ teaspoon freshly
  ground nutmeg
½ teaspoon pepper
1¼ teaspoons salt
¼ teaspoon cayenne
  pepper
2 egg yolks

Blend the ground pork with the next 7 ingredients. Form into cakes and fry until brown. This sausage will keep for several weeks in the refrigerator.

Fricasy of Double Tripe
(Tripe in Wine)

1½ pounds fresh tripe	2 tablespoons chopped
1 cup white stock	parsley
1 cup dry white wine	¼ teaspoon each
3½ ounces capers,	marjoram, basil,
drained	nutmeg
peel of ½ lemon,	¼ teaspoon salt
slivered	3 egg yolks, beaten

Wash tripe thoroughly in cold water and cut in 2-inch strips. Place in a heavy casserole and add the stock and the next 8 ingredients. Cover and simmer over low heat for 6 hours. Remove the tripe and keep warm. Reduce the liquid to 1 cup. Add the egg yolks, place over very low heat, and stir until thickened. Do not allow to boil. Add tripe and heat. Serve on a warm platter surrounded by toast points. Makes 4 servings.

Peppers with Risotto Filling

6 small green peppers	¼ cup chopped
4 tablespoons butter or	Canadian bacon
margarine	1½ cups cooked rice
1 large onion, chopped	salt and pepper
½ pound chicken livers,	
chopped	

Slice off the tops of the peppers and remove the seeds. Blanch the peppers by dropping them into boiling water for 5 minutes. Remove and drain. Sauté onion in butter until almost tender, add the livers and bacon, and cook until done. Mix liver-onion mixture into the rice; moisten with more butter if necessary and salt and pepper to taste. Stuff the peppers lightly and place them in a shallow baking dish; add a little water and cover with a piece of foil. Bake in a preheated 375°F oven for 15 minutes. For large peppers, double the recipe. Makes 4 to 6 servings.

Two menus from banquets prepared at Buckingham Palace for Elizabeth II

MENU

Crème Germiny

Sole Veronique

Filet de Boeuf Braisé Médicis

Petits Pois au Beurre. Pommes Fondantes

Salade Lorette

Soufflé Glacé à l'Empereur

Friandises

Fruits

WINES

Sherry-Tarifa 1890

Deidesheimer Grain Riesling Auslese 1945

Domaine de Chevalier 1937

Pol Roger 1934
Chateau Yquem 1928

Port—Taylor Vintage 1927

MENU

Charantais Melon

Barbue Saumonée Americaine

Carré d'Agneau Romarin
Petits Pois Frais
Haricots Verts
Pommes Nouvelles
Salade

Bombe Mocha

WINES

Niersteiner Schnappenberg 1966

Château Langoa Barton 1959

Krug 1959

Delaforce 1945

Elizabeth II and Prince Philip at a state dinner at Government House, Ottawa, Canada

Cumberland Sauce

6 tablespoons red
    currant jelly
2 tablespoons orange
    marmalade

¾ teaspoon dry English
    mustard mixed with
    a little water
pinch of cayenne
    pepper
2 ounces sherry

Mix all the ingredients together. If not smooth, rub through a sieve. Serve with cold meats and game. Makes about ¾ cup.

Cinnamon Peas

3 cups peas
4 tablespoons butter
    or margarine

2 teaspoons sugar
½ teaspoon cinnamon
½ cup heavy cream

Cook peas in boiling salted water until almost tender; drain thoroughly. Add butter and cook 3 minutes longer. Mix sugar and cinnamon together and sprinkle over the peas. Toss lightly, add the cream, and heat. Serve in a warm vegetable dish. Makes 6 servings.

Victorian Salad

1 large celery root
2 tablespoons lemon
    juice
1½ cups mayonnaise
3 tablespoons beet
    juice
2 teaspoons salt
½ teaspoon pepper

8 medium potatoes,
    boiled and cubed
celery root
6 artichoke bottoms,
    cut in small strips
12 cooked asparagus
    tips, about 3
    inches long
2 truffles, sliced

Peel and dice celery root. Cover with water add lemon juice, and boil 3 minutes or until tender crisp. Drain and cool. Mix mayonnaise, beet juice and seasoning together. Pour the dressing over potatoes, celery root, and artichokes. Toss together lightly. Arrange in a bowl and garnish with asparagus tips and truffles. Refrigerate until ready to serve. Makes 8 to 10 servings.

Duke of Windsor's Gingerbread

½ cup butter or margarine
⅓ cup brown sugar
1 egg
1 cup molasses
2 cups flour
1½ teaspoons baking soda
2 teaspoons ground ginger
1 teaspoon ground caraway seeds
2 teaspoons allspice
2 tablespoons chopped candied orange peel
1 cup chopped almonds
1 cup hot water

Cream butter and sugar until light. Beat in egg and molasses. Reserve ¼ cup of flour to be mixed with candied peel and nuts. Add sifted dry ingredients and beat until smooth. Mix in candied peel and nuts and blend in hot water. Pour into a 13 x 9 x 2-inch greased pan and bake in a preheated 325° F oven for about 30 to 40 minutes. Makes 24 two-inch squares.

Potato-Lemon Cheesecakes

puff pastry
¼ cup melted butter
⅛ teaspoon salt
rind of 1 lemon, grated
¾ cup hot mashed potatoes
½ cup sugar and 2 teaspoons
3 eggs, slightly beaten

Line 6 muffin tins with puff pastry. Add butter, salt, and lemon rind to the potatoes. Beat together ½ cup sugar and the eggs and mix into the potatoes. Fill each uncooked tart shell ¾ full, about 2 tablespoons in each tart, and sprinkle the tops with the remaining 2 teaspoons sugar. Cook in preheated 425° F oven for 30 minutes or until golden.

New College Pudding

1½ ounces fresh beef suet, finely minced
4 ounces soft bread crumbs
4 tablespoons sugar
⅛ teaspoon salt
½ teaspoon nutmeg
peel of ½ lemon, grated
2 to 3 tablespoons currants
1 egg, slightly beaten
1 tablespoon sherry

Work suet well into the bread crumbs with fingertips. Add sugar, salt, nutmeg, lemon peel, and currants. Mix together the beaten egg and sherry and add to the bread-crumb mixture. Let stand 15 minutes. Have ready a chafing dish over boiling water. Form mixture into 4 oval-shaped cakes flattened on the bottom. Rub chafing dish with a little butter before putting the cakes in. Cover and let steam about 1¼ hours or until the bottom is nicely browned. Serve hot. Makes 4 servings.

Queen Cakes

¼ pound butter
½ cup sugar
2 eggs, separated
½ teaspoon each nutmeg, mace, cinnamon
1 cup flour
⅓ cup currants

Cream butter, add sugar gradually, and beat until fluffy. Beat in egg yolks one at a time until thick and lemon colored. Mix spices and currants with flour and add to the first mixture, beating thoroughly. Whip egg whites until stiff but not dry, and fold into the batter. Grease small cupcake tins (which hold 2 tablespoons of batter), and fill almost to the top. Dust each one with a sprinkling of sugar. Bake in a 350° F oven for 20 to 30 minutes. Yields about 18 cakes.

Spode stone china selected by Charlotte, wife of George III

Royal Worcester dessert plate from a service made for George III

Comadore (Fruit and Nut Tarts)

Comadore
(Fruit and Nut Tarts)

½ cup sweet wine
10 dried figs, finely chopped
¼ cup raisins
½ tablespoon cooking oil
¼ cup pine nuts
⅛ teaspoon salt
¼ cup sugar
⅛ teaspoon ginger
⅛ teaspoon mace
⅛ teaspoon clove
¼ teaspoon cinnamon
1 firm apple, peeled, cored, and diced
1 firm pear, peeled, cored, and diced
puff pastry
cooking oil

Heat the wine and drop in the figs and raisins to soften for a few minutes. Lightly brown the pine nuts in the oil. Add the nuts to the wine with the remaining 8 ingredients. Stir over medium heat and cook until all the wine has evaporated and the apple and pear are soft but not mushy. Spread on a plate to cool. Roll out puff pastry to ¹⁄₁₆ inch thick. Cut in 3-inch squares and place not more than 2 teaspoons of the filling down the center of the square, leaving ⅜ inch on each end and ½ inch on the sides. With a pastry brush moisten the edges with water. Roll tightly and pinch the ends to seal. Fry in deep fat (375°) seam side down until golden, turn and cook the other side. Drain on paper towels. Makes about 40 finger-shaped tarts.

Queen Mary Pudding

¼ cup butter
¼ cup sugar
4 egg yolks
½ cup chopped
  almonds or
  hazelnuts
¼ cup chopped ginger

1⅓ cups fine bread
  crumbs
¼ cup golden raisins
2 small firm bananas
2 eggs whites
⅓ cup macaroon
  crumbs

Cream butter and sugar and beat until fluffy. Beat in egg yolks, one at a time. Stir in nuts, raisins, ginger, and bread crumbs. Slice bananas about ¼ inch thick and carefully fold into batter. Whip egg whites until stiff but not dry and fold in. Grease a 6-cup mold and coat the sides and bottom with macaroon crumbs. Lightly spoon mixture into mold. Tie a piece of foil securely over the top. Place in a pan containing hot water coming halfway up the side of the mold. Bake in a 350° F oven for 1½ hours. Unmold onto a hot dish. Serve with a lemon custard sauce. Makes 6 servings.

Rhenish Wine Cream

1 cup Rhine wine
⅓ cup granulated
  sugar
juice of ½ lemon
1-inch stick of
  cinnamon

4 eggs, separated
2 tablespoons con-
  fectioners' sugar
2 tablespoons orange
  flower water

Boil the wine, sugar, lemon juice, and cinnamon stick together for 10 minutes. Beat the egg yolks until very thick and lemon colored. Remove the cinnamon stick and add the hot wine slowly to the yolks. Blend well and stir in the confectioners' sugar and orange flower water. Beat egg whites until stiff but not dry. Fold into the wine mixture. Ladle from the bottom into goblets or compotes. Makes 6 servings.

Prince Charles' Summer Pudding

1 pound strawberries,
  washed, hulls
  removed, and
  chopped (any fruit
  in season may be
  used)

½ cup granulated sugar
  or to taste
2½ cups water
6 tablespoons corn-
  starch
¼ cup cold water

Simmer the strawberries, sugar, and water together for 5 minutes. Strain. Mix cornstarch and cold water to a smooth paste and add to the fruit

Elizabeth II and Prince Philip, with Princess Anne and Prince Charles

juice. Cook cornstarch and juice until thickened. Pour into 4 glasses and chill. Serve with cream. Makes 4 servings.

Chocolate Cake Made with Orange Marmalade

6 ounces semi-sweet
  chocolate
1 cup soft butter or
  margarine
1 cup sugar
5 eggs, separated

2 tablespoons orange
  marmalade
½ cup ground almonds
2 cups sifted all-
  purpose flour
3 teaspoons baking
  powder

Melt chocolate over hot water and cool. Beat the butter and sugar together until creamy. Add unbeaten egg yolks and continue to beat until thick and lemon colored. Blend in melted chocolate, marmalade, and almonds. Sift the flour and baking powder together; add a few tablespoons at a time while continuing to beat. Whip egg whites until stiff but not dry and fold in with a rubber spatula. Pour into a greased and floured 3 x 8-inch springform pan. Bake in a preheated 325°F oven for about 1¼ hours. Cool thoroughly before icing.

Icing

½ cup butter
4 cups confectioners'
  sugar

4 tablespoons double
  strength coffee
ground pistachio nuts
  (optional)

Cream butter and add sugar gradually. Mix in enough coffee to give a spreading consistency. Split cake and frost between layers, on sides and top. Sprinkle with pistachio nuts if desired.

FRANCE

St. Charlemagne from the *Belles Heures* of Jean de Berry

ET THEM EAT cake"—that apostrophe of Marie Antoinette's—has rung down through the ages as the definitive attitude of kings toward the well-being of their subjects, although Henry IV is said to have hoped that "all my subjects may eat stuffed chicken on Sundays."

Charlemagne, the great Frankish emperor (800–814), was a great trencherman if not much of a gourmet. He is honored for having spread the fame of Brie cheese beyond the borders of its village of inception. Charlemagne ate very much, if not very well; his food consisted mostly of meats cooked over open-hearth fires. If fish was available, it too was spit-cooked, or flung into capacious pots and stewed along with meat. His knights enjoyed long and exuberant feasts, sitting on bundles of hay before long, low, flat stones.

The meats and fish were served in copper vessels in the palaces, in wooden ones in the homes. The fingers were the approved utensils, although Charlemagne, or one of his lords, would carve the meat with a sword, reserving the best parts for himself or his favorites. The meat roasters were a select group, and to this day the *rôtisseurs* have perpetuated themselves into a renowned international gastronomic society of that name.

Manners, in medieval times, were as crude as the food, although the children of the nobility were admonished not to "hiccup nor belch" at table, nor were they "to wipe their noses on the towel which they used for drying their hands." The *Boke of Curtasye* also specified that one was not to put knife or dagger in one's mouth, dip meat in the saltcellar, nor, when sitting next to someone, "to put one's knee under his thigh nor spit upon the table." Such actions were characterized as those of "an incurtasye mon."

Perhaps Charlemagne's greatest contribution to the art of dining was to invite women for the first time to partake at table along with the men, so long as "they did not offend with nauseating odors nor noxious perfumes." Another splendid contribution to gastronomy was the inclusion of fruits to consume along with the meat. Birds of

58

various kinds also graced the royal table for the first time. Peacock was the favorite, although swan and stork were also on the menu. Young dormice stuffed with nuts and spices were considered a special treat!

While his companions in arms passed the flowing bowl of wine or mead, Charlemagne preferred cider from Normandy, believing in its medicinal value. Certainly, it did him little harm, as he had four wives and a bevy of mistresses.

Charlemagne died in 814. With him passed French cuisine—for five long centuries. In its place came famine and death by starvation. A few of the nobles and some of the religious holed up in their castles or cloisters. The commoners mixed earth and oxblood with their flour. Acorns, bark, leaves, buds, and berries were tried—and found wanting.

Gradually the famine abated. Illicit deals in grain were nipped and outlawed. Peddlers of food resumed their appointed rounds. Barges of fish arrived at quayside, and whale meat became the dish of the day. New spices—cinnamon, bay, rosemary—and shallots and scallions appeared. Soups were held in highest esteem, three and four different ones being served at the same meal, based on meat juices and veal stock. It is reported that Joan of Arc "put wine in the bottom of a receptacle and poured four or five soups over it. She took nothing else."

The Valois kings came to power in 1328, and with them appears the first of the procession of gifted French chefs: Guillaume Tirel, better known as Taillevent. A restaurant bearing the latter name is today one of the best in Paris.

Fortunately for Taillevent, vast improvements had been made in the technology of the kitchen. The open hearths were being fitted with turnspits, braziers, and damping devices to control heat. Taillevent created 17 sauces using bread as a binder. He wrote the first French cookbook, *Le Viandier*. He perfected ragoûts and hochepots. He even essayed vegetables, coaxing Charles V (1364–80) to eat his first cabbage. At Taillevent's death, his shield bore three cookpots rampant.

The methods of service and royal dining also displayed great changes, with emphasis on style and chic. The king's marshal or *maître d'* was in charge. He aired the dining halls, supervised the clearing and cleaning of tables, designated the seating, and planned the entertainment. He was assisted by the butler, who was in charge of bread and wine service, but more importantly in charge

of "assay"—he saw to it that tasters "assayed the wine and food for poison before the King tasted."

A "sewer" or steward, heading a retinue of squires and pages, served the dishes, usually on bended knee. The king or liege lords carved.

The *entremets* of the time were not dishes but acts—minstrels, magicians, jugglers, dancers. The chefs entered into the fun by producing elaborate "sotelties," such as one offered by the Duke of Burgundy in Lille: an immense pie opened to the strains of 28 musicians playing from within. Out of the pie came a captive girl representing the "captive" Church in the Middle East.

Francis I (1515–47) bridged the Middle Ages into the more halcyon days of French gastronomy. As a gourmet, Francis was pretty much

***Francis I* by François Clouet**

of a flop; in fact, retrogression to heavy drinking bouts alienated the ladies, who no longer attended the banquets on the excuse that the physical act of chewing "detracted from the ethereal appeal of their beauty." A rather modest credit may be given to Francis for his introduction of ass's milk to the tables of France. He took the milk on the advice of his physicians. Whether it was a greater contribution to gastronomy or to the ladies of the court, who bathed in it, is a matter of opinion.

Francis chose the 14-year-old Catherine de' Medici as the consort for his son, who later reigned as Henry II. Her dowry to Henry—and indeed to all France—was the battalion of Italian chefs she brought with her to the Court. She thus enriched the French cuisine with truffles, grated Parmesan cheese, quenelles of poultry, a taste for veal, macaroons, zabaglione, "iced cream," and melons—as well as the glass of Venice, the faience of Urbino, the silver of the great Renaissance smiths (including Benvenuto Cellini), and, above all, the fork. Thomas Coryate, an Englishman, is quoted as saying that the Italians always use at their meals a little fork "of yronn, steele, and some of silver," because they "cannot by any means indure to have his dish touched with fingers, seeing that all mens fingers are not alike cleane."

Catherine herself was at once a gourmet and a glutton. She was a true taste-maker, and, as the mother of three kings, she gave great state banquets, at which over-eating—but not over-drinking—was condoned. In 1571, we are told, a banquet was given in Paris to receive Elizabeth of Austria, the bride of Catherine's second reigning son, Charles IX (1560–74). Because the day was Friday, no meat was served; the assemblage had to make do with two barrels of oysters, 50 pounds of whale meat, 200 crayfish, 28 salmon, 10 turbot, 18 brill, 400 herring, 50 carp, 18 trout, 1,000 pairs of frog legs, lobsters, mussels . . .

Under Henry III (1574–89), Catherine's third son, the Italian influence continued. Apéritifs (some iced) came in, along with that greatest of innovations, iced cream, the triumph of a Sicilian, Francisco Procopio. Milk, butter, strawberries (the lovely little *fraises du bois*), oysters, salmon, and whale tongue roasted and served with an orange sauce graced the king's table. Garlic, to ward off disease, was much in vogue. The chefs, *rôtisseurs*, pastry cooks, caterers were riding high—so much so that their first guilds were founded.

***Louis XIV* by Hyacinthe Rigaud**

Of the reign of Henry IV (1589–1610) little of gastronomic moment is preserved, save the triumph of chicken-in-the-pot and the elevation of the lowly cabbage to regal rank. Cabbage was said to have such remarkable properties as "to provide milk for wetnurses, to stop hair from falling out, and to sharpen one's sense of smell." The use of table linen became prevalent, especially the napkin (tied around the neck to protect the ruffs and furbelows). The vogue for "dining out" was ushered in and continued to spread throughout the 16th century. The eating places were called "cabarets," not yet restaurants. They were a vast improvement over the inns and taverns of previous days. Princes and kings frequented these newfangled dining oases. Henry IV preferred Les Trois Maures in the Marais quarter. Villon and Rabelais selected La Pomme de Pine in the Rue de la Juiverie.

Henry IV was also noted for the elevation of La Varenne, his chef, to Minister of State. His great book, *Le Cuisinier François*, is still available, and includes the first clearly detailed instructions for making pastries. *Sauce poivrade* was his creation.

Louis XIII (1610–43) liked to cook. He made jam and cooked eggs. Nicolas de Bonnefons, later lackey to Louis XIV and great chef of his day, author of *Les Délices de la Campagne*, left these instructions for boiling a royal egg: "Put two pints of water in a casserole and when the water begins to bubble, put in your eggs. Remove the pan from the water and put it aside. When the water has cooled to the point where you can plunge in your hand without burning yourself, take out your eggs. They are done."

French cuisine reached its zenith under Louis XIV (1643–1715), even though Louis himself was more glutton than gourmet. The real credit devolves upon Oliver de Serres, who taught the meat-eaters the glories and benefits of the fruits of the soil. He helped popularize the potato, until then raised as an ornamental plant. He explained that the tomato (known as the "love apple" and considered poisonous) was mighty good eating.

The preparation of good food became an art. Cookbooks proliferated. Food supplies multiplied. The famous chef L. B. Robert wrote, "Pyramids of meats and heavily spiced broths and thick soups are no longer to our taste. Today we prefer an exquisite selection of meats, which each guest is served separately, the finesse of their seasoning, the courtesy and cleanliness of each course." Oysters returned to favor, raw or cooked. Coffee appeared for the first time, and with it the coffee house, or *café*.

Only Louis XIV remained a gourmand rather than a gourmet. His regular fare comprised three or four soups, a whole pheasant, a salad, two or three slices of ham, mutton with garlic, a nice selection of *gâteaux*, and to top it all, eggs prepared in various ways. The great dish of the day,

for those who could afford it, was *pot-à-oie*. To make it, one took a large goose and stuffed it with pheasants, quail, ortolans, woodcock, and pigeons, and roasted it in the oven. The swells ate the stuffing; the servants ate the goose!

The ices and *glaces* of Procopio became very popular, although the product of his imitators left much to be desired. The bakers took to making the new Hungarian conceit, the *croissant*. (This breakfast roll came about, it is said, because the bakers of Budapest, working in their cellars, heard the Turks burrowing under the walls of the city and gave the alarm. To reward them, the Hungarian government permitted them to make a new cake in the shape of a crescent or *croissant*.) Tea and chocolate became a vogue.

Even wine came in for a renaissance, thanks to a Benedictine monk, Dom Perignon in Champagne. He did not invent the secondary fermentation of wine in a bottle, but he did show the French how to capture "the stars" by the use of heavy bottles and the cork.

Faience pitcher decorated with a portrait of Henry IV

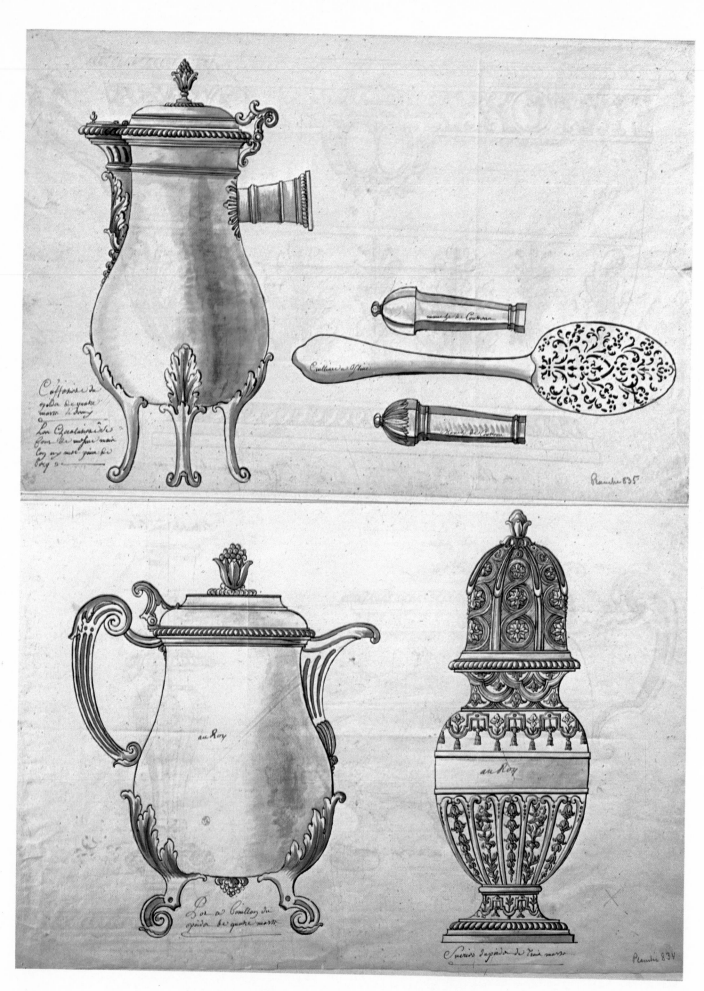

Patterns for silverware for the service of Louis XIV by Nicolas de Launay

Versailles, Louis' great pleasure dome, became the center of French cuisine, manned by more than 50 chefs, cooks, stewards, cellarers, and other professionals of the bottle and skillet. The great chef François Pierre de La Varenne did away with heavy spices and heaped dishes. Meats were served in their own reduced juices, fish in a rich *fumet* of heads and tails; *roux* (that sublime thickness of flour and butter), *pâtés*, and *duxelles* (of mushrooms) were introduced. In 1651 La Varenne wrote *Le Cuisinier François*, the bible of the new cuisine. In it, for the first time, appeared *Béchamel*, that subtle concoction of chicken or veal stock with *roux* and cream.

A typical day for Louis XIV began with a grand levée, with 100 courtiers in attendance to assist the king in donning his morning dress. Bread, wine, and water accompanied the ceremony. After mass, lunch followed with the "sewers" shouting "The king's meat!" as the dishes were carried in. At 10 o'clock came the main meal: soups, a still champagne or a syrupy "Hyppocras" (wine, honey, and aromatics), birds, meats, cakes, fruits, and jam. Mme. de Maintenon, Louis' mistress, said that if she ate half as much as Louis consumed, she would die within a week. To correct his gout, the king was regularly sweated and fed overripe fruit.

The enigmatic Vatel emerges as the great man of the era. More than a chef, he was an *officier de bouche*, the master of cooks, service, and cuisine. His dicta on the art of carving have gone into history: "A carver should be well-bred, inasmuch as he should maintain a first rank among the servants of his master. Pleasing, civil, amiable, and well disposed, he should present himself at table with his sword at his side, his mantle on his shoulder . . . he should make his obeisance when approaching the table, proceed to carve the viands, and divide them understandingly according to the number of guests . . . he should be very scrupulous in his deportment, his carriage should be grave and dignified, his appearance cheerful, his eye severe . . ."

Vatel's own serenity dissolved when the king arrived at Chantilly in April, 1671, with an entourage far larger than expected. Various meats and fish, though ordered, had not arrived. There was a shortage of food. Mme. de Sévigné wrote her daughter, the Comtesse de Grignan: "I have just learned of what passed at Chantilly. The king arrived on Thursday night. The walk, the collation which was served in a place set apart for

the purpose, and strewn with jonquils, were just as they should be. Supper was served but there was no roast meat at one of two of the tables. This affected Vatel's spirits and he was heard to exclaim 'I have lost my fame. I cannot bear this disgrace!' When during the night the fish for the next day's lunch did not appear in adequate quantity either, it was too much. Vatel ran himself upon his sword." Some say it was a bacon slicer, but the result was the same—poor Vatel was dead.

Probably the most oft-told tale of Louis at his height concerns the unfortunate Nicolas Fouquet, Louis' superintendent of finance. Thanks to acumen, a bit of conniving, and a lot of sharp dealing, Fouquet was able to rear a lovely country seat at Vaux-le-Vicomte. André Lenôtre, the great gardener, did the landscaping; the equally great Louis Le Vau was the architect. Vatel, then a rising *maître d'hôtel*, supervised the chefs in preparing a banquet for 500. Ortolans, quail, pheasant, partridge, bisques, and ragoûts were prepared. Champagne and the wines of Beaune flowed. Fireworks illuminated the sky. La Fontaine stated, *"Le ciel en fut jaloux"* ("Heaven was envious"). That may or may not have been so, but Louis was! Three weeks later Fouquet was arrested for embezzlement, stripped of his office and his fortune, and the 23-year-old Louis began to build Versailles!

Louis outlived his heir, the Dauphin, as well as the Dauphin's son and heir. He outlived an entire generation of his subjects. His great-grandson, the five-year-old Louis XV (1715–74), became king, and the late king's nephew, Philippe, Duc d'Orléans, became regent.

Philippe introduced elegance, but not grandeur, to French society. The *petits soupers* were his innovation—intimate, no-nonsense dinners for two or three couples. Gastronomy took the place of gluttony. Conversation, wit, and the *mot juste* took the place of fireworks and lavishness. The regent and eventually Louis XV both could cook. Louis' wife, Maria Leszczynska, was not to be outdone in the kitchens. He was served *bouchées à la Reine, poulet à la Reine, consommé à la Reine*. The court favorites also had dishes named after them: *cotelette à la Soubise* (the princess) and *gigot à la Mailly* (the duchess).

This was indeed an era of fine cuisine and glorified chefs. Brillat-Savarin, the historian of good living, epitomized the day: "A new dish confers more happiness on humanity than the discovery of a new star." The great chef Marin, *maître d'* of the Prince de Soubise, wrote, "Old cookery suffered from an excess of spices. Modern cookery is a sort of chemistry." He it was who created for Louis XV the omelette to end all omelettes, containing cock's combs and carp's roe.

The Duc de Richelieu produced the *tour de force* of all time while in the field during the Seven Years' War. As usual, he had his retinue with him, but unfortunately his larder contained only one carcass of beef and a few vegetables. Nonplussed for but a moment, his chef produced a small battlefield collation consisting of beef consommé, hors d'oeuvres of beef, rump of beef with vegetables, oxtail, beef tongue, *paupiettes* of beef, beef marrow on toast, and fritters of beef brain in orange juice!

The new culinary discoveries of the day included lentils, potatoes in all their guises, filet of sole (to which Mme. de Pompadour lent her name), and *chartreuse* of partridge (to which Mme. Du Barry lent hers). Voltaire warned, "Gluttony will numb the faculties of the mind." But he, himself, was a slave to coffee, consuming 50 cups a day.

Louis XV's court was one of mistresses, morganatic wives, and hangers-on. But instead of the traditional intrigue and mayhem, the great nobles were content if their name was attached to a new dish. Everybody went into the kitchen. The Duc de Villeroi, marshal of France, invented a sauce based on mashed egg yolks bound with butter—*poulet à la Villeroi*.

Louis XV was succeeded by his grandson, then but twenty years of age. Louis XVI (1774–92) was a dull and rather heavy man, full of good intentions. His great claim to gastronomic fame came through his accolade to the potato. It seems

The Picnic after the Hunt by Nicolas Lancret

that Antoine Parmentier, a renowned horticulturist, once presented the king with a bouquet of potato flowers. For a moment there was a hush. Then the king put one flower in his buttonhole and handed the corsage to his Queen, Marie Antoinette, who wore it. The potato was in; it became the national vegetable of France. It is even remembered that once Parmentier prepared potatoes in 20 different ways to regale a dozen guests, including Benjamin Franklin. And so Parmentier, the great gardener, is today remembered only for the potato!

The era is also noteworthy as the beginning of the age of restaurants. Cafés there had been, but never a dining-out place where one might order à la carte. A chef by the name of Beauvilliers is credited with opening the first true restaurant, the Grand Taverne de Londres on the Rue de Richelieu in 1782. It survived all upheavals and continued catering to the aristocracy until 1835.

With the Revolution, cuisine in France slowed down, but not for long. The new leaders tired of the spartan life. The revolutionary Directoire began to give dinners as lavish as the kings'. Great chefs were traded like diamonds. New restaurants opened.

It was said that Napoleon was better on a horse than at the table. He ate at military speed and whenever he felt like it. They tell the story of his poor chef putting six fat hens on the spit, one every half hour, hoping that at least one would be *à point* when the master chose to dine.

His ministers were less spartan. Talleyrand, Napoleon's chamberlain, and Cambacérès, his chancellor, vied with each other as to which could entertain the more lavishly. Once, *chez* Cambacérès, a huge 170-pound sturgeon was served to the guests. The servitors were instructed to pretend to trip, and allow the fish to fall to the ground. Cambacérès rose and shouted, "Bring another sturgeon!" Sure enough, in it came, larger than the one before. Not to be outdone, Talleyrand recruited Carême, with the possible exception of Escoffier the greatest chef of all time.

Mention should be made of the chef François Appert, the inventor of the canning process. In 1795 he conceived the idea of enclosing food in wide-mouthed bottles and then subjecting them to heat to destroy the fermentation that caused foods to spoil. Napoleon appointed him official purveyor to the *Grand Armée*. Several specimens of his handiwork fell into the hands of the Eng-

Marie Antoinette **attributed to Elisabeth Vigée-Lebrun**

lish, who improved on the bottles by substituting tin cans; they first appeared in 1814, and the English took the credit for this revolutionary idea.

The most famous dish associated with Napoleon was, without doubt, chicken Marengo. In the field, having defeated the Austrians at Marengo in 1800, the Little Corporal, instead of chasing the enemy, requested that dinner be served. Alas! there was no butter, no meat. Dunand, his chef, dispatched posses of soldiers. All they could "liberate" from the countryside were three eggs, four tomatoes, six crayfish, a small hen, a little garlic, some oil, and a saucepan. Dunand browned the chicken parts in the oil, and fried the eggs in the same oil with a clove or two of garlic and the tomatoes. He poured over this mixture some water mixed with cognac (from the

general's flask) and put the crayfish atop, to cook in the steam. The dish was served in a tin plate, the chicken surrounded by the eggs and crayfish. Napoleon feasted. He exclaimed, "Dunand, you must feed me like this after every battle!"

Inasmuch as Napoleon was more of a trencherman than gourmet, history leaves us little of his chefs' creations, despite the fact that he had a fantastic succession of chefs to serve him. Aside from Dunand, they included Gaillon and Danger (who accompanied him on his Egyptian campaigns), Venard de La Borde, Coulon, Farcy, Laguipière, Debray, Leconte, Heurtin, Lemoigne. Ferdinand cooked on the island of Elba; Dousseau during the "100 days," and Chandelier at St. Helena. Only Laguipière achieved fame, Carême himself proclaiming him his master. He died of cold on the retreat from Russia, and with him died all his recipes. One thing is certain, they all prepared pasta dishes, of which Napoleon was extraordinarily fond, even to demanding macaroni timbales *à la Milanaise* for dessert! Louis de Cussy, his faithful chief steward, though not a cook, wrote *L'Art Culinaire*. It was Cussy who was on hand at the Tuileries to welcome Napoleon back from Elba. *Fraises à la Cussy*—strawberries, cream, and champagne—was his triumph. Napoleon drank no spirits, save a little cognac in the heat of battle.

Another great gastronomic name of the Empire was that of Grimod de La Reynière, author of *Almanach des Gourmets,* a guide to the restaurants and food purveyors of Paris. He left a number of epicurean adages still worth remembering: "A real gourmet is never late; standing on ceremony at the table works to the detriment of the dinner; eat hot, nicely, and a great deal; a good dinner is one of the greatest joys of man's life; 13 at table is dangerous only when there is just enough to eat for 12." A final adage is more controversial: "Women, who everywhere else are the charm of society, are out of place at a dinner of gourmands!"

Another of the greats of the day was Anthelme Brillat-Savarin. He was born Brillat, but an aunt bequeathed money to him on condition that he add "Savarin" to his name. Outspokenly against the Revolution, he was forced to flee, first to Switzerland and then to America (where he played the violin on the streets). His great work, the *Physiologie du Goût,* appeared in 1825 and was an immediate and huge success. Among his famous aphorisms were these: "Animals feed, man

Napoleon in His Study by **Jacques Louis David**

eats; only a man of wit knows how to dine. The table is the only place where one is never bored —during the first hour. A dessert course without cheese is like a beautiful woman with one eye. To invite someone to your home is to take charge of his happiness all the time he is under your roof."

Probably the greatest name of all, however, was that of Antonin Carême, born in Paris in 1784. One of 25 children, he got his opportunity when he entered the service of the celebrated caterer Bailly. He became a great *pâtissier* but had no intention of remaining in such a restricted calling. He wanted to be the monarch of all (in the kitchen) he surveyed. As he put it, "One master: Talleyrand. One mistress: Cooking."

He served many masters, among them the Tsar of Russia, the Emperor of Austria, the Baron Rothschild, the English Prince Regent, and Louis XVIII, who granted him the soubriquet Carême de Paris. As Louis led a new regime in politics with the Restoration, Carême led a new regime in food. The glories of the French cuisine spread throughout Europe.

Louis XVIII (1814–24) was truly a gourmet king. He patronized the mushrooming great restaurants—Véry's, the Café Bignon, the Rocher de Cancale, Véfour, Café de Paris, Tortoni's. Louis was a master chef himself and was the inventor of a number of recipes that can hardly be recommended to the impecunious. For example, Cotelette Louis XVIII: Place three cutlets under the broiler, one atop the other. Eat the middle one, which has absorbed the juices from the other two; discard the top and bottom ones!

Or Ortolan Restoration: Place the little bird in the stomach of a partridge, having previously lined the cavity with *fois gras* and truffles. Again, discard the host bird!

Charles X (1824–30) was a dullard both in history and at the table. The only noteworthy gastronomic event of his reign was no fault of his. Marshal de Bourmont, a military commander of distinction, invaded Algeria and discovered the glories of *couscous*, that ubiquitous North African dish of crushed rice, mutton, and/or chicken. The French restaurateurs took the dish to their hearts and placed it on their menus.

Louis-Philippe (1830–48) was a gastronomic cipher. If he had any claim to fame, it was frugality. He learned to carve so as to get as many portions as possible from a roast or a chicken. He ordered dinners at prices to conform to his ideas of the importance of the guests. It was during his

reign, however, that the greatest of meat sauces—Béarnaise—was devised.

Napoleon III (1852–70) did little for cuisine; he was more concerned with public works than with public houses. His major contribution was in the construction of Les Halles, the great markets of Paris. Or, if this may be considered a contribution, the rise in acceptance of horsemeat as respectable provender dates from his time. At the very fashionable Grande Hôtel, where official receptions were often given, a menu of 1852 included vermicelli in horsemeat broth, boiled horsemeat, horsemeat *à la mode*, ragoût of horsemeat, and filet of horsemeat with mushrooms. Rum and horse-marrow cake was the dessert!

Aside from the monarch, however, gastronomy marched on. Alexandre Dumas wrote 301 books—the 301st was a cookbook. Gautier, Sainte-Beuve, the Goncourts, Georges Sand—gastronomic literati—all celebrated the *haute cuisine* in their books.

Toward the last years of the reign of Napoleon III, Mège-Mouriès, in the service of the Department of Agriculture, was awarded a patent for the production of margarine. Napoleon III personally congratulated him. Little came of it

Marquise de Pezé and Marquise de Rouget with Her Two Children by Elisabeth Vigée-Lebrun

until the War of 1870. Then he set up a factory, but—history has a way of preceding itself—the butter-makers issued a report that margarine was bad for the "bodily equilibrium." The sole concession: "Margarine may be utilized for stews and certain vegetables, never for cooking potatoes." On this sorry note is concluded the regal history of French food. Napoleon III was the last French monarch. Maurice-Edmond Sailland, known as Curnonsky, latter-day "Prince of Gastronomes," lived in a very republican France.

Not that French cuisine is likely to decline under the Republic. Although Charles de Gaulle is said not to have known what was placed before him, Georges Pompidou is noted as a gourmet *par excellence!*

French cookery has left its high marks on the world of cuisine and seems likely to continue to do so. A French chef, *toque blanche* at the ready, may always be counted on to create a dazzling new concoction. The kings are dead, long live the kings—of gastronomy!

Forest of Fontainebleau by **Jean Baptiste Camille Corot**

Royal Recipes

Oeufs en Meurette

2 cups water	2 sprigs parsley
2 cups dry white wine	beurre manié (1
1 teaspoon salt	tablespoon butter
1 medium onion,	rubbed into 2
sliced	tablespoons flour)
1 bay leaf	4 eggs

In a saucepan boil together, uncovered, the first 6 ingredients. Cook for 20 minutes and strain. Return to heat and add the *beurre manié* little by little until the sauce has thickened. Adjust seasoning and keep warm. Poach the eggs, drain well, and place on a warm serving dish. Pour over the sauce. Makes 4 servings.

Omelette Soufflé

3 macaroons, 2 inches	1 teaspoon orange
in diameter	flower water
1 ounce praline	⅛ teaspoon salt
powder	2 tablespoons clarified
¾ cup confectioners'	butter or
sugar	margarine
3 eggs, separated	

Pulverize the macaroons and praline powder in a blender. There should be about ¾ cup. Beat together in a bowl the sugar, egg yolks, and orange water. Add the pulverized macaroons and praline powder and mix well. Beat the whites of the eggs with the salt until stiff but not dry. Fold the egg whites into the macaroon mixture. Heat the butter in a 8-inch skillet over moderate heat. Do not have it sizzling, since the soufflé should cook and rise slowly. Turn the eggs into the skillet. Turn down the heat and shake the pan gently back and forth over the burner. When it looks just set around the edges remove and put under the broiler, 6 inches from the heat. Broil until just firm and slightly golden. Place a round silver platter or baking dish over the skillet and flip the soufflé over. Sprinkle a light coating of confectioners' sugar through a sieve evenly over the top Put under the broiler just a second to color the sugar. Serve immediately. Makes 4 servings.

Potage à la Condé
(Kidney Bean Soup)

2 cups dried red	1 carrot, grated
kidney beans	3 sprigs parsley
4 cups game or beef	1 bay leaf
stock	4 slices lean bacon,
3 cups water	blanched, fried
2½ teaspoons salt	lightly, and diced
1 medium onion, stuck	1 cup red wine
with a clove	4 tablespoons butter

Put beans in a large kettle and add the stock and water. Bring to a boil and cook for 15 minutes, skimming the surface if necessary. Add the remaining ingredients except the butter. Partially cover and simmer for 2½ hours or until beans are very soft. Drain into a colander and discard the vegetables. Purée the beans with some of the stock in a blender or food mill. Return to kettle. If thinner soup is desired add a little more stock. Bring to a boil and add 4 tablespoons butter. Makes about 6 cups.

Court-Bouillon with White Wine

1 quart white wine	1 stalk celery, diced
1 quart water	1 teaspoon thyme
1 medium onion,	1 bay leaf
diced	4 peppercorns
3 sprigs parsley	1½ teaspoons salt

Combine ingredients and simmer for 30 minutes. Strain.

Court-Bouillon with Red Wine

2 quarts red wine	2 teaspoons salt
1 quart water	6 peppercorns
3 carrots, chopped	1 green onion,
4 onions, chopped	chopped
6 shallots, chopped	2 bay leaves
2 sprigs parsley,	¼ teaspoon basil
chopped	2 cloves

Combine ingredients and simmer for 30 minutes. Strain.

Note: If court-bouillon has to be reduced by boiling, the quantity of salt should be proportionately less.

Shrimp with Sauce

1 pound fresh jumbo shrimp in shell	¼ teaspoon coriander
½ cup chicken broth	⅛ teaspoon rue
½ cup dry white wine	⅛ teaspoon caraway seeds
¼ teaspoon vinegar	⅛ teaspoon cumin
3 tablespoons olive oil	¼ teaspoon salt
½ teaspoon honey	⅛ teaspoon pepper
¼ teaspoon lovage	

Shell the shrimp but leave the tail shell attached. Devein the shrimp, wash, and pat dry with a paper towel. Mix broth, wine, and the remaining ingredients in a large saucepan. Bring to a boil and cook uncovered for 5 minutes. Drop in shrimp, return to a boil, and cook covered for 3 minutes. Place shrimp in a warm serving dish and pour over the sauce. May be served hot or cold, as a first course or as hors d'oeuvres. Yields about 23 shrimp.

Grand Espagnole Sauce

¼ cup butter or margarine	2 quarts brown stock
1 medium carrot, diced	3 sprigs parsley
1 medium onion, diced	1 bay leaf
1 stalk celery, diced	¼ teaspoon each thyme, marjoram, and whole allspice
¼ cup diced ham	½ cup flour
¼ cup diced veal	½ cup tomato purée
	½ cup white wine

In a large kettle sauté in butter the carrot, onion, celery, ham, and veal until tender. Drain off the butter and reserve. Add stock and seasoning. Simmer for 2 hours, skimming if necessary. Strain. To the reserved butter add enough to make ½ cup. Put butter into the kettle, stir in the flour, and cook until lightly brown. Stir in the strained liquid, tomato purée, and white wine. Simmer for 2 hours, skimming when necessary. Cook and refrigerate.

Note: This sauce may be frozen for future use. Salt when using for specific recipes.

Saumon à la Genevoise

2 tablespoons butter or margarine	3 pounds salmon, middle cut
2 shallots, chopped	water
2 carrots, chopped	1 cup Espagnole sauce
1 stalk celery, chopped	beurre manié (4 tablespoons butter rubbed into 4 tablespoons flour
2 cups Madeira wine	
2 sprigs parsley	
1 bay leaf	
¼ teaspoon thyme	salt and pepper

Sauté in butter the shallots, carrots, and celery until tender. Add wine, parsley, bay leaf, and thyme. Cover and simmer 30 minutes. Strain into a kettle just large enough to hold the fish. The liquid should cover no more than ⅔ of the fish. Add a little water if necessary. Cover and braise in a preheated 375° F oven for 30 minutes or until fish flakes easily. Remove salmon to a warm platter. To 2 cups of the wine stock add the Espagnole sauce and the *beurre manié*. Cook until the sauce thickens and is smooth. Salt and pepper to taste. Pour sauce over the salmon and garnish with parsley. Makes 4 to 6 servings.

Brown Stock

4 to 5 pounds of meat and bones (mostly beef but some veal and pork)	2 large stalks celery and leaves, chopped
6 quarts cold water	2 large carrots, chopped
2 medium onions, chopped	2 sprigs parsley
	1 bay leaf
	½ teaspoon thyme
	2 whole cloves

In an open roasting pan brown the meat and bones in a 500° F oven for about 1 hour. Transfer to a large kettle and pour in the water. Bring to a boil and skim. Add the vegetables and remaining ingredients and skim if necessary. Place the cover half on, turn the heat down, and barely simmer for 5 hours. Discard the meat and bones and strain the stock. Reduce the quantity to 2 quarts if there is more, or add water if there is not enough. Cool stock and refrigerate. Remove fat that has formed on top before using. The stock may be frozen for future use.

Fillets de Sole Pompadour

Merlans Entiers au Gratin
(Whole Whiting with Bread Crumbs)

6 shallots
6 ounces mushrooms,
  chopped
6 tablespoons chopped
  parsley
4 whole cleaned
  whitings weighing
  about 1 pound
  each

salt and pepper
nutmeg
1 cup soft bread
  crumbs
butter
3 cups white wine
lemon slices

Butter a shallow pan large enough to hold the fish without touching each other. Cover the bottom of the pan with shallots, mushrooms, and parsley and lay on the fish. Sprinkle the fish with salt, pepper, nutmeg, and bread crumbs, and dot with butter. Pour in the wine and bake in a preheated 375° F oven for 30 minutes. After 10 minutes of cooking, baste well with wine and continue to baste several times. Place fish on a warm platter and surround with mushrooms and shallots and any wine that has not been absorbed. Garnish with lemon slices. Makes 4 servings.

Pike à la Polonoise

2 tablespoons butter or margarine
3 onions, chopped
2 carrots, scraped and chopped
¼ cup chopped ham
3 sprigs parsley
¼ teaspoon each mace and thyme
2 whole cloves
2 bay leaves

2 cups boiling water
1 cleaned whole pike, striped bass, or similar white fish weighing 3 to 4 pounds
1 small turnip, peeled and cubed
¼ teaspoon sugar
Béchamel sauce

Sauté in butter the onions, carrots, and ham, cooking until tender. Add parsley, seasoning, and boiling water. Cover and cook 30 minutes. Strain. Wipe the pike with a damp paper towel and place in a kettle with a lid. Pour in the strained liquid to cover no more than ⅔ of the fish. Cover and braise for about 30 minutes or until the fish flakes easily. Remove, drain, and keep warm. Cook the turnip and sugar in a little of the fish liquid. Drain the turnip and add to the Béchamel sauce. Pour sauce over the fish. Makes 6 servings.

Vegetable dish from the service of Napoleon III

Fillets de Sole Pompadour

4 large fillets of sole
¼ pound fresh mushrooms, minced
3 tablespoons butter or margarine
3 tablespoons minced truffles
2 cups fine bread crumbs
1 teaspoon grated lemon rind
1 egg yolk

¼ teaspoon pepper
⅛ teaspoon ground nutmeg
1½ cups champagne or dry white wine
bouquet garni (sprig of parsley, ½ stalk of celery, bay leaf)
1 pound cleaned shrimp

Wipe fillets with a paper towel and cut in half lengthwise. Salt skin side lightly. In a saucepan cook the mushrooms in butter for 2 minutes. Add the truffles, bread crumbs, lemon rind, egg yolk, and seasoning. Mix together thoroughly. Spread mixture on each fillet, roll and tie with string. Place the fillets and the bouquet garni in a large skillet and pour in the champagne. Cover and poach for about 20 minutes. (Keep just below the boiling point). Cook the shrimp, drain and keep warm. Serve the fillets surrounded by shrimp and pour over the champagne sauce. Makes 8 servings.

Truite au Court-Bouillon
(Trout in Court-Bouillon)

2½ quarts water
1 cup vinegar
2 medium carrots, chopped
1 small onion, chopped
4 shallots, chopped
¼ teaspoon thyme

2 teaspoons salt
6 peppercorns
4 sprigs parsley
4 trout, weighing about 1 pound each, cleaned parsley
2 lemons

Boil the first 9 ingredients together for 20 minutes. Strain and pour liquid into a shallow pan large enough to hold the trout without touching each other. Immerse the fish in the bouillon and cook 5 to 7 minutes or until the fish flakes easily. Drain trout and place immediately in a napkin-covered dish. Garnish with parsley and lemon wedges. Makes 4 servings.

Trout in Wine

½ cup softened butter
2 tablespoons chopped parsley
6 trout, cleaned
3 cups water
1 cup white wine
1 carrot, stuck with 4 whole cloves
1 medium onion, sliced
2 slices white bread
1 teaspoon salt
¼ teaspoon nutmeg
2 tablespoons butter
parsley
lemon

Mix the butter and parsley together. Wipe the inside of the trout with a paper towel and salt lightly. Spread the butter-parsley mixture inside each trout. Place them in a large kettle with the water and wine. Add the carrot, onion, bread torn into fourths, and seasoning. Cover and cook 15 to 20 minutes, depending on the size of the trout. Remove the trout to a warm platter. Discard the onion and carrot. Pour 2 cups of the liquid and bread into a blender and blend until smooth; return to a saucepan. Reduce sauce to 1½ cups. Correct the seasoning and add the butter. If wine is very dry, add 1 teaspoon sugar. Pour over the trout. Garnish with parsley and lemon. Makes 6 servings.

Trout in Wine

Ballotine of Pheasant

1 pheasant	3 truffles, chopped
salt and pepper	1 veal bone
2 tablespoons butter	1 onion stuck with
or margarine	2 whole cloves
⅓ cup chopped	1 carrot
mushrooms	2 cloves garlic
3 ounces ground pork	6 peppercorns
3 ounces foie gras	bouquet garni
½ tsp. salt	sliced truffle

Bone pheasant and lay skin side down on a cloth. Salt and pepper the flesh lightly. Sauté mushrooms in butter for 3 minutes and mix with pork, foi gras, and salt. Spread stuffing over the flesh and sprinkle with the truffles. Roll the pheasant lengthwise into a firm roll and wrap the cloth securely around it. Tie at both ends and at intervals. Put pheasant roll in a large kettle and cover with water. Add veal bone, the carcass of pheasant, onion, carrot, garlic, peppercorns, and bouquet garni. Cover, bring to a boil, and simmer for 1 hour. Remove the ballotine from the stock and cool. Remove cloth and refrigerate for an hour or more. Reduce 6 cups of the stock to one half. Salt to taste. Strain stock, cool, and refrigerate for aspic. Cut ballotine in ½-inch slices and coat with aspic. Decorate each slice with a piece of truffle. Arrange on a platter overlapping and surround with chopped aspic. Decorate edge of platter with fancy cutouts of aspic if desired. Makes 6 servings.

Faience bowl with cover from the service of Henry II

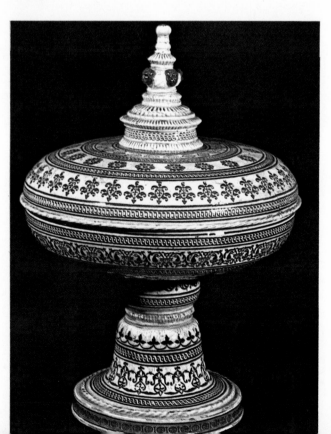

Fricassée of Chicken

1 roasting chicken, 3	4 cups water
to 4 pounds, cut	3 teaspoons salt
up	¼ teaspoon white
½ cup flour	pepper
3 tablespoons clarified	1 tablespoon chopped
butter or	parsley
margarine	beurre manié (6
1 cup chopped	tablespoons butter
mushrooms	rubbed into 6
2 tablespoons chopped	tablespoons flour)
onions	

Dredge chicken with flour. In a large kettle sauté chicken in butter until golden. Remove pieces and sauté mushrooms and onion for 5 minutes. Return chicken to the kettle and add water, salt, pepper, and parsley. Cover and cook gently for 30 minutes or until chicken is tender. Remove chicken to a warm deep serving dish. Reduce the liquid to 3 cups and stir in the *beurre manié* until thickened and smooth. Pour over the chicken. Makes 4 servings.

Boudin à la Reine
(Chicken Croquettes)

3 tablespoons butter	2 cups minced chicken
3 tablespoons flour	1 large egg, beaten
1 cup milk	1 cup fine bread
1 teaspoon salt	crumbs
⅛ teaspoon white	oil
pepper	Béchamel sauce
¼ teaspoon nutmeg	

Make a thick sauce with the first 6 ingredients. Mix in the chicken and spread on a plate to cool. Cover with plastic wrap and refrigerate until very cold and firm. Shape into 8 croquettes. Roll each one in crumbs, dip in egg, and again roll in crumbs. Fry in deep fat (365° F) until golden. Turn carefully so as not to puncture during frying. Drain on paper towel and keep warm in a 350° F oven until serving time. Serve with a thin Béchamel sauce. Makes 8 servings.

Béchamel Sauce

4 tablespoons butter	½ teaspoon salt
4 tablespoons flour	¼ teaspoon white pepper
	2 cups milk

Melt butter over low heat, add flour, salt, and pepper, and cook for 1 minute. Heat the milk and add, stirring, until thickened and smooth.

Ballotine of Pheasant

Wings of Fowls à la St. Laurent

4 half breasts of chicken with wings attached salt and pepper	1 cup very fine bread crumbs
2 egg yolks, beaten	½ cup melted butter or margarine

Season chicken with salt and pepper. Brush chicken all over with egg yolk, dust with bread crumbs, and dip in butter. Bake in a 375° F oven for about 45 minutes or until golden. Serve with the following sauce.

Maréchale Sauce

2 tablespoons butter or margarine	¼ teaspoon salt
¼ pound mushrooms, finely chopped	⅛ teaspoon white pepper
2 tablespoons flour	⅛ teaspoon nutmeg
1 cup milk, scalded	¼ cup heavy cream

Sauté mushrooms in butter for 3 minutes. Add flour and mix thoroughly. Stir in the hot milk, salt, pepper, and nutmeg. Cook until thickened. Add the cream just before serving. Makes 4 servings.

Carolingian ewer of "Charlemagne"

Chicken in the Pot

1 roasting chicken (4 to 5 pounds)	4 quarts water
1 slice ham about 1 inch thick (1 pound)	2 carrots
	1 parsnip
	1 turnip
1 cup toasted bread cubes	1 stalk celery
2 tablespoons chopped parsley	2 leeks
½ teaspoon dried tarragon	1 large onion, stuck with a clove
2 cloves garlic, minced	3 sprigs parsley
⅛ teaspoon pepper	1 bay leaf
2 eggs, slightly beaten	1 teaspoon thyme
	2 tablespoons salt
	½ teaspoon pepper

Chop the uncooked liver, heart, and gizzard of the chicken. Dice 6 ounces of the ham and mix all together with bread cubes, parsley, tarragon, garlic, pepper, and eggs. Stuff the chicken with this mixture, sew and truss tightly. Put 4 quarts of water in a large heavy pot and add the vegetables and seasoning. When the water comes to a boil, place the chicken on its side in the pot. Cover and let simmer slowly for 30 minutes. Turn the chicken on the other side and cook 30 minutes more or until tender but not falling apart. Remove the chicken, drop in the remainder of the ham cut in cubes, and cook the soup another hour. Adjust the seasoning. Serve the soup first and the chicken and vegetables separately if desired. Makes 6 to 8 servings.

Hen Hotch Potch

salt and pepper	¼ teaspoon cinnamon
1 chicken, about 3 pounds, cut in quarters	1 teaspoon salt
3 tablespoons clarified butter	4 slices white bread, toasted and cut in quarters
7 cups beef stock	6 sour grapes or 2 teaspoons lemon juice
1 cup red wine	
¼ teaspoon ground ginger	

Salt and pepper the chicken and sauté in butter until golden. Add the beef stock and wine and cook uncovered for 30 minutes, skimming the surface often. Add the seasoning, toasted bread, and grapes. Partially cover and simmer 1 hour. Remove the chicken to a platter and keep warm. Discard the grapes and put the liquid and the bread into a blender and blend until smooth. The soup is served first. Makes 4 servings.

Roast Duckling

1 duckling, 5 to 6 pounds, or 2 ducklings weighing about 2½ pounds each	4 teaspoons sugar
	1 tablespoon wine vinegar
	1 cup Espagnole sauce
1 large onion, chopped	peel and juice from 1 Seville or bitter orange
2 teaspoons sage	
½ teaspoon salt	orange
¼ teaspoon pepper	orange slices

Wipe duckling with a damp cloth and truss. Toss onion, sage, salt, and pepper together and fill cavity to flavor the duckling. Skewer the vent. Roast in a preheated 375° F oven about 2 hours or until done; 20 minutes to a pound. Remove duckling to a platter and keep warm. Cook the sugar and wine vinegar together until mixture becomes a pale caramel color. Add Espagnole sauce and any juice from the roasting pan after all fat has been removed. Cook 5 minutes over high heat and stir in the orange juice. Strain and add the blanched and drained rind of the orange cut in fine julienne strips. Garnish the platter with orange slices. Serve the sauce in a bowl. Makes 4 servings.

Compotte de Perdrix à Blanc
(Partridge in White Sauce)

3 slices bacon, chopped	1 bay leaf
3 tablespoons clarified butter	1 whole clove
	4 peppercorns
4 partridges or Rock Cornish hens	12 small onions
	½ teaspoon salt
¼ cup chopped mushrooms	¼ teaspoon sugar
	4 whole mushroom caps
4 tablespoons flour	
3 cups chicken stock	2 teaspoons lemon juice
2 sprigs parsley	
4 green onions, chopped	¼ cup water
	4 egg yolks, slightly beaten
¼ teaspoon thyme	1 cup heavy cream

Cover bacon with water and boil 1 minute. Fry bacon and reserve. Combine 3 tablespoons each bacon fat and butter in a large kettle and brown partridges or hens on all sides. Remove from the pan. Add mushrooms and sauté 2 minutes. Stir in the flour and stock and cook until smooth. Add parsley, onion, and seasoning. Lay in the birds, cover, and braise 30 to 40 minutes or until tender. Cook the onions with salt and sugar until done. Drain and reserve. Cook the mushroom caps in lemon juice and water until just tender. Remove the birds and arrange on a deep platter. Surround with the onions and keep warm.

Strain the sauce into a pan and stir in the combined egg yolks and cream. Cook over very low heat until thickened. Do not allow to boil after adding the yolks. Salt and pepper to taste. Pour the sauce over the hens and garnish with chopped bacon and mushroom caps. Makes 4 servings.

Soufflé of Chicken à la Crême

¼ cup butter	1 cup milk
¼ cup flour	1¼ cups finely minced chicken
½ teaspoon salt	
¼ teaspoon white pepper	4 egg yolks
	5 egg whites

In a saucepan melt butter, add flour, salt, pepper, and cook 1 minute. Stir in the milk and cook until thick. Add the chicken and the egg yolks beaten until thick. Allow to cool. Beat egg whites with a pinch of salt until stiff. Mix half of the whites thoroughly into the mixture and fold in the remaining whites. Pour into a 2-quart soufflé dish and bake in a preheated 350° F oven for about 40 minutes or until well puffed and golden brown. Makes 4 to 6 servings.

Gigot de Sept Heures
(Leg of Mutton Braised)

1 leg of mutton	2 small onions, chopped
4 cups chicken or veal stock	
	4 sprigs parsley
½ pound stewing veal	2 bay leaves
4 green onions, chopped	small whole onions
	potatoes
	salt and pepper

Brown meat on all sides. Remove to a roasting pan with a lid. Pour in stock and add the next 5 ingredients. Cover and braise in a 350° F oven for about 4 hours or until meat is tender. During the last half hour of cooking add onions and potatoes cut in ½-inch slices. Remove meat to a warm platter and surround with onions and potatoes. Reduce liquid to one half, add salt and pepper to taste, and pour over the meat and vegetables. Makes 12 to 14 servings.

Note: Lamb may be cooked in this way, reducing the cooking time.

Le Rognon de Boeuf au Vin de Champagne
(Beef Kidneys in Champagne Sauce)

2 beef kidneys	4 shallots
salt and pepper	1 cup champagne or
⅓ cup flour	white wine
1 tablespoon finely	6 tablespoons
chopped parsley	Espagnole sauce
6 tablespoons clarified	
butter	

Remove the skin and fat of the kidneys. Cut in ½-inch slices. Season with salt and pepper and dredge with flour and parsley mixed together. Sauté shallots in clarified butter, remove from pan and reserve. Sauté kidneys about 3 or 4 minutes on each side (kidneys become tough if over-cooked). Return shallots to the pan and stir in wine and Espagnole sauce. Blend well and heat. Remove kidneys to a warm platter and pour over the sauce. Makes 6 servings.

Note: To clarify butter, heat in a small pan; remove white froth as it forms on top; pour off butter, keeping back the sediment.

Jambon au Vin d'Espagne
(Ham with Espagnole Sauce)

1 pound veal bones	¼ teaspoon each nut-
2 medium carrots,	meg, mustard,
scraped and	ground ginger
chopped	2 cups beef stock
2 medium onions,	2 cups sherry
chopped	7-pound ready-to-
3 sprigs parsley	eat ham
2 bay leaves	2 cups Espagnole
	sauce

Put the veal bones in a saucepan with the next 9 ingredients. Cover and simmer for 2 hours. Strain. Trim off the skin of the ham. Score fat every ½ inch in a criss-cross pattern. Place ham in an open roasting pan and pour over the liquid. Bake in a preheated 350° F oven for about 1 hour or until fat is golden. Baste every 15 minutes with liquid in the pan. Remove ham to a warm platter. Skim all fat off the liquid and add the remaining liquid to the Espagnole sauce. Makes 12 to 14 servings.

Les Escalopes de Foie de Veau
(Scalloped Calf's Liver)

6 slices calf's liver,	2 tablespoons chopped
cut ¾-inch thick	parsley
2 tablespoons clarified	2 tablespoons flour
butter	1 cup beef stock
3 shallots, minced	juice of ½ lemon

Lightly salt and pepper the liver. Put butter in a large skillet and cook the shallots and parsley for 1 minute. Add the liver, brown it, and cook no longer than 4 minutes on each side; it should be firm and pink in the center. Remove the liver to a warm platter. Stir in flour and stock and cook until thickened. Add the lemon juice and continue to cook for a minute or two more. Adjust the seasoning. Mask the liver with the sauce. Makes 6 servings.

Potatoes à la Choiseul

3 large baking	¼ teaspoon nutmeg
potatoes	2 egg yolks
2 tablespoons butter	1 egg white
or margarine	cooking oil
1 teaspoon salt	confectioners' sugar

Peel potatoes. Cover with cold water and boil gently until done. Pour off water. Lay potatoes on a paper towel to absorb all moisture. Whip until very smooth and add butter, salt, and nutmeg. Beat in yolks one at a time and then fold in stiffly beaten egg white. With a teaspoon and rubber spatula make well-rounded little balls and drop in 375° F deep fat. Cook until they are golden brown on all sides, turning often. Sprinkle with sugar when ready to serve. Makes 30 to 36 potato balls, 8 servings.

Haricots Verds à la Poulette
(Green Beans with Chicken Sauce)

2 tablespoons butter	1 teaspoon lemon juice
2 tablespoons flour	1 egg yolk
1 cup chicken stock	1 tablespoon chopped
¼ cup chopped	parsley
mushrooms	salt and pepper
1 tablespoon chopped	1 pound cooked string
green onion	beans, cut French
	style

Melt butter, add flour, and cook 1 minute. Gradually add hot stock and cook until thickened. Add mushrooms and green onions and cook over low heat for 10 minutes. Strain, add lemon juice, egg yolk, and parsley. Blend thoroughly. Salt and pepper to taste. Put the well-drained beans in a warm vegetable dish and pour over the sauce. Makes 6 servings.

Choux-fleurs au Parmesan
(Cauliflower with Parmesan Sauce)

1 large cauliflower	4 tablespoons freshly
2 teaspoons butter	grated Parmesan
½ cup soft bread	cheese
crumbs	2 cups Béchamel
	sauce
	3 tablespoons medium
	cream

Wash cauliflower well and remove leaves. Leave the head whole with ½ inch of stalk. Place in a saucepan just large enough to hold the head, and add 2 inches of unsalted water (salt darkens cauliflower). Cover and cook until fork tender. In a small frying pan, melt butter and toss the crumbs until golden brown. Mix in 1 tablespoon Parmesan cheese. Drain the cauliflower and place on a warm serving dish. Pour over ¼ cup of the hot Béchamel sauce. To the remainder of the sauce add cream and Parmesan cheese. Stir until smooth and hot. Pour the sauce around the cauliflower and sprinkle bread-crumb mixture on top. Makes 6 servings.

Brioche au Fromage

2 packages yeast	1 teaspoon salt
½ cup lukewarm water	2¼ cups finely grated
3 tablespoons sugar	Gruyére cheese
5 cups sifted flour	(5 oz.)
½ pound soft butter	1 egg yolk mixed with
7 eggs	1 tablespoon milk

In a large bowl soften yeast in lukewarm water and add 1 teaspoon of the sugar. Beat in 1 cup of the flour and mix well. Turn out on a lightly floured cloth and knead about 5 minutes until smooth. Form into a ball and put into a small greased bowl. Cut a cross in the top, cover with a towel and leave in a warm place to rise. Put into the large bowl 2 cups of the sifted flour;

add ¼ pound of the soft butter, the remaining sugar, salt, and 2 of the eggs. Mix and knead until it is perfectly smooth. Add another ¼ pound of butter, 2 more eggs, and the remainder of the flour. Mix and knead until the dough is no longer sticky. Work in 1 more egg and half the cheese. Mix in another egg and the remaining cheese. Add the ball of sponge, which should be double in bulk, and mix well. Stir in the last egg and work all together to a smooth dough, which will be sticky. Put the dough in a greased bowl, cover and let rise in a warm place until double in bulk. Stir dough down, cover with plastic wrap and put in refrigerator overnight. Grease 2 conventional 5- and 7-inch brioche molds and form the dough into balls large enough to fill the molds ⅔ full. Make a cross on top of each ball with a knife and place a smaller ball of the dough, tapered to a point at the lower end, in the incision. Cover the molds and set in a warm place. When double in bulk, brush the surfaces lightly with egg yolk and milk. Bake in a preheated 375° F oven for about 50 to 60 minutes or until done. Remove from molds and cover with a cloth to keep the crust soft. This dough may be used in the small brioche molds also.

Lemon Biscuits

3 eggs	1 tablespoon grated
1¼ cups granulated	lemon peel
sugar	2 cups sifted flour
	confectioners' sugar

Whip the eggs until fluffy and add the granulated sugar slowly until they are very thick and white, about 5 minutes. Add the lemon peel and fold in the flour with a spoon. Line a baking sheet with brown paper and sprinkle it with confectioners' sugar. Drop the batter by spoonfuls onto the paper and sieve a dusting of confectioners' sugar over each biscu't. Bake in a preheated 325° F oven for about 30 minutes, until lightly colored. Remove from paper immediately. If they should stick, place the paper on a wet towel. The biscuits should be very dry and should be stored in a tin box. Serve with stewed fruits or ice cream. Makes about 2 dozen 1-inch biscuits.

Almond Macaroons

1½ cups blanched almonds	2 egg whites
2 cups confectioners' sugar, sifted	2 teaspoons orange flower water or almond extract

Pulverize half the almonds in a blender, dropping in a few at a time. Add 1 egg white and 1 teaspoon orange water. Blend to a smooth paste. Remove to a bowl and repeat with remaining almonds, egg white, and flavoring. Mix in the sugar until the almond-sugar mixture is very smooth. Line a baking sheet with brown paper and drop almond paste by tablespoons onto the paper. Leave 1 inch or more between macaroons. Sift a little sugar over the top and bake in a 300° F oven for about 30 minutes or until golden. Remove from oven and immediately take the macaroons off the paper. If macaroons should stick, place the paper over a moist cloth. Makes about 20 macaroons 2½ inches in diameter.

Crème au Thé

½ cup boiling water	4 eggs
1 tablespoon tea leaves	½ cup sugar
2½ cups medium cream	⅛ teaspoon salt

Pour boiling water over the tea leaves and let steep 10 minutes. Scald the cream over low heat and add the tea essence. In a bowl mix together the eggs, sugar, and salt and beat very slightly. Pour about a third of the cream into the eggs and mix until well blended; return to the remaining cream. Put 6 custard cups in a pan and pour in enough hot water to come half way up the side of the cups. Pour in the custard and bake in a preheated 350° F oven for about 30 minutes or until custard is firm. Serve warm or very cold. Makes 6 servings.

Puff Pastry

2 cups all-purpose flour	½ pound sweet butter, at room temperature
1 teaspoon salt	
¾ cup ice water	

Work the flour, salt, and water together. Turn out on a lightly floured cloth. Roll out dough to about a 15-inch square. Work the softened butter into the form of a brick about 3 by 5 inches and place it in the middle of the dough. Fold up the dough, bringing the right and left edges together, and then the top and bottom edges to meet. Wrap the dough in plastic wrap and then in a cloth. Refrigerate for 30 minutes. Remove the dough and carefully roll out in a long strip about 20 inches long by 8 inches wide. Fold the top end down toward you to the middle of the dough and fold the bottom end up over it. Turn it so the open edges are at the top and bottom. Roll it out again in a long strip. Fold again as above, wrap and refrigerate 30 minutes. Repeat, 2 rollings, 2 foldings. Refrigerate. Repeat again for the last time, making a total of 6 rollings and 6 foldings. This will make pastry enough for 8 patty shells made with a 3½-inch cutter and rolled out ⅜ inch thick. The cut-out dough must be refrigerated for at least an hour before baking, or it can be frozen for future use. After baking, shells may be kept in a covered container for several days.

Gâteaux à la Madeleine
(Madeleine Cakes)

3 whole eggs	½ cup clarified butter
1 egg yolk	1 cup cake flour
⅛ teaspoon salt	1 teaspoon grated lemon rind
½ cup confectioners' sugar	

Beat eggs and salt for 5 minutes until very thick. Add sugar, 1 tablespoon at a time, while continuing to beat. Pour in butter in a steady stream and continue to beat until all the butter has been incorporated. Fold in the flour gradually, shaking in a little at a time. Add the lemon rind. Grease madeleine molds and flour lightly. Fill just short of the rim. Bake in a preheated 350° F oven for 8 minutes until the edges are slightly golden. Remove from the molds at once. Makes 3½ dozen.

Porcelain plate, cup, and saucer made by Grellet and Massié

Louis XII of France and Anne of Brittany, from the Sixth Tapestry of The Unicorn Tapestries

Oeufs à la Neige
(Snow Eggs)

2 cups milk
6 egg yolks
3 tablespoons sugar
⅛ teaspoon salt

2 teaspoons orange
flower water or
vanilla

Heat the milk in the top of a double boiler. Mix the egg yolks, sugar, and salt together. When the milk is scalded pour about 1 cup slowly into the egg mixture, beating constantly. Pour back into the double boiler. Cook, stirring constantly, until custard thickens and coats the spoon; about 10 minutes. Stir in orange flower water and cool. Pour the custard into a glass bowl or individual dishes and float poached meringues on top. Chill. Makes 6 servings.

Meringue

2 egg whites
pinch of salt
3 tablespoons granu-
lated sugar

½ teaspoon orange
flower water or
vanilla
simmering water

Beat egg whites until frothy; add salt. When they start to get fluffy shake in the sugar very slowly while continuing to beat. Continue beating until the meringue forms sharp peaks. Have the water simmering in a large skillet. Shape the meringues with 2 tablespoons into oval mounds. Push off into the water with a rubber spatula and cook until set, about 2 minutes, turning once or twice. Lift out with a slotted spoon and drain on a paper towel. Place on the custard. Makes 6 servings.

Pissaladière
(Anchovy Tomato Pie)

1 package dry yeast
¼ cup lukewarm water
olive oil
½ cup milk, scalded and cooled
1½ cups flour (approximately)
1½ pounds onions, thinly sliced
1 large clove garlic, minced

8 medium tomatoes, peeled, seeded, and chopped
1½ cups freshly grated Parmesan cheese
2 2-ounce cans flat anchovy filets
1 4-ounce can black olives

In a mixing bowl combine yeast and water, stirring to dissolve. Add 2 tablespoons olive oil and lukewarm milk. Stir in half the flour and beat until smooth; add enough remaining flour to make a soft firm dough. Round up in a greased bowl, cover with a cloth, and let rise until double in bulk, about 1 hour.

In a skillet sauté onions and garlic in 2 tablespoons olive oil and cook uncovered over low heat for about 1 hour, until tender and golden brown. In a saucepan cook the tomatoes, uncovered, over low heat for about 1 hour, until the liquid is almost absorbed, stirring often.

Punch the dough down and gather into a ball. Roll out into a circle 12 inches in diameter. Place on a baking sheet and press dough to make a slight rim. Bake in a preheated 425°F oven for 10 minutes. Remove and reduce oven to 350°F. Sprinkle the Parmesan cheese on the crust. Spoon on onions and tomatoes. Lay the anchovy filets on top of the tomatoes to form a lattice over the top. Fill each space with half an olive. Brush with oil and cover the filling with foil. Return to oven and bake 20 minutes more or until crust is deep golden. Makes 10 to 12 appetizer servings.

Rainier III of Monaco and Princess Grace with their children, Caroline, Albert, and Stephanie

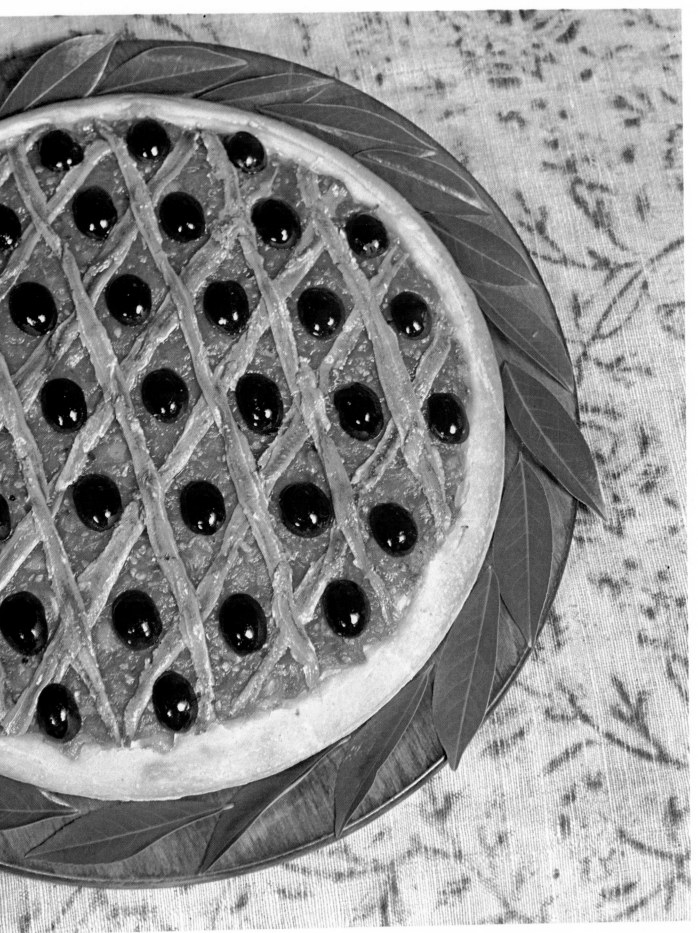

Pissaladière

ITALY

Francesco IV Gonzaga, Prince of Mantua
by Peter Paul Rubens

HE ITALIAN cuisine, born in the royal kitchens and foster child of the Roman gastronomy, in turn propagated the French *haute cuisine*. Thanks to great families such as the Medici, Italian cooking developed in grandeur and sophistication, and, with the betrothal of Catherine de' Medici to the Dauphin Henry in 1533, Italy's royal cuisine was "married" to the French.

It began in Rome during the heyday of the Empire. One of the first cookbooks, written by Apicius in the 1st century A.D., became an important hand-me-down for the Italian aristocracy a millennium later. Certain Roman dishes similar to those still eaten, such as *gnocchi, sformato,* and *agrodolce* sauces, may have been passed on via the royal kitchens of the Gothic kings Odoacer and Theodoric the Great.

No significant development appeared in the royal cooking until the 9th century, when the Arabs invaded Sicily. The Saracen influence spread to the royal kitchens of a fragmented nation. Islamic desserts, such as ice cream and sherbet, and sweets based on honey, almond paste, and marchpane or marzipan, were adopted. Although cane sugar was also introduced, it was not used in desserts until centuries later. In the 11th century, as the First Crusade marched on the Holy Land, the royal households used cane sugar as a spice for meat and fish sauces. Meanwhile, the lemon, known to the Romans, and buckwheat (called *sarraceno* in Italy) were brought back by the Crusaders.

Italy was throughout the centuries a divided land, consisting of kingdoms, duchies, counties, republics, and the papal states. Therefore it had no national cuisine. Both the common and the royal kitchens produced regional dishes, and a sense of regionalism continues to pervade Italy's culinary art.

Italy's rulers were unique. The Duke of Naples, the Count of Sicily, the King of (Northern) Italy, or the Doge (Duke) of Venice shared one thing in common—they established no dynasties such as developed in England, France, Germany, and Spain. Because of the turbulence of the times, these rulers apparently had little inclination to reflect on their stomachs; consequently, little is known about what they ate.

But it is known *how* one royal personage ate —the princess Theodora Ducas, daughter of a Byzantine emperor, and wife of the Venetian Doge Selvo. In 1071, this delicate Greek brought the fork to the Venetian court. When she ate, she had a eunuch slave cut her meat and feed her with the golden, two-pronged implement. This was too much for the Venetians, however, and the fork did not reappear in Italy for another 400 years.

While the table service of most royal houses lacked forks, their kitchens contained a plethora of equipment. In the 11th century, and on through to the 18th, labor-saving devices consisted of spits, tongs, shovels, andirons, and trivets for the fire; saucepans made of copper, bronze, and stone; ewers, rolling pins, kneading troughs, frying pans, pots, buckets, cauldrons, jugs, basins, and pails. Yet, for all the apparent crudeness of the kitchen service, fine feasts were prepared and elegant dishes managed.

By the 13th century, pasta had made its appearance on the royal menu, but scarcely with its current importance. A cookbook of that period lists *vermicelli*, *tortelli*, and *tortelletti* recipes and also tells how to make egg pies, milk tarts, and vegetable tarts similar to the current Genoese *torta pasqualina*. As only the wealthy and the aristocracy were literate and able to afford cookbooks (handwritten and hence expensive), it is safe to assume that the 13th-century royalty enjoyed at least some of those dishes. Leavened bread reappeared on the tables, and the basic recipe was much elaborated upon. Often, it was flavored with honey and spices, and ultimately, gilded with gold dust, which was believed to be good for the heart!

After Marco Polo returned to Venice from Cathay in 1295 with the routes to the Oriental spice trade, his city became the center of culinary development as a consequence. With the spices that the Romans had once so avidly used came a return to the elaborate multicourse meal, the artistic arrangement of food, and the custom of disguising food—to make a fish look like a roast, or a roast like a fish. The more effective the disguise, the greater was the guests' delight.

With the Renaissance, Italians became more literary and less taciturn. Food was featured not only in their cookbooks, but in their literature as well. Boccaccio, in his *Decameron* (1353), tells of

the queen who, after *breakfast,* asked that instruments be fetched so that she and her dining partners could tread the measures of a dance.

Sometime in the 1400's the fork reappeared in Venice. This time its use spread, and the homes of the aristocracy (and the bourgeois wealthy) used elaborately patterned gold and silver two-tined pieces. Not until the 1600's did the use of the fork spread to the rest of Europe. In 1611 the English traveler Thomas Coryate wrote in his *Crudities:*

"Here I will mention a thing that might have been spoken of before in discourse of the first Italian towne. I observed a custom in all those Italian Cities and Townes through which I passed and is not used in any other country that I saw in my travels, neither do I thinke that any other national of Christendome doth use it but only Italy. The Italian and also most strangers that are Cormorant in Italy doe always at their meals use a little forke when they cut their meat. For while with their Knife, which they hold in one hand, they cut the meat out of the dish, they fasten the Fork which they hold in their other hand upon the same dish, so that whatsoever he be that, sit-

Giovanni II Bentivoglio **by Ercole Roberti**

ting in the company of any others at meale, should inadvisedly touch the dish of meat with his fingers from which all at the table doe cut, he will give occasion of offence unto the company as having transgressed the lawes of good manners, in so much that for his error he shall be at the least brownbeaten, if not reprehended in wordes. This form of feeding I understand is generally used in all places of Italy, their Forkes being for the most part made of yronn, steele, and some of silver, but those are used only by Gentlemen. The reason of this curiosity is, because the Italian cannot by any means indure to have his dish touched with fingers, seeing all mans fingers are not alike cleane. Hereupon I myself thought good to imitate the Italian fashion by this forked cutting of meate, not only while I was in Italy, but also in Germany, and oftentimes in England since I came home. . . ."

Cleanliness was uniquely important to the avant-garde Italian aristocracy. Diners cleansed their hands in bowls of rose water and dried them with scented towels before beginning a meal and after each course. Such cleanliness was unknown in the rest of Europe, which was, hygienically speaking, in the Dark Ages.

The culinary development of Venice in the 14th century only presaged the development of Florence in the 15th. The Medici were in power, and the Renaissance was upon them. Lorenzo the Magnificent, the patron of Michelangelo and Botticelli, politician and patrician par excellence, was the epitome of the Renaissance Prince. He fostered art and literature in a way that dazzled all Europe, and his banquets, feasts, carnivals, and entertainments were unsurpassed.

This love of the *dolce vita* brought Italian cuisine to its prime. But credit did not belong to Lorenzo alone—other princes, the doges of Venice, the cardinal princes of an ever-more-secular church, and other rulers shared the lavish tastes of the 15th-century Renaissance. All were concerned with beauty—in art, in literature, in architecture, and in a well-prepared table.

The tables were dressed with sweet-smelling plants; live fish swam in tanks hidden among them; gilded baskets laden with fruit were hung from the branches; leverets, rabbits, and birds were tied with silk ribbons. Gold and silver bedecked the table in the forms of candlesticks, beakers, tableware, and fountains; plates made of majolica and porcelain, flagons of transparent, sparkling glass and graceful shape completed the service. Copper wine coolers were damascened,

Paola Adorno, Marchesa Brignole Sale, and her Son by Sir Anthony Van Dyck

and there were even golden toothpicks.

Much of this decor was inspired by classical models, as was the food. What Apicius had left to posterity in the 1st century, Bartolommeo de' Sacchi, or Platina, revised and modernized. His cookbook, inspired not only by Apicius, but also by Pliny the Elder, Varro, Columella, and others, was printed in 1475. It was called *De Honesta Voluptate ac Valetudine* ("Concerning Honest Pleasure and Well-being"), and its recipes were in Latin, which was to be expected from a humanist of the time who had also written the *Lives of the Popes*. Platina counseled moderation and, decrying the excessive use of spices, recommended instead the use of lemon and orange juice and verjuice to season food. One of Platina's suggestions, the serving of fruit as a light beginning to a meal, remained popular. Although Platina did not address himself directly to royalty, it is reasonably certain that they were his principal audience.

The princes did not, for all of Platina's good counsel, follow his advice concerning moderation. When Lorenzo de' Medici married in 1469, *before* Platina, the wedding feasts lasted three days, and of sweetmeats alone, 5,000 pounds were consumed. At the wedding of Caterina Sforza of the ruling family of Milan, in 1477, *after* Platina, a 22-course wedding feast lasting five hours was held. At one point in this banquet, six children dressed in hunter's regalia brought the 14-year-old Caterina a variety of game "all served in their natural forms"—hardly a move toward moderation.

Between-course entertainments were a very important part of the banquet. The Trionfi, outdoor spectacles staged by Lorenzo in Florence, eventually moved indoors to entertain the prince's dinner guests. (The *intromesso* provided by the dance, drama, and other diverse spectacles eventually became part of the classical ballet and opera.)

Dinner in the Ducal Palace in Venice was "served to the sound of music . . ." and ". . . song, epithalamiums, comedies, and melodrama enlivened the official ducal banquets," of which the first known in official records was celebrated in 1485. Music was an important part of the feasting of royalty.

Bust of Lorenzo de Medici by Andrea del Verrocchio

Giuliano de Medici **by Sandro Botticelli**

A parallel existed between high cuisine and great art: Both served to enhance the prince's reputation. Thus, the entertainment extravaganzas were intended not to aid the digestion, but to increase the ruler's glory. A competitive spirit existed among the princes in the giving of banquets and feasts, as it did in the patronizing of great artists. It could be asked, were the princes gourmets, or impresarios?

The parallel carried over to the 16th-century Mannerist period of the Renaissance. As art became more complex, elaborate, and even contrived, so did the banquets. With the loss of gracefulness and refinement, however, came an increased inventiveness, originality, and sophistication. The way to France's *haute cuisine* was paved.

The Renaissance reached the tables of France with the arrival of Catherine de' Medici, the 14-year-old great-granddaughter of Lorenzo the Magnificent, who brought the high cuisine of her forefathers with her to the Court at Avignon as an ostensible part of her wedding dowry. Her pastry cooks introduced such Italian delicacies as frangipane, macaroons, and Milan cakes, cream puffs, ice cream, and sherbet. Other of her cooks prepared artichokes, broccoli, small peas (now *petit pois*), and truffles for the first time in France. One dish, stuffed guinea hen, is still to be found in French cookbooks as *pintade à la Médicis*. Catherine became queen on the accession of Henry II and ruled over the best-fed court in French history.

Back in Italy, cookbooks became popular. The Cardinal of Ferrara's cook, Cristofaro de Messisbugo, in 1549 wrote *The New Book Which Shows How to Arrange Banquets (in Princes' Households)*, which was still in print in the year 1600. It provided instructions for staging banquets and listed recipes and other items as well. The menus of some great banquets were also included.

One banquet, a private dinner given in Mantua by Duke Alfonso of Ferrara in honor of the Commendatore de Leone, had eighteen guests and four courses with a total of 55 separate dishes. The first two courses were as follows:

Gold saltcellar by Benvenuto Cellini

First Course: a large simnel bread; truffle salad with raisins; endive salad with herbs; pheasant salad with oranges; butter, dressed with a sugar coating; five large stuffed capons, served cold with sliced salt tongue.

Second Course: thirty *tomaselle* or "hogge's pudding," with meatballs and sausage; ten roast pheasants; a sort of paste covered with *tortelletti* and Neapolitan macaroni; five forced-meats of *prosciutto* and *mortadella;* fifteen partridges with white cole; *cervelat* sausage and small *ducati;* venison in black sauce with cinnamon; five dishes of lemons, oranges, and olives; wine.

Between courses, perfumed water was provided for washing the guests' hands, while violin and vocal music was performed. And so it went for the remainder of the 55 dishes.

Such a repast was not an everyday affair, of course—only on special occasions were banquets held. For that matter, it is known that the private life of the Medici was almost austerely simple.

It is not difficult to imagine a typical menu in the Medici or any other royal household similar to the one given below, from a cookbook by Romoli, who pedantically suggests the day-by-day menu for *every* day of the year. The following is for the first Saturday in September:

Antipasto: dried figs, sweet melon, soft-shelled crabs, Pergolese grapes, ravioli, and marinated fish. Boiled Foods: tunafish, scalloped eel, onion stew, salmon, white sauce. Fried Foods: *fascioli riconci* (literally, "put-together bundle"), pickerel tails marinated in vinegar and garlic, snails in green sauce, tench fish, sliced lemon. Fruit: herb-stuffed tarts, cooked apples, peaches in wine, fennel.

The 16th was the didactic century; books on banqueting, everyday eating, and so on were typical. The intended audience was the new royalty—the merchants and bankers who had become the rulers of city-states, such as the Medici; and the *condottieri*, or mercenary soldiers, who took power by coup and ruled as dukes, such as the Sforza of Milan. As these men became princes, they sought to behave like princes. A book by Liberato on how to run a royal household admonished its readers about the importance of a clean kitchen. The prince was not to hire a cook "with the itch, or suffering from ulcerated legs." It also recommended a carver of "moderate height and good appearance, and above all things, tidy, smart, and skillful."

Actually, the carver was important to the prince's household—he was expected to cut a joint so that his master would have the best meat, and the rest would be distributed according to the guests' ranks! Order was the order of the day. At such meals, cardinals, princes, dukes, and kings were served by young noblemen. To serve the great was held to be an honor.

At the end of the 16th century, the table service, once elegant, became spectacular. Napkins, like the *origami* of Japan, were folded in a multitude of shapes, perfume scented everything, silk bouquets decorated each place setting. Occasionally the flag or family coat of arms of each guest was placed at his seat. On rare occasions a gala banquet would have an entire table setting carved out of sugar. So perfectly imitated were the bread, knives, napkins, and dishes that Henry III of France, on a visit in 1580, was actually startled when the napkin he picked up crumbled in his hand.

The art of pleasing the palate was further perfected, and new dishes were constantly created and made to fit the season of the year. The favorite savories were truffles, oysters, sausages, carrots, and greens. Soups of the day were vinegar soup, kid broth, Imperial and Neapolitan pottage. After these antipasti came entrées derived from regions famous for the quality of their produce or its preparation. *Mortadella* came from Cremona, Milan supplied sausage made from pig's brains; cheese came from Piacenza, tripe from Treviso, lamprey from Binasca, sturgeon from Ferrara, macaroni was prepared in the Genoese style, and sausage was made in Modena. There were Peruginian thrushes, Lombard quails, and geese from Romagna. Only the finest fish from the Adriatic graced the royal tables. The turbot, red mullet, and fresh sardine, once singled out by Boccaccio for special praise, were favorites. Fruits of all kinds were available in abundance. The royal epicures so gorged themselves that the household physicians became wealthy from the overeating induced.

Sugar was still used as a base for many sauces, and strong spices were pervasively employed. The thirst ensuing from the heavy seasoning was quenched with numerous wines, both Italian and foreign. Favorite regional wines were frequently doctored with spices or scented with perfumes. Bread and oysters were served gilded.

By the year 1600 the Renaissance was over, the Italian cuisine had passed its zenith, and Marie de' Medici followed in Catherine's footsteps by marrying another French king, Henry IV, and again bringing to France a retinue of cooks and new dishes. The torch of high cuisine passed to the French. Italy began its culinary—and artistic —decline in the 17th century.

In the traditional manner of empires before their fall, the ancient Italian royal cuisine declined into decadence and excess. Its great days were nearly over when, in 1755, Venice gave one of the most sumptuous feasts of all time. The Duke Clement Augustus of Bavaria was entertained in the Great Hall of Venice. One hundred eighty guests, in the latest *Paris* fashions, were regaled with a three-course dinner of 125 dishes each, making a total of 375 separate dishes. The dessert, designed by Marco Francheschi (his name was duly recorded), consisted of 35 sculptured centerpieces and 48 different sauces to flavor them.

Lapidary jug with lid and vessel in the form of a bird

The House of Savoy

Marchesa Brigida Spinola Doria **by Peter Paul Rubens**

The house of Savoy, the only dynasty to reign over a united Italy, had as its founder Umberto Biancamano (Humbert of the White Hands), who in the 11th century established in what is now the region of Savoie in France a small independent state that commanded the three main Alpine passes between France and Italy. In the course of the next three centuries the Counts of Savoy gradually expanded their domains into neighboring Piedmont.

Savoy became a dukedom in the 15th century. In the 18th, by the acquisition of the island of Sardinia, it turned into the Kingdom of Sardinia. Its final status as the Kingdom of Italy was achieved in 1861, but it was not until 1870, with the annexation of Rome, that Italy became completely united under Victor Emmanuel II.

In examining the somewhat slender records of the eating habits of the members of the House of Savoy, one is impressed by the frugality of the cuisine. The meals were at the same time luxurious and rough-and-ready. There are notes about gala dinners and wedding feasts, but also about impromptu meals served within sight of the trenches or just behind the lines during World War I.

One eating spot in Turin is indissolubly linked with the House of Savoy. In the square behind the Carignano Palace, for many years the official residence of the kings of Sardinia before they became kings of Italy, is the Grande Ristorante del Cambio ("Great Exchange Resturant"), famous as far back as 1665 as the inn that sheltered D'Artagnan, the fourth musketeer of the king of France, when he went to Piedmont on a secret diplomatic mission. This may be only a legend, but it is no legend that this restaurant frequently served, at the outset of the 18th century, as a favorite lounging spot for the princes of the House of Savoy. Its café specialized in coffee, soft drinks, sweet cordials, *marrons glacés,* and oranges.

In 1854 there appeared an interesting *Treatise on Cooking, Modern Pastry Making, and the Preparation of Sweets* by Giovanni Vialardi, assistant head cook and pastrymaker for Charles Albert (1831–49) and Victor Emmanuel II (1849–61), kings of Sardinia. But the times did not call for luxury; the fatal battle of Novara, during the war of 1848, was still too much alive in men's memories. The subtitle of the book is a program for parsimony: "An Economical, Simple, Aristocratic and Middle-Class Way of Preparing Foods."

Victor Emmanuel II, who became the first king of Italy (1861–78), was himself a man of simple, almost lower-class tastes; his weakness was not refined dishes, but excellent wines, which he collected from all parts of Italy and foreign lands as well. Long after his death innumerable bottles continued to repose in the royal cellars, "a silent memorial," adds the historian, "to a Latin warrior King."

But at the great court receptions, even those held in Florence (the intermediate capital between Turin and Rome), in the sumptuous decor of the Pitti Palace, simple lemonades and ices often prevailed over wines and liqueurs. Francesco Grandi, Prince Demidoff's cook, in his *Economical Cookbook*, published in Florence in 1870, describes the "Cavour Lemonade," which Grandi himself had perhaps invented in honor of Italy's great statesman: "Half a tumbler of lemon juice, one tumbler of orange juice, half a tumbler of *anacrone* [a word found in no Italian dictionary], one pound of sugar in small pieces, two tumblers of good vermouth; place everything in an earthenware pot with several orange and lemon peels, stripped of all their white inner layer, and left to steep for two hours; then pour in twenty tumblerfuls of water, stirring well until the sugar is quite dissolved; lastly, strain the beverage through a silken sieve."

During the time when Florence was the capital, several fancy balls were held in the Pitti Palace, two during the carnival season, the others scattered throughout the year in accordance with a special dynastic calendar. Chief among these festive occasions were the ball held during the visit of the king's daughter, Queen Maria Pia of Portugal, and the one in 1868 that celebrated the arrival of Crown Prince Humbert's bride, the future Queen Margherita. Among the many legends that circulated about her was one indicating that she, like so many of us, was reluctant to use knife and fork on chicken wings. Even today Italian mothers remind their children that *"Pure la Regina Margherita mangia il pollo colle dita"* ("Even Queen Margaret eats chicken with her fingers").

Although Florence is the cradle of the Italian language, and King Victor Emmanuel II tried to lose his Piedmont accent, his menus were invariably written in French, as was the custom of the period. A sample is supplied by the dinner menu for May 31, 1870, one of the last dinners that the royal family of Savoy ate in Florence. The royal diners began with a *riz à la jardinière au consommé* (rice and vegetables in broth), followed by *Kiffel à la normande* (Kiffel Norman style), *noix de veau piqué aux champignons* (pope's-eyes of veal larded with mushrooms), *poulardes à la française* (chicken French style), *filets de soles en Bellevue* (filets of sole Bellevue sauce), *haricots verts au beurre* (green beans in butter sauce), *rôti de canard* (roast duck), and *salade* (salad). Four desserts concluded the repast: *charlotte à la polonaise* (charlotte Polish style), *pâtisserie* (pastry), *fromage de Hollande* (Dutch cheese), and *crème et fraises* (strawberries in cream).

The reign of Humbert I (1878–1900), abruptly ended by the hand of an assassin, lived

Dish inscribed with the arms of the Buonaparte and Mornovi families in center

on in the memory of the earthquake victims whom he helped and consoled like a true father. One gastronomic note comes down from his days, "Soft Boiled Eggs Humbert I Style," the recipe for which was given in 1905 by Carlo Molina in the Rome *Messaggero della cucina*: The eggs are boiled for three minutes, removed from their shells, and laid on a bed of artichoke hearts puréed in butter, with a garnish of chicken crests and force-meat, asparagus tips and black truffles, and covered with a sauce *suprême* with white truffles.

Humbert's son and successor, Victor Emmanuel III (1900–46), soon found himself faced with the dark days of World War I, which Italy entered in May, 1915, on the side of the Allies. Amedeo Pettini, the king's chief cook, relates in the first (December, 1929) issue of *La Cucina Italiana* the story of the king's Christmas day at the battlefront.

"The King's open military car dashes across the Paduan plain, over ice-covered roads, around military trucks and pieces of artillery, on its way to the front lines. It makes a hurried halt for coffee at a field kitchen, where an Air Force colonel is desperately trying to obtain some condiments for his men's macaroni, finally settling for an ancient chunk of moldy green cheese, the only thing available.

"The King's car moves on to Villa Giusti, where two years or so later the armistice was to be signed that put the final seal of victory on Italy's war effort. The kitchen was cold, but the King's cook and his helpers managed to get it going. The Christmas Day luncheon came out of a large basket in the car's trunk compartment. It consisted of a cup of warm consommé out of a thermos bottle, followed by a cold omelet and an equally cold veal cutlet *alla milanese.*

"But more abundant provisions were coming up for the evening Christmas dinner. This time the menu included a Roman-style soup, roast beef and roast chicken, a Treviso style salad, and that peculiarly named but popular Italian dessert known as *zuppa inglese* [literally, "English soup"; the link is with the English trifle, a remote and distant ancestor]."

The chef even gives recipes, after a fashion:

"Roman style soup: beat up one fresh egg per person with a spoonful of grated Parmesan cheese and a *soupçon* of powdered nutmeg; have ready on the fire one dishful of broth for each egg used; bring the broth to a boil, and pour in the mixture, stirring as you pour; serve at once." The chef does not specifically say so, but any good Roman knows this soup as *stracciatella,* or "rag soup."

Meat and fowl were turned on the spit, to the accompaniment of the chirp of a cricket hidden away among the hearthstones.

Salad Treviso is served warm. Wash some good red Treviso wild chicory, and dress it with lots of oil, salt and pepper. Then spread it out on the grate and cook it over burning embers, turning it over from time to time, until it crackles. Serve it piping hot with lemon.

For the "English soup," lay out a dough made of fine flour in a pie dish about five inches in diameter, and spread it over with lots of apricot marmalade. On top of this place an inch-thick layer of sponge cake having the same circumference as the pie dish. The sponge cake is next soaked with a sweet-smelling syrup composed of rum and alkermes (a brandy flavored with spices and colored red with cochineal, used mainly for coloration). Over this place a layer of custard made of egg yolks, flour, sugar, and water, and flavored with vanilla. Then comes another layer of sponge cake and custard. Last of all is a final layer of sponge cake. Next beat three egg whites with a quarter-pound of sugar, and wrap this around the *zuppa,* covering its surface with the same meringue. Sprinkle with powdered sugar, put into the oven for a few minutes, and draw it out when it is blond in color.

All this was consumed to the accompaniment of the rumble of distant guns, which were nevertheless close enough to cause the ground to tremble.

But chief cook Amedeo Pettini had far greater potentialities. The royal dinner of 1916, served at the front, which he described in a later issue of *La Cucina Italiana,* displays far greater variety and possibilities of enjoyment, due no doubt to the presence of Queen Elena, who had joined her spouse at the front. This time the menu ran as follows: Consommé with *gallozzole* (dumplings); prosciutto in gelatine; fried chicken Florentine style; loin of veal with *certosine;* steaming "hunt-

Dining room of Villa Barbaro-Giacomelli at Maser, designed by Andrea Palladio

er's foam"; artichoke hearts Italian style; roast squab and peacock; salad; peaches Marengo; and timbale of wafers with vanilla ice cream.

This war dinner is one of the most comprehensive menus known for banquets of the House of Savoy. Needless to say, the king and his consort were unaware of what was being plotted in the kitchen by their chef and his aides until the courses began to appear on the table.

By way of explanation: *gallozzole* are small dumplings of *pasta reale* (royal dough); prosciutto in gelatine was served with a black currant sauce, diluted with Marsala wine, and flavored with orange and lemon peels cut pine-needle fashion, and with a touch of mustard; the fried chicken was served with a tomato sauce on the side; the *certosine* were small timbales of carrots, turnips, and peas, with a core of chicken and veal forcemeat, all closed up into small molds and cooked in a double boiler. The "hunter's foam" was a purée of hare-meat, truffles, and cream, held together with beaten eggs, surrounded by mushrooms cooked in butter, and glazed over with a wild game sauce. The artichoke hearts were steeped in a Spanish sauce with white wine and finely chopped mushrooms, parsley, tongue, and prosciutto. The salad came out of the hothouses of Turin's hard-working Capuchin monks, and is described as the one that was always preferred by the royal couple; its dressing consisted of yolks of hard-boiled eggs put through a sieve, mustard, pepper, white vinegar, and a few slices of Alba truffles. The Marengo peaches had an underlayer of rice cooked in milk and slightly sweetened, and an over-veil of apricot marmalade, topped with a meringue, and baked a few minutes in the oven; they were served with a sauce of apricot preserves flavored with Marsala wine.

The Fascist era ushered in an ever-increasing number of "wholesome, autarchic" banquets. ("Autarchy" was Mussolini's name for economic self-sufficiency, with expanded use of domestic products and imports of foreign foodstuffs reduced to a minimum.) One of the first victims of the autarchic program was the gastronomic vocabulary, which had been traditionally French, and had then acquired, by reason of Italy's alliance with the Western powers during World War I, a few Anglo-Saxon elements. It is characteristic of the ignorance of those who insist on mingling politics with language that the old French-sounding but Latin-based *menu* (from the root of Latin *minuere*, "to restrict, make less" in the sense of

"details" or "items") was replaced by an Italian-sounding but Germanically derived *lista* (*delle vivande*).

Pettini gives a description of the wedding banquet offered at the Quirinal Palace in Rome on the occasion of the marriage of Prince Humbert and Princess Maria José of Belgium. The "list of foods" served on January 4, 1930, and reprinted in the April 15, 1930, issue of *La Cucina Italiana*, runs as follows: Eggs *alla Montebello*, lobster with Tartar sauce; pheasants on the spit; Princess salad; asparagus in foamy sauce; ice cream Palermo style; Dutch bread sticks.

The efforts made by the faithful chef to italianize French names are both amusing and pathetic: what is evidently a *mousseline* becomes *salsa avorio* ("ivory sauce"); an *aurore* becomes *aurora*, but is described as having drawn its inspiration from the colors of Guido Reni, while the sauce that goes with the lobster is not really Tartar, but *remoulade;* the vegetable *julienne* of the Princess salad turns into a *macedonica;* and the *hollandaise* sauce for the asparagus into a "foamy sauce."

As for the wedding cake, "destined, by reason of the symbolism of the orange blossoms with which it is girded, to represent a sweetly dedicatory role in the banquet," it is specified that it is really a "Margherita cake with vanilla flavor, covered with a frozen glaze of white *fondant* (sugar paste), and flavored with the most Italian liqueur in existence, maraschino."

As can be seen, royal luxury and Spartan austerity are happily blended in these court repasts. The only criticism that may be made is a certain lack of imagination and innovation. If the court Christmas dinner of 1930 is compared with that of 1932, the monotony becomes obvious:

1930	1932
Timbale of macaroni	Timbale of *tagliatelle* Florentine style
Boiled spider fish	Creamed lobster
Roast breast of turkey with watercress	Roast turkey with early vegetables
Salad	Treviso style salad
Artichokes Milan style	Lettuce Piedmont style
Nubian cake	Congress cake with cream

The Nubian cake is defined as "something dark, with a chocolate frosting," that bears a striking resemblance to Vienna's *Sachertorte*.

Notably absent from House of Savoy dinners are antipasti. The normal opener is a timbale (the *tagliatelle* Florentine style in this menu are a reconstructed version of *pappardelle* with hare), or a soup (there is a wonderful turtle soup listed for the 1933 New Year's Day dinner); this is followed by a meat course, a fish course, and a dessert, with some vegetable preparation in between.

The New Year's Day dinner also included filet of sole with peas, roast veal and capon with dressing, Milan style salad, and kohlrabi Cadore style.

Pettini died some years ago. But Nino Borgese, who knew him well, and had occasion to serve members of the Savoy dynasty, particularly Humbert II, still runs one of Genoa's finest restaurants, "The Saint." He began his career as a kitchen helper in 1919 at the house of the Duke of Bonvicino, where the Duke of Aosta was a guest at least twice a week, at luncheons and dinners that featured butlers in knee-breeches and white wigs.

Later Borgese became head chef at the home of Emmanuele Filiberto, Duke of Aosta, who commanded Italy's Third Army during World War I and was the father of Amedeo, commander of the Italian forces in Ethiopia in World War II. In 1928, Borgese joined another master cook, Barbano, to take care of the gastronomic wants of the famous "historical carrousel" that took place in Turin and drew the aristocracy of all Europe, the very flower of the *Almanach de Gotha*.

"It was a pleasure to cook for those people," he reminisces, "because they were able to appreciate your efforts. On one occasion, at the home of Count Carù della Trinità, both the King [Emmanuel III] and Fuad I of Egypt, King Farouk's father, were among the guests. For them we prepared lamb chops à la Pompadour, prosciutto mousse, and salmon Princess style. Prince Humbert [later Humbert II] enjoyed my ministrations at least a hundred times. He was a man of very refined tastes; he loved my creamed *risotto*, my pheasant in salmis or *chaud-froid*, my mixed fries à la Villeroy. His favorite sauces were Béarnaise and Bordelaise. King Humbert and I were born in the same month and year, September of 1904, as well as in the same township (he in Racconigi castle, I in the town of Saluzzo down below). When he was a guest at the home of the Counts of Sant' Elia, I prevailed upon the Countess to allow me to prepare for him a chocolate birthday cake, on which I inscribed 'Long live 1904!' He enjoyed the cake and asked to make my acquaintance. From that day on we were friends, if that is the proper term where a Prince and a chef are involved. He presented me with a pair of silver cuff links with the emblem of the House of Savoy. On one occasion I brought the birthday cake to him in person at Cascais; at other times I have sent it to him. Humbert of Savoy never fails to write and thank me."

Courtesy is indeed the mark of a true king!

A page from Domenico Romoli's *La Singolare Dottrina*

Q V A R T O.   40

Alesso

Anguilla grossa in pasticcio alla francese, testa di Storione coperta di mangiar bianco semplice con granella di melagrane forte di sopra, laccie di fiume lattinate coperte di herbette & fiori con sapor di noci, trotte salì prese con aceto rosato & pepe, mirausto di pancia di Storione, lampredozze coperte di ginestrata torte di gambari, riso maritato, gielo di color d'ambra in boccone & pasticci de tartarughe alla francese.   *Fritto*

Aligoste ripiene, Rombi & linguatte con fette di cedro con fette conditi di budelorbi & pesciolini con salsa uerde, calamaretti di latte & gambaretti con limoni trinciati, anguilla arrosta con una fresca, teste di dentali in gelatina schiauona, ostreghe alla tedesca, spinaci alla fiorentina, torte di prugnoli, et oliue.

Torterie

Vermicelli di ricotta di latte di Amandole, melangoli ripieni di prune damascene & zibibi stufati, pasticci di pere cottogne, torte di spinaci, et melerose, frutte di Sardegna piene di pasta, marsapani pasticcetti di fegati di ranocchi, uisrole stufate con le suppe ostreghe in bragia, & melezane di Genoua.

Fruttarie.

Mandole monde, pignoli freschi con acqua rosa & zuccaro, noci monde con uino rosso & sale, carciofi, cardi, tartufi intieri asciutti con pepe & sale mandole uerdi, palmetti, pistacchi, & finocchio fiorentino abbrustato.

Royal Recipes

Stuffed Omelette

3 whole eggs
   pinch of salt
3 tablespoons butter
   half a Marzipan recipe

1 egg yolk, beaten
2 tablespoons
   granulated sugar
½ teaspoon cinnamon

Beat the whole eggs with a fork and salt lightly. Heat 1 tablespoon butter in an 8-inch skillet; when it starts to sizzle pour in the eggs. Stir gently with a fork until the egg has heated evenly and the surface has just set. Remove immediately from the stove. Cut into thirds and slip the three pieces onto a board or plate. Take a piece of Marzipan the size of a walnut, form into a sausage shape, and roll in a strip of the omelette. Repeat with the other pieces. Melt the remaining butter in the skillet; dip the omelette rolls quickly in the beaten egg yolk and cook until heated and golden, turning each roll while cooking. Remove to a warm plate and sprinkle with cinnamon and sugar mixed together. Makes 2 to 3 servings.

Soft-Cooked Eggs Humbert I Style
(Eggs on Puréed Artichoke with Sauce Suprême)

½ cup fresh bread
   crumbs
3 tablespoons milk
   salt and pepper
2 ounces raw chicken,
   cut in small pieces
   butter or margarine
2 tablespoons flour

⅛ teaspoon white pepper
¾ cup chicken stock
¼ cup heavy cream
4 artichoke bottoms,
   fresh or canned
4 eggs
8 cooked asparagus tips
4 slices truffle (optional)

Soak crumbs in milk and mix in ¼ teaspoon salt and ⅛ teaspoon pepper. Put chicken into blender and process until it becomes a paste. Combine the two mixtures and beat together. Drop 8 tablespoons of the chicken forcemeat, one at a time, into barely simmering salted water and poach for 1 or 2 minutes on each side. Drain on paper towel and keep warm while making the sauce. Melt 2 tablespoons butter, add flour, ½ teaspoon salt, and ⅛ teaspoon white pepper. Cook for 1 minute; add hot stock and cook until thickened. Add cream and stir in 1 tablespoon butter. Cover and keep warm.

Purée artichoke bottoms and mix with 2 tablespoons melted butter and salt and pepper to taste. Boil the eggs for 3 minutes and remove the shells. Divide the artichoke purée between 4 small heated individual baking dishes. Place an egg on top of the purée and a forcemeat ball on two sides. Spoon over the sauce and garnish each dish with 2 asparagus tips. Place in a 350°F oven just long enough to heat through if necessary. Place a slice of truffle on top. Makes 4 servings.

Tortellini

2 cups sifted all-
   purpose flour
½ teaspoon salt
2 eggs
2 tablespoons cold
   water

¾ cup cooked,
   chopped, and
   seasoned spinach
¾ cup ground cooked
   meat—veal, pork,
   or chicken
¼ cup grated Parmesan
   cheese

Mix flour and salt on a pastry board or in a bowl. Make a well in the center and add the unbeaten eggs and water. Blend together well with the fingers and form into a ball. If necessary, add more water. Turn dough onto a lightly floured cloth and knead for 10 to 12 minutes until the dough is smooth and elastic. Place a bowl over the dough and let rest 10 to 15 minutes. Divide the dough in half and roll out paper-thin; cut with a 2-inch cutter.

Make the filling by mixing together the spinach, meat, and Parmesan cheese. Place ½ teaspoon of the filling in the middle of each circle of dough. Moisten edges with water and fold over, pressing edges together to seal. Bring the ends together around the index finger to form a ring. Drop tortellini into a pot of boiling water and cook for 7 to 8 minutes. Drain in a colander. Serve with melted butter, grated cheese, or a sauce. Makes about 90 tortellini, 6 to 8 servings.

Polenta

1 cup fine polenta or
    yellow cornmeal
4 cups water
1 teaspoon salt
½ cup butter, melted

1 cup grated Parmesan
    cheese
½ cup grated Gruyére
    cheese

Mix 1 cup of the water with the cornmeal. Bring the remaining water and the salt to a boil; stir in the cornmeal, stirring constantly, and cook until thickened. Cover and cook over low heat for 15 minutes, stirring frequently. Stir in the butter and Parmesan cheese. Put in a low 5-cup baking dish, sprinkle with Gruyère cheese, and bake in a 375° F oven until cheese is bubbly. Place under the broiler until golden brown. Makes 6 servings.

Stracciatella
(Rag Soup)

3 eggs, slightly beaten
2 tablespoons cold
    water
2 tablespoons finely
    chopped parsley

¼ cup freshly grated
    Parmesan cheese
¼ teaspoon nutmeg
6 cups well-seasoned
    chicken broth

Mix the eggs and the next 4 ingredients together. Bring the broth to a boil and pour in the egg mixture in a steady stream, while stirring with a fork. As soon as the egg has set, remove from heat and serve. Makes 6 servings.

Aragosta
(Creamed Lobster)

2 1½-lb. lobsters
¼ cup olive oil
2 tablespoons butter
½ teaspoon salt
⅛ teaspoon pepper

4 tablespoons brandy
4 tablespoons cream
2 egg yolks, slightly
    beaten
lemon garnish

Split the lobsters lengthwise; remove and discard black vein and sac. Heat the oil in a large skillet, add the lobsters flesh side up, and cook 10 minutes over low heat. Turn, cover, and cook 10 minutes more. Remove the lobsters to a board, pick out the meat, and cut it into small pieces. Melt the butter in a medium saucepan, add lobster meat, salt, and pepper, and sauté 5 minutes. Pour in brandy and set it aflame. When flames die, gradually add the cream that has been mixed with the egg yolks, stirring steadily. Remove from heat and fill 2 lobster shells. Place on a small warm platter and garnish with lemon wedges. Makes 2 servings.

Aragosta (Creamed Lobster)

Snails in Red Wine

Snails in Red Wine

48 canned snails and shells	¼ cup finely chopped parsley
½ cup red wine	2 teaspoons minced garlic
½ teaspoon salt	
½ teaspoon freshly ground pepper	5 tablespoons very fine dried bread crumbs
¼ teaspoon nutmeg	
1 cup sweet butter	

Rinse the snails in a strainer and put into a bowl. Pour over the wine and add the salt, pepper, and nutmeg. Let marinate for 15 to 20 minutes. Rinse shells, invert to drain, and wipe dry. Add parsley and garlic to butter that has been melted in a large skillet. Cook for 2 minutes over low heat but do not boil. Remove snails from the wine with a slotted spoon, drain on a paper towel. Roll each snail lightly in bread crumbs and add them to the butter. Cook for 1 minute on each side. Remove the skillet from the stove, spoon a little garlic butter into each shell, and place a snail in the shell. Spoon in more garlic butter and put all the filled shells in the skillet. Pour in the wine, cover, and cook 5 minutes. Remove cover and simmer 5 minutes more while basting each snail with the wine sauce. Place 6 snails in each soup plate or in the conventional snail plates and pour over the wine sauce. Makes 8 servings.

Lingue Arroste Peverone
(Roast Tongue with Pepper Sauce)

1 smoked beef tongue, about 3 pounds	1 bay leaf
	4 whole cloves
2 large cloves garlic, crushed	5 whole allspice
	2 cardamom seeds
1 carrot	6 slices bacon
1 small onion	

Wash tongue and place in a kettle with the next 7 ingredients. Cover with water and simmer slowly for 2 hours. Cool, and remove the skin. Trim away the fat. Wrap the tongue, covering completely, with the slices of bacon and lay in a shallow pan. Roast in a preheated 350°F oven for 1 hour, turning on other side after 30 minutes. Remove the bacon and serve the tongue in a warm deep platter or casserole with Pepper Sauce poured over. Makes 6 servings.

Pepper Sauce

1 teaspoon freshly ground pepper	1 cup dry white wine
	2 cups Béchamel sauce

Boil pepper and wine together over high heat until reduced to ¼ cup. Strain through a fine sieve into the hot Béchamel sauce, and boil for 1 minute. Yields 2 cups.

Rice Salad

3 tablespoons olive oil
1 tablespoon wine vinegar
1 large clove garlic, crushed
½ teaspoon freshly ground pepper
2 teaspoons salt
1 tablespoon fresh oregano leaves, chopped, or 1 teaspoon dried
2 tablespoons large capers
peel of ½ lemon, cut in slivers
1 cup julienne-cut celery root or chopped celery
½ cup finely chopped green peppers
12 black olives, sliced
4 medium tomatoes, peeled and seeded
4 chopped scallions (including green tops)
1 cup freshly cooked cold rice

Prepare salad dressing by combining the first 8 ingredients. Marinate the celery root, green peppers, olives, tomatoes, and scallions in the dressing for 1 hour or more. When ready to serve, remove the garlic and toss with the rice. Serve with cold meat. Makes 6 servings.

Umberto's Salad

tender garden salad greens (for 6)
2½ tablespoons olive oil
1 tablespoon vinegar
¼ teaspoon mild mustard
¼ teaspoon salt
⅛ teaspoon freshly ground pepper
2 filets anchovy, cut into small pieces
1 hard-cooked egg, chopped
3 truffles or 5 small raw mushroom caps, thinly sliced
6 or 8 small green nasturtium seeds

Wash and dry greens; wrap in cloth and refrigerate. Beat together oil, vinegar, mustard, salt, and pepper. Mix in anchovy and chopped egg, and pour dressing into a small bowl. When ready to serve, place the greens in a salad bowl with the truffles or mushrooms arranged on top. Sprinkle on the nasturtium seeds. Pour over the dressing and toss lightly until all the leaves are coated. Serve immediately. Makes 6 servings.

Rice Salad

Pheasant Salad

1½ cups cold pheasant or chicken cut in small cubes	¼ cup olive oil
	1 tablespoon orange juice
4 seedless oranges, peeled and sectioned	1 teaspoon lemon juice
	1 clove garlic, crushed
1 medium onion, thinly sliced	¼ teaspoon salt
4 tablespoons chopped fresh mint	¼ teaspoon freshly ground pepper
	lettuce

Mix together the pheasant, oranges, onions, and mint in a bowl. Blend the oil, juices, and seasoning together and shake well in a bottle. Pour over the salad just enough dressing to coat it well and toss lightly. Chill and let marinate in the dressing for an hour before serving in a lettuce-lined salad bowl. Makes 2 to 4 servings.

Cream Puffs

Peaches Marengo

1 cup uncooked rice	8 peach halves
2 cups hot milk	2 egg whites
1 teaspoon salt	10 tablespoons sugar
2 tablespoons butter	¼ teaspoon almond extract
sugar	
½ cup orange juice	

Wash rice and cook in top of double boiler with milk and salt for 1 hour without removing the cover. Mix together in a saucepan the butter and ¼ cup sugar. Cook over low heat, stirring constantly, until slightly browned. Add orange juice and cook only until well blended. Pour into the rice and toss with a fork until all grains are coated. Butter a round 8 x 1½-inch baking dish and fill with the rice. Place peaches on top. Make a meringue of the egg whites and 10 tablespoons sugar, flavored with almond extract. Cover the dish with the meringue

or pipe through a pastry tube. Place in a preheated 350°F oven until golden, about 15 minutes. Serve with Apricot Sauce. Makes 8 servings.

Apricot Sauce

½ cup apricot preserve	1 tablespoon Marsala
¼ cup water	wine

Mix apricot preserve and water together in a saucepan and boil for 5 minutes. Remove from heat and add the Marsala wine. Yields ¾ cup.

Cream Puffs

½ cup water	⅛ teaspoon salt
¼ cup butter or	½ cup sifted flour
margarine	2 whole eggs

Bring the water, butter, and salt to a boil. Add the flour all at once and stir vigorously with a wooden spoon until the mixture leaves the sides of the pan. Remove from the stove and add 1 egg at a time, beating well after each addition. The mixture must be very smooth. Drop dough from a spoon onto a greased baking sheet, leaving 2 or 3 inches between. Bake in a preheated 400° F oven for 10 minutes. Turn heat down to 350° F and bake about 30 to 40 minutes more or until double in size and golden brown. Turn oven off, remove puffs, slit the sides with a sharp knife, and return to the oven for 10 minutes with oven door ajar. Cool the puffs on a rack. Makes 6 large cream puffs or 8 medium ones.

Filling

1 pound Ricotta cheese	4 tablespoons grated sweet chocolate
3 teaspoons finely grated orange peel	½ cup heavy cream
	⅓ cup orange marmalade
1 teaspoon finely grated lemon peel	6 glacéed cherries

Mix first 5 ingredients together and refrigerate. When ready to serve, fill the puffs, slitting the sides more if necessary. Melt marmalade, brush the top of each puff, and top with a cherry.

Marzipan

½ cup blanched almonds	1 egg white, slightly beaten
1 cup sifted confectioners' sugar	½ teaspoon almond extract

Grind almonds in a blender until very fine; mix with the sugar. Add beaten egg white, a spoonful at a time, to the almond-sugar mixture until just moistened. Add almond extract and mix with the fingers until smooth and pliable, like clay. If sticky, dust with sifted sugar.

Marzipan may be used in desserts, rolled between wax paper to be used on top of fruitcakes, or tinted and shaped to resemble fruits, vegetables, and flowers. Marzipan will keep well in an airtight jar in the refrigerator. To be used as filling for Stuffed Omelette.

Note: Marzipan is an ancient confection believed to have come from Persia and was a favorite of the young Persian princes. It was brought to Europe by the returning Crusaders and became very popular.

Granite
(Cherry Sherbet)

1 cup water	2 cups fresh ripe pitted cherries, puréed in blender or food mill
½ cup sugar	
2 tablespoons lemon juice	

Bring water to a boil, add sugar, and stir until sugar is dissolved. Boil for 5 minutes and remove from the stove. Add the lemon juice and cool. Combine the puréed cherries and syrup and pour into an ice cube tray, divider removed. Freeze for 2 to 3 hours. Break up the frozen mixture several times during the freezing for a smoother texture. Spoon into a stemmed glass or compote. Makes 4 servings.

Cavour Lemonade
(Wine Punch)

½ cup orange juice	peel from ½ orange and ½ lemon, white part removed
½ cup lemon juice	
½ pound fine granulated sugar	9 cups water
2 cups dry vermouth	

Mix orange and lemon juice with the sugar and vermouth. Place in an earthenware crock with the peel. Let steep at least 2 hours or longer. Pour in the water. Remove the peel and either pour over an ice block in a punch bowl or serve on the rocks in individual glasses. Makes 3 quarts.

SPAIN
and
PORTUGAL

Philip II by Titian Vecelli

PAIN WAS SUBJECTED in ancient times to many foreign cultures—Phoenician, Greek, Roman, Carthaginian, Visigothic, and Arabic—and its cuisine, like other of its national characteristics, necessarily reflected these influences. As a result, many culinary variations appeared at the Spanish royal table.

The first rulers of Spain were the Visigothic kings, who eventually adopted the Romanized customs of the Iberians. There is not sufficient evidence to indicate how these monarchs ate, other than what appears in the writings of St. Isidore, Bishop of Seville (7th century), and especially those of Apollinaris Sidonius (5th century), son-in-law of the Emperor Avitus. Apollinaris, who was received at the Court of Theodoric, king of the Visigoths, speaks of the unusually frugal and excellent service that was observed at the king's table; drunkenness was not tolerated. Among the dishes that the king ate and offered to his guests were *pulmentum*, a thin gruel of wheat and cooked vegetables, mixed with cured, dried beef; and *minutal, isicia,* and *martisia,*

which all were prepared with fish. However, the indispensable victual was meat; fowl was especially esteemed, and was always prepared with lard rather than oil. Some of the Visigothic monarchs were great imbibers of beer and cider, although the people preferred wine and *cecia,* a fermented drink made from barley. Other sovereigns preferred mead (water with honey), which was the traditional drink of the Germans.

Around A.D. 718 the Visigoths were defeated by the Arabs, who attained a high level of civilization during this period, eventually considering themselves as the dispensers of Western knowledge, first at Córdoba and later at Seville. The courts of the Cordoban caliphs and of the Sevillian kings were distinguished by a refinement and luxury that sharply contrasted with the simplicity and coarseness of the contemporary Christian monarchs. A great deal is known about the eating habits of these Moslem sovereigns, thanks to the works of Abdul Kasim, teacher of the Caliph Abd-er-Rahman III (929–961), and those of the famous Rhazes, physician of Baghdad in the 10th century. These works also preserved some contemporary recipes.

In that distant epoch between the 9th and 12th centuries, a set of standards was observed in the royal cuisine that could be compared to those which Anthelme Brillat-Savarin described many centuries later in his *Physiologie du Goût* (1825). Ziryab of Baghdad introduced the finest recipes of the Orient to the Cordoban court. He also established the rules to be followed in serving a sumptuous meal. Among the favorite dishes of these monarchs were *alboronia,* a stew of eggplant, onion, garlic, and pumpkin, seasoned with spices, almonds, and filberts, all chopped and mixed; *altamandria,* a dish prepared wth fowl, chopped and mixed with rice and seasoned with spices and melted lard; *jota,* a type of porridge with wild amaranth, borage, and other greens, seasoned with aromatic herbs and cooked in a beef consommé; and *aletria,* a dough made with wheat, water of orange or lemon blossoms, and rose water. All of these were eaten accompanied by an abundance of fruit and delicacies.

The life of the Christian monarchs of medieval Spain was very hard. Since they were entirely preoccupied with recovering the territories seized by the Arabs, they had no time to enjoy the pleasures of a good table. Moreover, since both agriculture and animal husbandry had been practically abandoned by all able-bodied men, in order to fight against the Saracens, it was necessary to pass laws proscribing luxury and to provide a model of behavior. For all of these reasons, the royal cuisine during the Spanish medieval times was simple, yet substantial.

The king preferred to eat alone, and it was considered a great and rare honor to be invited to the royal table; such an invitation was reported to have been once refused by the Cid. It was the custom to present all the courses on the table at the same time, and a ceremony known as the *salva* was observed to provide proof that the food

The Family of Philip V by Louis Michel Van Loo

had been prepared by a nobleman before being served to the monarch.

Frequently, at gala banquets, entire roasted steers were placed on the table; these were carved in the presence of the king and his guests. The art of carving and wielding the knife had to be perfectly mastered by those charged with this service. To this end, the Marques de Villena wrote *Arte Cisoria, o Tratado de Cortar con el Cuchillo* ("Art of Carving, or How to Cut with a Knife") around the middle of the 14th century. After having been cut, the pieces of meat were arranged on large slices of bread called *trincheros* (trenchers), and then presented to the diners.

The food limitations imposed on the common citizenry even reached the king's table, as far as can be determined in various legislative documents, such as the *Partidas* ("Records") of Alfonso X of Castile and León (1252–84). The depositions of James I of Aragon (1213–76) established that the king was to partake of only two meals a day. In the orders of Alfonso XI of Castile (1312–50), it was authorized to serve the king but four courses in a meal. Pedro I of Castile and

Charles III by Goya

León (1350–69) also issued restrictive norms regarding luxury and squandering, even though the nobility did not take them too seriously. This can be seen from the ostentatious banquet given by Don Álvaro de Luna in his castle at Escalona for Don Juan II, his wife Doña Isabel of Portugal, and many guests.

Among the dishes that appeared frequently at the king's table were *sopa de oruga,* prepared from a plant no longer used in cooking; *cazuela mojí,* a favorite of Alfonso the Wise; and *porriol,* a stew of onions, chopped and cooked and accompanied by pieces of salt pork, flavored with white wine, a preference of Pedro I. There was never a scarcity of meat at the king's table, except during Lent. Mutton was the most appreciated, although game was highly esteemed. One widely accepted dish, which was served at court at the end of Lent, was *broete lardero,* a complicated preparation composed of various meats, pieces of salt pork, bird livers, and an abundance of herbs and spices. Alfonso V of Aragon (1416–58) enjoyed *janete,* a dish of chicken, which was first cooked with onions in bacon fat and later stewed in a complex sauce of almonds, pears cooked in honey, liver of fowl, spices, sugar, and parsley. But the most delicate dish, a true luxury of the Middle Ages, was unquestionably the so-called *manjar blanco* (blanc mange) in all its variations—a dish made of shredded chicken with sugar, milk, and rice flour. The best Spanish cooking of the medieval period is collected in the famous *Libro de Guisados* ("Book of Stews"), published in Catalan at the end of the 15th century by Ruperto de Nola, the cook of King Ferdinand I of Naples (1458–94). Charles I of Spain, who was also the Holy Roman Emperor Charles V, had the book translated into Spanish.

The discovery of America brought about an important change in Spanish cooking, although its effect was not immediately realized. The change began in the kitchens of the royal palace, which was the first to make use of the new foods that arrived from the New World—important foods such as the tomato, pimento, potato and sweet potato, certain types of beans, and such exquisite fruits as the pineapple, cherimoya, avocado, and many others. In addition, there was the Mexican *guajolote,* which is known today as turkey—a festive dish in all the kitchens of the world.

Charles I (1516–56) so loved good eating as to be a virtual glutton. He totally modified the table service that was developing in the palace,

***The Family of Charles IV* by Goya**

and established in Spain the Burgundian etiquette of his forebears, which was to remain in fashion for a long time. The king's dinner was converted into an important event, especially on the days when the monarch ate in public. This ceremony was held once a week, and it was considered an important privilege to watch. Usually the king ate alone, but on many occasions he had the company of his wife and children. The queen ate in private, accompanied by her children, even though at times she had to put up with the presence of some ladies-in-waiting who attended her and rendered homage.

Meals at Court tended to be substantial and varied, although there has been much exaggeration concerning them, depicting as a daily bill of fare what was served only at banquets and gala meals.

Charles finally withdrew from the pomp of the Court and became a recluse in the monastery of Yuste, but he managed to have the finest dishes available in the kingdom sent to his retreat. His son, Philip II (1556–98), was very sober concerning his food and liked simple dishes and good

stews. Philip III (1598–1621), a pious and austere man, did not pay much attention to the pleasures of the table. Philip IV (1621–65) was a refined and demanding gastronome. Charles II (1665–1700), the unhappy, sick, and childless king who was the last Spanish Hapsburg, scarcely had the strength even to enjoy a good meal.

Many documents exist that give minute details concerning the cuisine of the Hapsburg dynasty, particularly the *Arte de Cocina* ("The Art of Cooking") by Francisco Martínez Montiño, the chef of Philip III. As an example of a gala early 17th-century meal in the Royal Palace of Madrid, a menu from the month of September follows:

First Course: ham with the entrées; young turkey cooked with its sauce; hodgepodge (*ollapodrida*) in large black-dough pies; molded pastry puffs; plates of pigeon with stuffed pumpkin; roast partridges; hat-shaped penny loafs; roast chopped veal; pigeons in sweet-dough pie with slices of bacon; veal tarts with shoots and almonds; small thrushes with shredded bread over gilded bread slices; fresh trout; roasted fattened rabbits.

Second Course: roast capons, plates of veal with small meatballs of veal, sweetbreads, and livers; roast turtledove; plates of quince and stuffed chickens cooked in a batter; *cazuelas mojis* (pie casserole) of eggplant; plates of sausages and

Ferdinand VII by Goya

corned beef; plates of stuffed capons, cooked with tartlets on white-bread slices; teat pie; marzipan sweetmeats; lion-shaped pastries stuffed with hare; shank pies; roasted pigeons with mutton spareribs and grated bread.

Third Course: young roasted hens; plates of shoots with fluted eggs; roast chickens with verjuice; peach tarts in marinade; cold meat pies of roast larded kid; plates of pigeon with greens; *manjar blanco;* pork sausages cut in the shape of a

wheel, mixed with other sausage and tongue; pineapple; for dessert, grapes, melons, figs, plums, sweet whipped cream; raisins and almonds, peaches, sugarplums and preserves, olives, cheese, and rolled waffles.

After Charles II died without leaving an heir, the manners of Versailles were introduced to the Spanish court by Philip V (1700–46), nephew of Louis XIV of France and founder of the Spanish Bourbon dynasty. He began a process of Frenchifying the kitchen of the Spanish court—a process continued into the reign of the last sovereigns. Ferdinand VI (1746–69), melancholy and lovesick, cared little for food. Charles III (1759–88) was a great hunter but abstemious in his meals, which comprised a frugal breakfast of chocolate, a simple lunch, and an early supper that always consisted of soup, a piece of roast, a fresh egg, and a cup of sweet Canary wine into which he dipped two pieces of toast and then drank the rest. For dessert he always selected from a big plate of fancy cake coated with sugar and a basket of unripe fruit. A sample from the records of this monarch's court, signed by his cook, Juan Tremonille, follows:

Food of Our Lord the King: three soups—one of lobster with their claws, one of herbs and young fowl, and one of rice and veal broth; 10 dishes for the carving board—roast partridge, fried animals' testicles, veal sweetbreads garnished with cockscombs and *botoncillos,* a kettle of macaroni, filets of young rabbit cooked in champagne, pigeon cutlets, roast fattened duck, veal ribs with pickled pork, encrusted chicken in white sauce, and little pies Spanish style; two entrées—cooked shortribs and three chickens with ham; two roasts —one of fattened young chickens, one of three chickens or three pigeons; four final dishes—cooked lobster, sweet cherry tarts, chicken-liver tarts, and serpentine fritters.

Charles IV (1788–1808) was a glutton, obese and sluggish, who liked the strong flavor of wild game. Ferdinand VII (1808 and 1814–33), like his daughter Isabel II (1833–68), liked the simple dishes enjoyed by the good citizens of Madrid, such as the *cocido* and the *callos.* They favored many other dishes with disconcerting names written in that French which constitutes the lingua franca of the universal kitchen. Simple appetites, with preference for game without any complicated preparation, were characteristic of Spain's last kings preceding the Republic, Alfonso XII (1874–85) and Alfonso XIII (1886–1931).

Portugal

For centuries Portugal and Spain shared a common history, but Alfonso Henriques, son of Henry of Burgundy and of Theresa, the Spanish Infanta, proclaimed himself ruler of an independent kingdom on July 25, 1139. Thereafter the history of the former County of Portugal developed under four dynasties: the House of Burgundy (1139–83), the House of Aviz (1383–1578), the House of the (Spanish) Hapsburgs (1578–1640), and the House of Braganza (1640–1910); and finally the present Republic was established.

During the first of these periods, the kings ruled a land torn by constant strife against the Arabs or the Christian princes. They fought from the safety of their castles or from embattled encampments. The members of the Court suffered from boredom in the fortresses or royal *alcázares*, with their chilly and empty spaces; the men played with their dogs or their swords; the women spun by the warmth of the fire, while listening to the sage advice of a *dueña*, or bartering with a peddler over his wares. When it was time to eat, the servants arranged the silverware, took out tablecloths, napkins, and towels, and set the royal table. It had *tigelas* (bowls) of carved wood, or *chávenas* (teacups) of silver or pewter, spoons carved out of bone or made of metal, and table knives; in addition, *saleiros* (salt shakers), *galhetas* (cruets), and *cálices* (chalices) dressed the table. The king drank from one of the chalices, which was usually beautifully fashioned from silver or gold. Before the king drank, the ceremony of the *proba* ensured that the drink was not poisoned.

After the food was on the table, pages presented the *bacia ou jarro* (washbowl) to the diners, so that they could clean their hands. Then the food—succulent and of great quantity—was served, generally commencing with a *potagem* or pottage (stew) made with onions, dried beef, pork fat, and strongly seasoned with pepper and garlic. A bishop blessed the table and the king began the meal—substantial dishes of meat, fowl, and fish, garnished with vegetables, fruit, and savory sweets. Everything was washed down with quantities of wine made from imported French vines planted by Henry of Burgundy, and kept in the royal wine cellars.

When the king was on campaigns in the field,

he dined simply but well. The forces ate "off the land," and any unexpected dish was considered providential. Once, when Celorico, in Beira, was under siege by Sancho II (1223–48), and the city's resistance began to falter because of imminent starvation, an eagle flew over the city and dropped a magnificent trout that it was carrying in its beak. The lord of Celorico had his cook broil the fish and sent it to Sancho, who, moved by the generosity of his enemy, gave up the battle and lifted the siege.

Pedro I (1357–67) was a glutton, who loved long banquets and ostentatious feasts. Thus, when he knighted Don João Alfonso Tello, he wanted the entire populace of Lisbon to participate in the celebration. He had kitchens improvised, which roasted entire steers whole and then distributed them among the people, accompanied by mountains of bread and fruit and hundreds of barrels of rich Minho wine.

Ferdinand I (1367–83) married Doña Leonora Telles, after breaking his engagement with a daughter of King Henry II of Castile, and then waged war upon Castile. But upon the behest of the Pope, who negotiated a marriage between Ferdinand's daughter Beatriz and Henry's son John, Ferdinand ended hostilities. The nuptials were performed in Elvas, and the king was represented by his faithless queen, who was accompanied by her lover, the Count of Andeiro, a Galician nobleman. The wedding feast was fabulous, with huge tables laid for the nobility. The most regal foods graced the service: sweetmeats of fowl and game; wild boar adorned with truffles; plank-roast tuna pies; entire roasted steers; partridges and pheasants; and bear-meat hams, brought down from the mountains of León. These alternated with the popular dishes of the Alentejo, such as the renowned *acordas* (panadas), *chourizos de sangue* (blood sausages), *coelho cum pepinos* (neck with peppers), partridge stew, egg dishes—which play such an important role in the Portuguese gastronomy—and vegetables from the gardens of Crato, accompanied by fruit from Andalusia and the Algarve. The wine cellars held barrels of good wines from Beiras, Bucelas, Carcavelos, and Voleres. Among the guests at this banquet were the famous military hero Nuno Álvares Pereira and his brothers who, upon approaching their table, found it occupied by courtiers. Nuno kicked the table upside down, strewing the plates and food all over the ground, and then marched off with his family to eat elsewhere, to the astonishment of the queen and Court.

While the dynasty of Aviz was on the throne in the last decades of the 15th century, other royal weddings were held at the Portuguese Court that are still memorable for their splendor. At a time when Bartholomeu Dias had already rounded the Cape of Good Hope and Columbus was just dreaming of sailing to the West, John II of Portugal (1481–95) sealed the marriage contract between his son Ferdinand and the Infanta Isabella, daughter of Ferdinand of Aragon and Isabella of Castile, thus uniting the crowns of Spain and Portugal. John wanted the wedding to be truly regal, and he brought together so many birds to Évora, in Portugal, where the wedding was to take place, that the crops in the region were obliterated. Unfortunately, an epidemic of plague struck the city, and the wedding took place by proxy in Seville, Spain. When the infanta finally arrived, the nuptials were celebrated with feasting that lasted until Christmas. According to the story, the banquet was held in a pavilion erected expressly for the purpose, to which fabulous dishes were borne on golden carts, or in coaches disguised as ships, from which were released flocks of doves and song birds. Only a short time later Ferdinand was thrown from his horse and killed, ending the celebrations.

At the beginning of the 16th century, as a result of the discoveries by the Portuguese of new routes in the Orient, the monopoly held by Venice in the spice trade was transferred to Lisbon, which attained a splendor it had never known before. The usually moderate Portuguese began to demand the most expensive spices for their kitchens and to perk up their wine and beer. King Manuel the Fortunate (1495–1521), homely and prematurely aged, surrounded himself with great pomp at mealtime and was served exotic and expensive victuals. He hardly touched a bite and drank only water—served in a richly engraved gold cup.

The last king of the House of Aviz was the unfortunate Sebastian (1557–78), who, obsessed with becoming a champion of Christianity, became a recluse in his palace at Cintra and dreamed of adventurous feats in Africa, while he tamed horses, hunted, ate a soldier's repast, and turned away from all amorous pursuits. Philip II of Spain unsuccessfully attempted to dissuade him from his fancies during a conversation in the monastery of Guadalupe. The friars of the monastery presented

Hunt Room of the ducal palace, Villa Viçosa

Hall of the Spanish Tapestries in the National Palace of Ajuda, Lisbon

the young sovereign with a New Year's or Christmas gift, which consisted of six baskets of bread, two wild boar, 50 chickens, 100 pairs of partridges, 12 hams, 24 cheeses, 12 measures of wine from Ciudad Real, 25 pounds of butter, 37 pounds of assorted confections, 50 pounds of pumpkin, 25 pounds of nougat candy, 50 marzipans, six baskets of rolled waffles, 200 bunches of large grapes, six baskets of oranges, lemons, and limes, a quantity of different preserves, three platters of pan-fried fruits, and 50 pounds of apples.

Embarking upon his adventure, the young king disappeared in the battle of Alcazarquivir, although many believed that he survived to live anonymously in the village of Madrigal as a baker.

John IV (1640–56), who founded the House of Braganza, ruled in a period of wars and blights; crops were sparse, but the royal kitchens produced a cuisine that featured eggs (*ovos*) with monotonous regularity: *ovos mexidos, ovos estrelados, ovos enformados, ovos moles de Aveiro, de Chares, de Mirandela, de Vianha*. The cuisine also was remembered for the discovery of chocolate sweets and bonbons of liquor.

Alfonso VI (1656–83) was an obese, gluttonous king. He liked to partake of complicated dishes whose recipes originated in Goa, Mozambique, Macao, or Timor. He was deposed by his brother, Pedro II (1683–1706), who suffered from melancholia and preferred to eat a good meal in the solitude of his chambers rather than to attend his own wedding banquet.

John V (1706–50), amorous and adventuresome, who had been made as rich as Midas by the wealth of Brazil, celebrated the marriages of his daughter Maria Magdalena Barbara to Ferdinand, heir to the Spanish throne, and of his son José to the Infanta Maria Victoria, in an unusual way. The infanta entered Portugal on her father's arm, across a specially constructed bridge built for the occasion over the Caia River, and then partook of lavish banquets in which the most exotic dishes alternated with the most traditional of the Portuguese cuisine, accompanied by the greatest wines. These displays of luxury at a time when the country's soldiers were begging for a bowl of soup at monasteries caused great consternation. Yet on other occasions the kings set an example of sacrifice and austerity for their subjects. Joseph Emanuel (1750–77), the former Prince José, did just that when, on November 1, 1755, a violent earthquake destroyed the city of Lisbon. And his daughter, Maria (1777–1816), wallowed in melancholy and ordered such frugal meals as would be found in a convent's kitchen: *cabidela de frango* (giblet stew), *caldeirada de sardinhas* (sardine pot), *desfeita de bacalahau* (codfish stew), or a simple *caldo de castanhas* (chestnut broth).

After Napoleon's Peninsular Campaign broke out and Junot's cavalry trampled the beautiful Portuguese countryside, the Court fled in 1807 to distant Brazil and there John VI (1816–26) awaited his opportunity to return to Lisbon. Meanwhile, beneath the palms of Rio, he savored the delicious *bananinhas fritas* (fried plantains), *vatapa* (a Brazilian Creole stew), or the rather plebeian *feijoados* (a black bean casserole). He returned to his homeland in 1821, and he was eventually poisoned while enjoying a snack in Belem, and died, along with his physician and cook.

John was succeeded by some heartless, wretched monarchs, persecuted by adversity, which eventually resulted in the crumbling of the Portuguese empire. The monarchy ended, without pain or glory, in 1910.

Kitchen of the National Palace of Cintra, Portugal

Royal Recipes

Royal Eggs

1 cup flour	6 eggs, poached
2 egg yolks	1 cup Béchamel
¼ teaspoon salt	sauce
2 tablespoons butter, at room temperature	¼ pound small shrimp, cleaned, sautéed, and seasoned
ice water	

Put flour in a bowl. Make a well in the center and put in the egg yolks, salt, and butter. Quickly mix in with fingertips and add gradually about 3 tablespoons ice water to make a smooth but not sticky paste. Roll out on a lightly floured cloth to ⅛ inch thick. Cut out 6 rounds with a 4-inch cutter. Fit over bottom of baking cups and prick with a fork. Bake in a preheated 400° F oven for about 12 minutes or until golden. Have poached eggs ready and place one in each pastry cup. Cover

Cocido (Meat and Chick-pea Stew)

with Béchamel sauce. Place shrimps on top to form a crown. Makes 6 servings.

Eggs Portuguese

3 eggs	juice and grated peel of 1 lime
1 egg yolk	
1 cup and 2 tablespoons sugar	½ cup butter
	⅛ teaspoon salt
3 tablespoons orange flower water	

In the top of a double boiler mix together the eggs, yolk, and 1 cup of the sugar. Stir in the orange flower water and the juice and peel of the lime. Add the butter and salt. Cook over simmering water, stirring frequently, for 30 to 40 minutes or until very thick. Pour into a baking dish. Sprinkle the remaining 2 tablespoons of sugar over the top and place under the broiler. Broil until the sugar is glazed and a medium brown. Serve hot or cold. Makes 4 servings.

Mutton Soup

2 quarts water	¼ cup ground almonds
1 pound mutton or lamb, all fat removed, cut in 1-inch cubes	1-inch cinnamon stick
	4 tablespoons rice flour, mixed with ½ cup water
1½ teaspoons salt	
4 medium pears, peeled, cored, and quartered	2 tablespoons orange flower water

Put the water, mutton, and salt into a large kettle. Bring slowly to a boil and simmer for ½ hour, skimming the surface frequently. Add the pears, almonds, and cinnamon stick. Partially cover and cook for 1 hour. Remove the mutton and cinnamon stick. Mix a little hot soup with the flour and water paste and stir into the soup. Cook until slightly thickened; add the orange flower water. Purée the soup in a blender or press through a sieve. Correct the seasoning and reheat if necessary. Makes 6 servings.

Cocido
(Meat and Chick-pea Stew)

12 cups water	1 onion or leek stuck with a clove
2 pounds beef brisket	
½ stewing chicken	4 carrots, cut in ½-inch slices
4 ounces salt pork	
¼ pound chorizo (Spanish sausage)	1 4-ounce blood sausage
5 ounces ham	1 small cabbage, coarsely shredded
½ pound chick-peas, which have been soaked overnight with 1 salted pork foot	2 tablespoons olive oil
	1 large clove garlic, minced
	6 small whole potatoes, peeled
	3 ounces fine noodles

Put the first 6 ingredients into a very large kettle. Bring to a boil and simmer 15 minutes, skimming the surface often. Add the chick-peas, pork foot, and onion and simmer over low heat, partially covered, for 2½ hours or until meat is tender. Put the carrots in during the last 30 minutes of cooking. In the meantime prick the blood sausage with a fork and cook with the cabbage in just enough water to cover for 20 minutes. Remove the sausage, peel off the casing, and chop. Drain cabbage and reserve the liquid. Heat the olive oil and add the garlic and cabbage and cook until golden; cover and keep hot. Boil the potatoes. Drain the stock from the meat; there should be 6 cups; add some cabbage broth if necessary. Cook the noodles in the stock and adjust the seasoning. Serve the soup with the noodles and shreds of chicken in a tureen as the first course. Put the chick-peas in a warm serving dish with the meats and carrots on top. In another dish arrange the cabbage with the potatoes around the edge and the chopped blood sausage in the center. Serve with a thick tomato-onion sauce such as Salsa de Tomate. Makes 6 servings.

Salsa de Tomate

2 pounds ripe tomatoes	2 teaspoons sugar
1 cup water	1½ teaspoons salt
2 tablespoons olive oil	¼ teaspoon freshly ground pepper
1½ cups chopped onions	
4 large cloves garlic, minced	2 tablespoons chopped parsley

Wash tomatoes, cut in quarters, and simmer in a covered saucepan until very soft. Press the tomatoes through a sieve and discard the seeds and skin. Fry the onions in olive oil until tender and golden, adding the minced garlic in the last 5 minutes of cooking. Stir in the purée, sugar, salt, and pepper; cover and simmer 10 minutes. Mix in the chopped parsley. This is a thick sauce; if desired, it may be diluted with beef or chicken stock or water and used with various pasta dishes. Yields about 4 cups.

Wild Fowl Montino

2 whole breasts of fowl, pheasant or chicken	¼ teaspoon nutmeg
	2 tablespoons lemon juice
4 hard-cooked eggs, diced	1 egg, slightly beaten
2 tablespoons chopped fresh mint	4 slices uncooked bacon, finely chopped
⅛ teaspoon salt	¼ cup chicken broth
⅛ teaspoon white pepper	¼ cup clarified butter or margarine
¼ teaspoon ginger	

Bone the breasts and remove the skin. Pound the pieces with the back of a knife to flatten slightly and form into similar shapes. Mix diced eggs, mint, seasoning, lemon juice, and beaten egg together. Cover each breast with the chopped bacon and spread on the stuffing, patting down and rounding slightly over the sides. Place in a small baking dish. Mix the broth and butter together and pour half of it over and around the breasts. Cover the dish with foil and bake in a preheated 350° F oven. Baste carefully with the broth every 15 minutes, adding more broth and butter if necessary. Bake for about 1 hour or until fowl is done when tested with a knife. During the last 15 minutes remove the foil and let brown slightly. Serve from the baking dish. Makes 4 servings.

Pheasant Alcantara Style

6 truffles or 12 small mushroom caps, coarsely chopped	8 ounces chicken livers and 1 pheasant liver, coarsely chopped
3 cups port wine	3 tablespoons chopped parsley
2 tablespoons butter or margarine	salt and pepper
½ medium onion, minced	1 cleaned pheasant or partridge
	2 slices bacon, cut in half and blanched

Simmer the truffles or mushroom caps in the wine for 10 minutes. Strain, cool the wine, and reserve the truffles or mushrooms. Sauté the minced onion in butter until tender; remove onion and sauté livers about 10 minutes. Purée the livers in a blender or press through a sieve. Mix the livers with the truffles or mushrooms, parsley, and onion. Salt and pepper to taste. Fill the cavity of the pheasant with the liver mixture; close with skewers. Truss and refrigerate for several hours, spooning the wine marinade over the pheasant from time to time. When ready to cook, place pheasant on a rack in a shallow pan. Cover the breast with slices of blanched bacon and pour in the marinade. Roast in a preheated 350°F oven for 1 hour, basting several times with the marinade. Remove the slices of bacon and continue to cook for 15 minutes more or until pheasant is brown and tender. Remove pheasant to a warm platter and keep hot. Reduce the marinade to one half, skimming off any fat. Serve the sauce in a bowl. Makes 2 to 4 servings.

Partridge in Spiced Sauce

partridge giblets	1 tablespoon grated Seville orange rind
2 cups water	
½ cup sherry	⅛ teaspoon pepper
1 teaspoon salt	⅛ teaspoon salt
2 medium garlic cloves	4 partridges or squabs, cleaned and trussed
1 bay leaf	
½ carrot	softened butter
½ small onion	4 orange slices
1 cup stale bread crumbs	2 egg yolks
¼ cup melted butter	

Put the giblets and the next 7 ingredients in a saucepan, partially cover, and simmer 45 minutes. Toss together the bread crumbs, butter, grated orange rind, pepper, salt, and enough water to moisten. Loosely stuff the birds and close the openings with poultry pins; rub the birds with butter. Place on a rack over a broiler pan and broil, 6 inches from the heat, on all sides until golden. Remove birds to a casserole which has been lined with the orange slices. Pour in half of the strained stock. Cover and bake in a preheated 350° F oven for 1¼ hours or until tender, basting frequently. Remove the birds to a warm platter. Discard orange slices and pour the liquid into a saucepan with the remaining strained stock. Thicken with egg yolks over low heat. Do not boil after adding yolks. Garnish each bird with a slice of orange. Pour some of the sauce over the birds and serve the remainder in a bowl. Makes 4 servings.

Chuletas de Cordero à la Farnesio (Lamb Chops and Dumplings)

3 cups water	salt and pepper
½ chicken breast	1 egg yolk
½ carrot	6 lamb chops
1 celery stalk	4 cups cooked peas
1 small onion	½ pound mushrooms, chopped and sautéed (optional)
1 teaspoon salt	
2 tablespoons butter	1 truffle, sliced (optional)
½ cup blender bread crumbs	

Simmer the first 6 ingredients together until the chicken is tender. Remove chicken, strain broth and reserve; discard vegetables. Remove skin and bone from chicken, cut in pieces, and put into a blender; or mince and pound to a paste. Heat butter, add bread crumbs and chicken, and mix well. Add about 1 tablespoon broth to make a stiff paste. Salt and pepper to taste and mix in the egg yolk. Form dumplings into 2 rolls 3 inches long and wrap in foil. Refrigerate for 30 minutes or longer. Just before cooking the chops, remove rolled dumplings to a lightly floured board and cut each roll into 3 pieces. Reshape if necessary to make 6 rounds. Bring the chicken broth (there should be 2 cups) to the boiling point and put in the dumplings. Poach a few minutes on each side, keeping the broth just under a boil. Drain on a towel and keep warm while cooking the chops. Place chops in a circle on a warm round platter and put the peas mixed with the mushrooms in the center. Place a dumpling on each chop and top with a slice of truffle. Makes 6 servings.

Chuletas de Cordero à la Farnesio (Lamb Chops and Dumplings)

Pa de Carneiro
(Shoulder of Mutton or Lamb in Wine)

shoulder of mutton or lamb (about 3½ pounds)	2 strips blanched bacon
	1 small onion
	½ stalk celery
salt and pepper	½ carrot
garlic	2 sprigs parsley
1 cup port wine	6 peppercorns
	2 tablespoons flour

Bone the mutton or lamb and remove fat. Salt and pepper the meat, and rub the inside with garlic. Place in a flat dish just large enough to hold it, and pour over the wine. Let marinate in refrigerator for 2 hours or overnight. When ready to cook, roll the meat tightly and tie with string in several places. Place meat, seam side down, in a shallow pan or casserole just large enough to hold it. Pour over the marinade and place the bacon on top. Put in the onion, celery, carrot, parsley, and peppercorns. Roast in a preheated 350°F oven for 1½ hours. Cook mutton 45 to 60 minutes longer than lamb. Baste often with the liquid in the pan, adding a little water if necessary. Remove the meat and place on a hot platter. Discard vegetables and strain liquid into a saucepan; there should be at least ½ cup. Stir in 2 tablespoons flour and cook 2 minutes. Add 1 cup water and cook until thickened. Season to taste. Pour sauce over the roast. Makes 4 servings.

Peito de Vitela Entolado (Rolled Breast of Veal)

Peito de Vitela Entolado
(Rolled Breast of Veal)

breast of veal, about 3½ pounds before bones are removed	2 tablespoons chopped parsley
salt and pepper	1 teaspoon thyme
garlic	½ teaspoon basil
8 hard-cooked eggs	¼ teaspoon cayenne pepper
½ cup minced ham	1 small onion
1 truffle, chopped (optional)	½ carrot
3 tablespoons chopped raisins	1 stalk celery
	1 bay leaf
	water

Bone the breast of veal, trim off any fat, and reserve the bones. Lay veal skin side down, and rub on salt, pepper, and garlic. Finely grate the hard-cooked eggs and add the ham, truffles, raisins, parsley, thyme, basil, cayenne, 2 teaspoons salt and ½ teaspoon pepper. Toss together and spread on the veal. Roll and tie with string at both ends and in the middle. Wrap in a double thickness of cheesecloth and tie the ends securely. Place the bones in the bottom of a large kettle, place the roll on top, and surround with the vegetables. Pour in 4 cups water and add 1 teaspoon salt. Cover and simmer over low heat for 2 hours. Cool the roll in the broth. Discard bones and vegetables and remove the cheesecloth. Put the roll on a plate with another to cover it and a weight on top of the upper plate. Remove any fat from the top of the broth, reduce to 2 cups, and strain through a double thickness of flannel cloth. Refrigerate meat and broth for 24 hours. A couple of hours before serving, remove any fat from the broth, melt the broth but do not heat it, and pour through the double thickness of flannel cloth again. Refrigerate until almost set. Repeat as often as necessary to make a smooth aspic. Spoon over the roll, and decorate the top with truffles if desired. Makes 8 servings.

Ensalada de la Reina
(The Queen's Salad)

3 endives	1 tablespoon olive oil
1 large tart apple, peeled and chopped	1 tablespoon lemon juice
¼ cup diced celery	¼ teaspoon salt
6 small mushroom caps, diced	mayonnaise
sections from 2 grapefruit, skin and membranes removed	

Separate the endive leaves and soak in ice water. Mix the apple, celery, and mushrooms together. Drain endive and dry on a paper towel. Place the leaves around the edge of a platter, the points outward. At the base of the leaves arrange grapefruit sections overlapping. Fill the center with the apple mixture that has been tossed with the oil, lemon juice, and salt. Serve the mayonnaise in a bowl. Makes 4 servings.

Ensalada del Rey Martín
(King Martin's Salad)

1 medium globe artichoke	½ cup olive oil
8 celery stalks	2 tablespoons vinegar
½ small cabbage, cut in fourths and core removed	½ teaspoon salt
	¼ teaspoon freshly ground pepper

Discard any tough outside leaves of the artichoke and cook in boiling salted water to which a wedge of lemon has been added. When tender drain, cut in fourths, remove the choke, and submerge in cold water. Refrigerate until ready to serve. Cut celery into 4-inch pieces and make cuts 1 inch deep at each end to fringe it. Place in ice water and refrigerate to curl the ends. When ready to arrange the salad, place the cut cabbage on a round platter with the tips touching in the center. Between each piece of cabbage place a quartered artichoke and a piece of celery. Mix the oil, vinegar, salt, and pepper together and pour over the salad. Makes 4 servings.

Almond Honey Turnovers

dough of Honey Nut Bread	1½ cups honey
Nut Filling	½ cup chopped almonds
1 egg, slightly beaten	½ cup chopped walnuts
olive oil	

Roll out the dough paper-thin and cut with a 3½-inch cookie cutter. Place 2 teaspoons of the nut filling on each circle. Fold over and seal edges with a sharp-tined fork, first dipped in the beaten egg. Fry in 375° F oil until golden. Drain on a paper towel and keep warm. Put the turnovers in a dish close together and pour over the hot honey and nuts that have been boiled together for 1 minute. Baste the turnovers several times to get them well coated. Serve warm. Makes about 24.

Honey Nut Bread

1 package active dry yeast	¼ cup olive oil
½ cup warm water	1 egg, slightly beaten
2 to 2½ cups flour	½ cup hot honey
½ teaspoon salt	¼ cup pine nuts

In a mixing bowl dissolve yeast in warm water. Stir in 2 cups flour and salt and mix until smooth. Add enough remaining flour to handle easily. Turn onto lightly floured cloth; knead until smooth and elastic, about 10 minutes. Round up in greased bowl, bring greased side up. Cover with cloth. Let rise until double in bulk, about 1½ hours. Punch down; let rise again until almost double, about 35 minutes. Roll dough into an oblong about 9 by 15 inches. Brush olive oil over the surface and spread on the nut and sugar filling. Starting at wide side of the oblong, roll up like a jelly roll. Pinch edges to seal. Place on a greased baking sheet. Let rise about 1 hour. Bake in a 375° F oven for 35 to 45 minutes or until golden. Place the bread on a plate and pour over the heated honey; sprinkle the top with pine nuts. Cool before slicing.

Nut Filling

½ cup almonds, ground in blender or crushed with rolling pin	½ cup granulated sugar

Mix the almonds and sugar together.

Monte Blanco
(Puréed Chestnut Whip Cream)

1 pound fresh chestnuts	1 egg white
water	3 tablespoons sifted confectioners' sugar
1 cup milk	½ cup whipping cream
⅛ teaspoon salt	grated sweet chocolate (optional)
1 teaspoon vanilla	
¼ cup granulated sugar	

Make a cross with a sharp knife on the flat side of the chestnuts. Cover with water and boil 15 minutes. Drain and while chestnuts are hot remove the shell and skin. Place the chestnuts with the milk, salt, ½ teaspoon vanilla, and the granulated sugar in the top of a double boiler and cook until the chestnuts are very soft. Drain off the milk (use for a custard at a later date) and press the chestnuts through a ricer, food mill, or coarse sieve directly into a serving dish or on top of a sponge cake such as Bizcocho. Whip egg white until stiff but not dry and add the confectioners' sugar while continuing to beat. Whip the cream, add remaining vanilla, and fold the egg white into the cream. Top the chestnut purée with the cream mixture. If desired, sprinkle grated chocolate on top. Chill before serving. Makes 4 to 6 servings.

MIDDLE EUROPE

Francis Joseph I **by Hermann Wasmuth**

 HARLEMAGNE WAS FOR a few decades the ruler of all of western Europe, and at his table gathered German as well as French noblemen. Never happier than when united around the table with his friends and advisers at court, Karl der Grosse, as he is known in German, took particular interest in the food and drink offered at the imperial palace at Aachen and at his other residences. From his palace at Ingelheim he noticed that the winter snow melted first from the steep hill of the village of Johannisberg and accordingly saw to it that grapes were planted there; these vines still produce the world-famous Schloss Johannisberg wines. Charlemagne also owned vineyards in the village of Aloxe-Corton, which still produce some of the most extraordinary wines of Burgundy, the red Corton Clos-du-Roi and the white Corton-Charlemagne.

The wines accompanied great roasts of ox and venison prepared in the imperial kitchens on huge spits over open fires. The chief dish, however, was roasted peacock prepared in a manner that began a tradition throughout the Middle Ages. The roasted bird arrived at table decked with an ornate peacock-shaped cover made of the partially gilded head and feathers of the peacock. The cover may have been made by the royal artists, whose studio was situated within the palace complex. Charlemagne's meals were never complete without the rich creamy cheese that he had brought from the abbey of St. Germain-des-Près. Each year two cartloads of this cheese, very much like Brie or Camembert, were ordered for the imperial table.

Although later German nobles and kings of the medieval period have left few reminiscences of their dining habits, one of the staples of princely households must have been the sausage. The name itself descends from the Latin word *salsus,* "salt"; for one of the steps in the manufacture of sausage was the mixing of the freshly chopped meat with large quantities of salt before it was stuffed into the casing. The meat used was pork, and the casing was the intestines of the animal, cleaned and cut into suitable lengths. The slaughter of the porkers took place during the cold months in order to protect the meat from spoilage while the sausage was being made. The raw meat was cut into small chunks and thrown into a huge wooden tub, in which it was mixed with salt and other ingredients, some of which also acted as preservatives. Wine, garlic, herbs, and— if available—whole peppercorns were mixed with the meat, which was then forced into the casings. The sausages were sometimes placed in a smoke-house, where a fire of beechwood imparted a fine flavor and golden color to the sausage and further aided its preservation. After a week or so in the smokehouse, the sausages were hung in a cool, airy room to complete the curing process.

As important as sausage was for daily suste-nance in the castle of the medieval noble, the lord of the house loaded his banquet table with more lavish productions. Roasted pheasant, swan, and peacock were well known in medieval Germany and Austria. The removal of the peacock's gor-geous cover was always the occasion for the men around the table to swear "by God, by the Holy Virgin, by my lady, and by the Peacock" to do a knightly or pious deed.

A medieval feast must have been a confusion of sights, sounds, and smells, as musicians and jesters vied for attention with the food itself and the lord's dogs begged for scraps among the diners. The guests were equipped with little other than their appetites to cope with the job of con-veying the food from table to mouth. Pieces of meat were hacked off the roast or more often ripped away with fingers. During this period the custom became established that a knight was seated beside his lady so that he could serve her —again with the fingers, for the fork did not come into general use in Germany and Austria until the 18th century. Etiquette decreed that only the first three fingers were to be used in conveying food to the mouth; the ring and little finger were ex-tended away from the others—a custom that still lingers. Greasy fingers were a sign of poor breed-ing, and the nobly born never wiped their fingers on their clothes—the tablecloth was to be used for this purpose.

Medieval diners found the table set with drinking glasses or ornately mounted drinking horns and a saltcellar, but little else. The men sup-plied their own knives and cut pieces for the ladies; meat thus separated from the roast was placed on small wooden platters or on a thick slice of bread.

The records show that staggering quantities of food were consumed. In 1500, at the very end of the medieval period in Germany, Prince George

the Rich of Landshut gave a feast during which the guests consumed 3,000 roast oxen, 5,000 roast geese, more than 60,000 chickens, 80 boar, many thousands of crayfish, 200 hogsheads of domestic wine, and 300 barrels of imported wine.

The coming of the Renaissance to Germany and Austria brought with it the craving for food seasoned with rare spices from the East and herbs, such as parsley, that Italian cooks had introduced into the European cuisine. These spices and sea-sonings became the mark of the princely table, for few others could afford them. At the close of the Middle Ages, pepper was quite literally worth its weight in gold, and a pound of saffron cost considerably more than a good field horse. The tremendous desire to heighten the tastes of fa-miliar foods and to create exotic new flavors con-stituted one of the stimuli for the voyages of exploration that changed the history of Europe in the latter part of the 15th and the beginning of the 16th century.

Bronze bust of Charles V by Leone Leoni

The Holy Roman Emperor Charles V (1519–56) was well known for his partiality to highly seasoned food. At the convocations of the Imperial Diet he dined alone in state, served by young counts and princes of the realm. While his musicians played from a platform behind the royal diner, he sliced away at roasted meats, calf heads, and suckling pig. The roasts were probably basted with a sauce consisting of honey, large quantities of pepper, garlic, and asafoetida, a pungent herb tasting like a blend of onion and garlic. Charles was a moderate drinker, according to the taste of the times; he drank only three times at each meal. When he was ready to imbibe, he beckoned to his physicians, who apparently attended him as wine stewards as well, and they poured from two silver flasks into a crystal tankard that held nearly a quart. Charles downed it without setting the vessel down; contemporary chroniclers report, however, that he was forced to stop two or three times for breath.

The 18th century in Germany marked the rise of Prussia, the greatest of whose rulers, Frederick the Great, was not only a military strategist, a formidable intellect, and a friend of Voltaire, but also a lover of fine food. The king dined each day at noon, and upon rising he personally wrote out the menu for the day and indicated which chef was to prepare it. One of the frequently selected dishes, *boulettes de moelle,* a kind of meat patty made with beef marrow, was prepared by the chef Schliger. Henaut, another of Frederick's chefs, made the *bisque d'écrivisses,* a creamy soup made with the crayfish that still abounded in German rivers. If the king ordered only five courses, this was a signal that he wished to dine alone or at most with two or three persons. Gala dinners consisted of as many as 30 courses. A menu for one of the simpler meals consisted of *soupe aux salsifis, ailes de perdreaux glacés aux cardons* glazed wings of young partridge with artichokes, *petits pâtés à la romaine,* and *escalopes à l'ang-*

A Prince of Saxony and **A Princess of Saxony** by Lucas Cranach the Elder

laise. At the Prussian court, under the influence of the cosmopolitan Frederick, French-inspired cooking began to supplant native German cuisine. At other German courts, however, old-time German food and eating habits continued. During the first years of the 18th century, Liselotte, the Princess Palatine and wife of the Duc d'Orléans, wrote from her adopted home in Paris of her affection for the foods of her homeland and of her disdain of French food. For her a dish of sauerkraut and smoked sausage was superior to anything French cooking could produce. It was she who introduced to Paris pickled herring, raw cured ham, and blood sausage. The same lady also wrote of her proud adherence to the centuries-old habit of using only a knife and her fingers for eating. In fact, the nobles of Germany resisted the fork as an instrument dangerous to the user— many were wary of spearing themselves as well as their food—until the end of the 18th century.

The love of wine and of its effects still added color to German feasting. Drinking glasses were often made without flat bases so that they could not be set down until empty, and those who could drain their glasses at a single pull—glasses contained a mere pint—were considered masters of the grape.

By the 19th century the dining room was more clearly separated from the wine cellar, and in February, 1833, Helmuth von Moltke, a Prussian noble, presented a more refined picture of court activities at the Prussian capital of Berlin. Upon arrival at 11 in the morning the guests danced a waltz and then separated into two rooms, where each guest chose a flower; partners for the "breakfast" found each other by their matching flowers. The breakfast turned out to be a full-scale dinner, commencing with turtle soup, oysters, and caviar, followed by a truffled pâté and, as Moltke described them, "other delightful melanges of culinary art." After this refreshment, dancing continued until eight, when the Court went to the theater.

Vienna, one of the radiating centers of the brilliant culture of *fin-de-siècle* Europe, the capital of the vast Austro-Hungarian Empire, cultivated the life of the senses with brilliance and abandon. A reverence for eating was an elegant obsession of the Viennese, and to Vienna came the nobility of the empire—Czechs, Magyars, and Austrians— to sample these pleasures. The international quality of the city created a cuisine that blended adaptations from French cooking with highly sea-

soned East European food. Paprika, the chief seasoning of traditional Magyar cooking, and dishes such as *gulyàs* (goulash) and *paprika Händel* came into the vocabulary of European cooking through the kitchens of Vienna. The Austro-Hungarian court kitchens, comparable in size and activity to a small city, turned out fantasies of pas-

Mariana de Austria, **daughter of Ferdinand III of Austria who became queen of Spain, in a portrait by Velázquez**

try and confection as well as elegantly decorated roasts, fish, and fowl. The city itself, on the other hand, boasted establishments such as Sacher's and Demel's, where the aristocracy and the middle class met to enjoy elegant dining and the traditional Viennese *Jause,* something more than a snack and only slightly less than a meal. The chic

Strawberry Meringue

restaurants also furnished the backdrop for the scandals that titillated Viennese society; the Archduke Rudolf often took his mistress, Baroness Maria Vetsera, to an intimate supper at Sacher's.

At Schönbrunn, the vast court kitchens and bakeries were kept busy preparing for balls and state banquets. At the heart of the formal routine of the ball was the buffet set up in the *Redoutensaal*, one of the largest reception rooms of the palace. Here the dancers quenched their thirst with champagne, mocha, Roman punch, ice cream, and almond milk. The young officers crowded around the tables, offering their caps to be filled with *petit fours* from the Schönbrunn bakeries. After a short supper of five courses the imperial family left the ball at midnight; then began the famous *Zuckerschlacht*, the so-called sugar battle, as the guests eagerly snatched up the contents of tray after tray of sugar sculptures. Here the art of the chef transformed itself into that of the sculptor and painter. Gorgeous bonbon imitations of classical statues, effigies, and miniature portraits of the emperor and his family were prized as souvenirs of the court balls.

At the court banquets, however, the gastronomic brilliance of the court shone most brightly. Here the emperor entertained his generals, leading political figures, and the commanders of the various regiments stationed around Vienna. Ceremony ruled all; as the Master of the Kitchen escorted the emperor from his chambers, the guests stood in a half circle, with the highest in rank nearest the door. After the emperor had greeted each guest according to protocol, the party moved to the dining hall. The table was set in an open square, and white tablecloths contrasted with the masses of flowers in golden vases interspersed with the famous sugar sculptures. At each place, in front of a veritable wall of wine glasses of various shapes and sizes, reposed a menu handwritten in French. The meal always consisted of 12 courses and usually began with crabs and oysters, the latter brought from Venice. Next came the soup, accompanied by beer; then the hors d'oeuvres and Rhine wine. With the fish was served Bordeaux and with the entrées champagne; with the roast or game either sherry or Madeira; and finally, with dessert, the emperor's fabled Hungarian Tokay. By the end of the emperor's life this wine was all but unobtainable except in the tunnel-like mazes of the imperial wine cellars. This Tokay from the vineyards at

Dürer goblet, of silver gilt, from the collection of Archduke Ferdinand of Tirol

Hegyalja—one of the most magnificent sweet wines in the world—was presented to Queen Victoria on the occasion of her Diamond Jubilee by the Emperor Francis Joseph.

Among the most famous delicacies of the imperial table was a braised beef called *Tafelspitz*. Taken from the hindquarters of the beef, close to the thigh bone, this cut was considered by Viennese gourmets to be the tastiest part of the animal. The meat was quickly seared in a pan similar to a dutch oven and then braised slowly

The Castle of Nymphenburg by Bernardo Bellotto

until very tender—the trick of knowing just when the roast was done was one of the secrets of the great Viennese chefs—while the juices were reduced and thickened and flavored with a touch of paprika, cognac, and orange juice. The *Tafelspitz* rode to the table on an elegantly decorated mound of potatoes and was served with baked celery, purée of young peas in potato jackets, or spears of baked squash.

Court etiquette decreed that the guests could continue eating only as long as the emperor did, and inasmuch as he ate sparingly as he grew older, the guests very often left the table with appetites not yet dulled. This necessitated a visit after the banquet to places such as Demel's,

where the late-night snack would almost certainly include *Eiskaffee*, a rich, soft coffee ice cream, and *indianer Krapfen*, a delicate shell of pastry filled with sweet whipped cream and a touch of apricot marmalade, topped with a glaze of chocolate icing. The Viennese saw nothing incongruous about consoling themselves with sweets for the loss of a slice of *Tafelspitz*, for sweets were more than the finish of an elegant meal—they were one of the joys of living.

Austria has changed greatly since World War I; the empire has been dismembered, the aristocracy dispersed, and the monarchy replaced by a republic. But Vienna lives, and so do the joys of her food.

Royal Recipes

Vegetable Stew

butter
1 pound onions, sliced
4 cloves garlic, minced
salt
pepper
4 carrots, cut in 1-inch
   pieces
2 large green peppers,
   cut in ½-inch slices
8 whole small tomatoes,
   peeled

2 medium zucchini, cut
   in ½-inch slices
½ eggplant, cut in
   ½-inch slices
10 ounces each cauli-
   flower flowerets,
   Brussels sprouts,
   string beans, peas,
   and asparagus tips
1 cup water

In a large kettle sauté the onions and garlic in butter until tender and golden. Salt and pepper lightly. Add all the vegetables except the asparagus tips, tossing them to mix well. Salt and pepper again and add the water. Cover and cook in a preheated 350° oven for 20 to 30 minutes, adding the asparagus tips the last 10 minutes of cooking. Correct the seasoning. Makes 8 servings.

Magyar Gulyàs Leves (Goulash Soup)

Vegetable Stew and Bárány Pörkölt (Lamb Goulash)

Borju Paprikas
(Veal Paprika)

4 pounds shoulder or
  breast of veal
boiling water
1 cup soft bread crumbs
2 eggs, slightly beaten
  melted butter

2 teaspoons fresh
  chopped marjoram
  or ½ teaspoon dried
3 tablespoons chopped
  parsley
paprika
salt
pepper

Have the butcher slit a long pocket in the meat for stuffing. Pour boiling water over meat and pat dry. Mix the bread crumbs, eggs, and ¼ cup melted butter together. Add marjoram, parsley, ½ teaspoon paprika, ½ teaspoon salt, and ¼ teaspoon pepper and toss lightly. Stuff the pocket with the filling and close with skewers. Sprinkle top of veal generously with paprika. Place the meat in a shallow pan and roast in a preheated 450°F oven for 30 minutes. Reduce temperature to 325°F, pour over ½ cup water mixed with 3 tablespoons melted butter, and cook for 30 minutes more. Baste frequently with ½ cup water and the pan juices for another 30 minutes (total cooking time 1½ hours).

Remove to a warm platter and pour over the pan juices. Serve with tarhonya or cracked wheat. Makes 6 servings.

Barány Pörkolt
(Lamb Goulash)

4 strips bacon, chopped
2 large onions, chopped
2 pounds lamb, cut in
  1-inch cubes
2 to 3 tablespoons
  paprika

1 medium green pepper,
  cut in ½-inch strips
1 1-pound can tomato
  purée
1 cup beef stock
½ teaspoon pepper
1 teaspoon salt

Fry the bacon and onions together in a large skillet until the onions are golden; remove. Dust the lamb in paprika and cook about 5 minutes over medium heat, moving the meat rapidly to keep it from burning. Add green pepper, tomato purée, and stock; return onion and bacon and add salt and pepper. Cover and cook over low heat for 30 to 40 minutes or until lamb is tender. Correct the seasoning. Makes 4 to 6 servings.

Borju Paprikas (Veal Paprika)

Dining room of the villa, Bad Ischl, of Francis Joseph I

Magyar Gulyàs Leves
(Goulash Soup)

1½ pounds round steak, cut into 1-inch cubes	2 medium tomatoes, peeled and chopped
salt and pepper	1 green or red pepper, seeded and cut into 2-inch strips
3 medium onions, chopped	
1 to 2 tablespoons paprika	3 medium potatoes, peeled and cut into 1-inch cubes
1½ teaspoons marjoram	
1½ teaspoons caraway seeds	2 ounces medium egg noodles
8 cups water	

Trim meat and render fat to make 2 tablespoons. Salt and pepper meat and brown on all sides in a large kettle in the fat. Remove meat and brown the onions. Stir in paprika, marjoram, caraway seeds, and 2 tablespoons salt. Add water and return meat to the kettle. Cover and simmer for 1½ hours over low heat. Add tomatoes and green peppers and cook 30 minutes more. Put in the potatoes, and when the liquid has returned to a simmer add the noodles. Cook until the potatoes and noodles are done, about 10 minutes. Correct the seasoning. Makes 6 to 8 servings.

Esterhazy Rostelyos
(Sirloin Steak and Sour Cream)

1 2-pound sirloin steak	1 tablespoon small capers
salt	
pepper	1 pound carrots, cut in 2-inch julienne
2 medium onions, sliced	
1 tablespoon flour	1 tablespoon chopped parsley
1½ teaspoons paprika	1 tablespoon butter
1 teaspoon marjoram	4 tablespoons sour cream
1½ cups beef stock	
2 lemon slices	

Trim fat from steak and render to make 1 tablespoon. Salt and pepper the steak lightly and brown on both sides in the fat. Remove meat and sauté the onions until golden. Stir in flour, paprika, and marjoram. Add 1 cup of stock, lemon slices, and capers and return the meat. Cover and simmer over low heat for 30 minutes. In a small skillet sauté carrots and parsley in butter for 5 minutes. Pour in the remaining stock; add salt and pepper to taste, cover, and cook until tender. When ready to serve, drain the carrot liquid into the meat pan and arrange the carrots on a warm platter. Place the steak and onions on the carrot bed, discard lemon slices, and stir the sour cream into the meat pan. Correct the seasoning. Pour over the steak. Makes 3 to 4 servings.

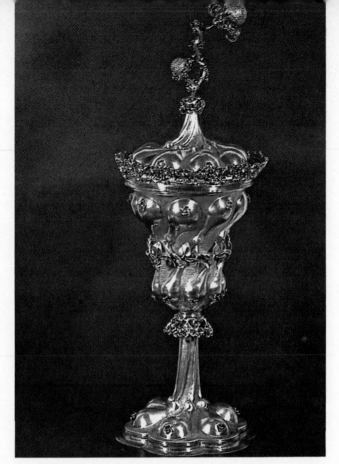

Burgundian court goblet from the collection of Maximilian I

The Maximilian goblet, of silver and gilt

Hirn mit Zwiebeln
(Brains with Onions)

1 pound calf's brains	2 cups chopped onions
salt and pepper	2 tablespoons butter
1½ tablespoons vinegar	

Soak brains in ice water with 2 teaspoons salt for 30 minutes. Drain and remove all membranes with a sharp knife. Place brains in a saucepan with enough water to cover; add 1 teaspoon salt and 1 tablespoon vinegar and simmer gently for 15 minutes. Remove brains with a slotted spoon and plunge again into a bowl of ice water with the remaining vinegar for a few minutes until firm and white. Drain, pat dry with a paper towel, and chop into ½-inch pieces. Sauté onions in butter until tender and lightly browned. Add brains and cook until well heated. Salt and pepper to taste. Makes 2 servings.

Kaiser Gugelhupf
(Raisin Cake)

1 package dry yeast	1½ cups confectioners'
¼ cup lukewarm water	sugar
sifted flour	½ teaspoon salt
2 eggs	¾ cup raisins
1 cup milk	⅓ cup ground almonds
⅓ cup butter	

In a mixing bowl soften yeast in lukewarm water and stir in ½ cup sifted flour. Sift 1½ cups flour over the sponge, cover with a towel, and put in a warm place until the sponge rises through the flour, about 2 hours. Break in the eggs, add milk, and beat thoroughly until smooth. In a small bowl cream butter until light and fluffy and add the sugar and salt. Mix a little of the batter into the butter mixture until smooth and then combine the two. Toss the raisins and nuts with 1 tablespoon flour and add to the batter. Turn the batter into a 6-cup Gugelhupf mold or angel food cake pan. Bake in a preheated 375°F oven for 30 to 40 minutes. Unmold on a cake rack and dust with confectioners sugar.

Wiener Eiskaffee
(Coffee Parfait)

½ cup fresh coffee	1-inch vanilla bean
beans or 1 table-	or ¼ teaspoon
spoon freeze-dry	vanilla extract
coffee dissolved	2 egg yolks
in 1 tablespoon	1 cup confectioners'
boiling water	sugar, sifted
1 cup medium cream	1 pint whipping cream

Roast coffee beans in a preheated 375°F oven for 15 minutes. Heat the cream, coffee beans, and vanilla bean to the boiling point. Let stand 20 minutes or more. Strain and discard the beans. Beat the yolks until lemon color; slowly add the sugar and beat until very thick and almost white. Stir in the coffee-cream mixture. Refrigerate for 1 hour or more. Whip the cream and fold into coffee mixture. Serve in tall glasses. Top with plain whipped cream if desired. Makes 6 servings.

Linzer Torte
(Raspberry Tart)

1½ cups butter
1 cup sifted
   confectioners' sugar
1 egg
2¾ cups flour
⅛ teaspoon salt
½ teaspoon cinnamon

¼ teaspoon ground
   cloves
1¼ cups ground almonds
   grated rind of 1 lemon
1½ cups raspberry jam
1 egg white, slightly
   beaten

Cream the butter and sugar until light and fluffy. Add the egg and beat in well. Sift together the flour, salt, cinnamon, and cloves and gradually add to the butter mixture. Stir in almonds and lemon rind. Chill for 1 hour or more. Roll out dough to ¼ inch thick and line the bottom of a 10½ x 1-inch spring-form pan. Press a 1-inch strip of the dough against the side of the form to make a rim ¼ inch thick. Spread dough lining with raspberry jam. Roll out the remaining dough and cut into 1-inch strips to form a lattice over the top. Brush with egg white and bake in a preheated 375°F oven for 30 to 40 minutes or until golden brown. Remove and sprinkle the edge with confectioners' sugar. Makes 8 to 10 servings.

Strawberry Meringue

6 egg whites
1 cup sugar

1 pint strawberries
1 pint whipped and
   sweetened cream

Cut out four 7-inch circles from a piece of brown paper and place on a baking sheet. Make a meringue from 3 egg whites and ½ cup sugar. Insert a plain tube in a pastry bag and, starting in the center of one of the circles, pipe the meringue in a spiral, covering the entire circle. Pipe a 1-inch border of meringue on the remaining circles of paper. Bake in a preheated 250°F oven for about 45 minutes. Remove from oven, let cool, and slip the rings off the paper. Lay the rings on top of each other on the filled-in base. Make more meringue, using the remaining egg whites and sugar. Frost outside and top edge of the shell with meringue. With a fancy tube, pipe rosettes on the top edge and outside. If any meringue is left over, lightly coat the inside where the rings join. Return to the 250° oven and bake for 1 hour. Turn off the heat and leave in the oven for 2 more hours. Chop the smaller berries and fold into the whipped cream. Fill the shell with the whipped cream just before serving, and place the largest strawberries on the top. Makes 6 servings.

The Kitchen of Archduke Albrecht of Austria by David Teniers the Younger

Schlosserbuben
(Prune Fritters)

5 dozen prunes	2 teaspoons melted
water	butter
juice and peel of 1	⅛ teaspoon salt
lemon	¼ cup sifted all-purpose
5 dozen almonds,	flour
blanched and	oil for deep frying
toasted	¾ cup grated sweet
1 egg, slightly beaten	chocolate
¼ cup white wine	sifted confectioners'
	sugar

Cover prunes with water and add juice and peel of the lemon. Simmer 15 minutes. Drain and pat dry on a paper towel. Remove the pit from each prune, insert an almond, and press to close. Mix the egg, wine, butter, and salt together. Stir into the flour and blend until very smooth. Dip each prune into the batter and fry in 375°F oil until golden. Roll in grated chocolate and dust with confectioners' sugar. Makes 60 fritters.

Edam Cheese Tart

2 cups sifted flour	1½ tablespoons butter
salt	2 cups light cream or
4 egg yolks	milk
5 tablespoons soft	4 whole eggs
butter or	¼ teaspoon white
margarine	pepper
water	½ pound Edam cheese,
1 medium onion,	grated
grated	

Put flour and 1 teaspoon salt in a bowl. Make a well in the center and add egg yolks and butter. Work all together and add enough water to moisten. Roll out on a pastry cloth and line a 10-inch pie plate with the dough. Refrigerate for 1 hour or more. When ready to bake, line the dough with wax paper and cover with uncooked rice to hold the pastry flat. Bake in a preheated 375°F oven for 10 minutes. Remove rice and wax paper and return to the oven for 5 or 6 minutes more. Sauté onion in butter until tender; stir in 1 tablespoon flour, cook 1 minute, and add cream. Cook 5 minutes more, stirring constantly. Cool to lukewarm. Beat the whole eggs until light and fluffy, add ½ teaspoon salt and ¼ teaspoon white pepper, and stir into the cream. Sprinkle cheese into the pie shell and pour over the egg mixture. Bake in a preheated 375°F oven from 30 to 40 minutes or until a knife inserted in the center comes out clean. Serve hot. Makes 10 to 12 servings.

Covered jug made for Rudolph II from a palm nut mounted in silver gilt

Tomerl Pfannkuchen
(Cornmeal Pancakes)

2 cups diced onions	½ cup cornmeal
1 tablespoon butter or	¼ teaspoon salt
margarine	2 eggs, slightly beaten
1 cup sifted all-purpose	1¾ cups milk
flour	

Sauté onions in butter until tender. Mix the flour, cornmeal, and salt together. Combine eggs and milk and slowly stir into the flour; the batter should be medium thick. Add the onions. Heat a 5-inch greased skillet and pour in about ¼ cup of batter. Swirl batter to cover bottom of the pan and cook until golden; turn and cook the other side. Serve with butter or gravy in place of potatoes or rice. Makes 8 pancakes.

Jasper tankard with gold mounts, inscribed with the device of Rudolph II

SCANDI-NAVIA and the LOW COUNTRIES

Christian II, King of Denmark by Lucas Cranach

NY CONTEMPORARY SCANDINAVIAN king with a proclivity for food and drink comes by it honestly. The ancestral Viking kings were renowned as topers and trenchermen. It would indeed take considerable appetite to eat through one of the enormous roasted animal haunches they favored, or one of the immense loaves of black barley bread. Those kings also had a penchant for porridges and gruels, usually sweetened with honey and laved with cream. (These were undoubtedly the forerunners of the many more delicate porridges of today, such as Danish buttermilk soup fragrant with vanilla and lemon; or a sweet-and-tart berry fruit soup; or the Norwegian national cream porridge, *Rømmegrøt*, of smooth sour cream blended with hot butter, brown sugar, cinnamon, and black currant juice.)

In the early 10th century, Rollo the Dane and his piratical partisans settled in conquered Normandy and learned to like two of the lovely local dishes: fresh Dover sole, marinated in apple brandy and poached in cream; and a dessert tart of apples baked in cream within a buttery pastry shell.

Some say that the present-day joys of the smörgåsbord were bequeathed to us by the Viking kings. The Vikings were great hosts; whenever they held a real party, it went on for days. The celebrants traveled far to get there, brought whatever foods they could from their home territories, pridefully placed them upon the banquet table, and settled down for a few days of frolic and feast.

In the later Middle Ages, the kings began to pay more attention to the niceties of the banquet hall. In Norway, Haakon the Old was crowned in Bergen in 1217 to the accompaniment of a prodigious three-day celebration banquet. He ruled "ably and generously," and an Italian cardinal who traveled to his Court in 1247 was delighted at the unexpectedly excellent manners he found there.

During the Renaissance, court life took on more elegance, and so did the manners of eating. France became the model, and cooks in the Scandinavian royal kitchens borrowed freely from the French culinary wizards. But if a French sauce was rich, the Scandinavians made it richer—with their own superb butters and creams. Whereas a

French banquet design plotted certain courses with certain sauces, and some without, the Scandinavians preferred to sauce them all, and lusciously. And while the French perfected their classic presentations of classic dishes, the Scandinavians embellished those ideas with their own further flourishes. Cooks in the court kitchens at Stockholm refined the art of cake baking at this time. They could not have done so previously, because until the mid-16th century sugar was not available even at a price royalty could pay.

The Vasa kings initiated a period of notable eating in Sweden. In fact, royal household records suggest that the Courts of the Vasa kings must have operated under a regimen of massive eating and drinking.

Gustavus I Vasa (1523–60) started it off by importing foreign master chefs. He personally began each day with beer soup served in bed before 6 A.M. He took his dinner at 9 or 10 A.M. and his supper from 4 to 5. His first son, Eric XIV (1560–68), in his first reigning year, cured a sneeze by drinking claret spiced with anise and licorice—210 half-gallon cans of it. He also managed to indulge his fondness for sweets. During that same first year of power, his court used 3,000 pounds of sugar, 99 pounds of dates, 621 pounds of figs, 876 pounds of almonds, 1,469 pounds of prunes, 95 pounds of currants, 2,165 pounds of raisins, and 15 barrels of citron. One of his special passions was pears preserved in candy sugar. He was an avant-gardist of table fashions, too; he is said to have owned 12 gilded forks and 12 spoons—several decades before forks first appeared in French courts.

John III (1568–92) was also fond of sugar. On one occasion, when his order of sugar failed to arrive on time, he sent soldiers off to arrest the negligent supplier and to buy or steal or seize whatever sugar they could from whatever sources they could; unconditionally, they had to return with 100 pounds of sugar by nightfall. John also had a hankering for fish. His favorite dish was *gravad lax* (fresh salmon marinated with salt and fresh dill); and he relished a dish of special bits of the dried halibut from Bergen, and pike mousse molded in the shape of a pear. He imported live crayfish and carp from Germany and stocked them in the castle ponds at Kalmar. During one month of John's reign, his table devoured 63 oxen, 28 calves, 298 lambs, 26 rabbits, 63 geese, 980 hens, 950 game birds, seven tons of preserved game, 858 salmon and pike, six tons of salt pork, and many beef tongues, hams, and pork backs.

John is said to have invented an aquavit good for dealing with both "poison and plague," distilled from Rhine wine, red coral, unicorn horns, white ivory, burnt deer horns, and spices and herbs. His Court recorded astounding wine consumption, not so much French wine as Rhenish and Hungarian. The wines served were seldom untampered with; white wines were often mixed with honey in proportions of ten to one. Always on hand were at least three different kinds of spiced wines—spiced with such as "cardamom, cinnamon, sugar, nutmeg, cloves, saffron, egg white, milk, and many other things." The beer consumption was even greater. It was taken for granted that each individual at court would need at least six liters of beer to get through each day; a marshal of John's Court is recorded to have drunk, in one day, four liters of beer for breakfast and 22 during the rest of the day.

In the Court of Norway and Denmark, Christian IV (1588–1648) drank beer so heartily that he once proposed 35 toasts in brisk succession, and subsequently had to suffer the indignity of being carried out of the banquet hall in a chair. Credit goes to that same ebullient toaster for bringing efficiency to the skoaling ritual. Previously, the toasting vessel had been a large bowl passed from person to person, but King Christian innovated individual drinking vessels.

Olaf V of Norway

At the Oslo gala honoring the accession of Frederick III (1648–70), 1,000 guests were seated in three separate buildings. The countryside was previously combed for birds, eggs, pigs, sheep, and fish for the affair; barrels of specialties were imported from England, Germany, France, and Holland. Eight years later another royal feast recorded the consumption over 12 courses of 1,387 chickens and 78 oxen.

During the 18th century in Sweden, the royal compulsion toward gourmandism continued. Charles XII (1697–1718) and his warriors discovered stuffed grape leaves (*dolma*) in Turkey and adapted them for Sweden as cabbage rolls; today those *kåldomar* are traditional for Father's Day. A Swedish-German historian records that Charles, who ate whatever was put on the table and never complimented the cook, preferred hot and heavy dishes and enjoyed candied bitter orange peel. He is said on one occasion to have imbibed too much wine and accepted a challenge to ride out stark naked in the middle of the day; upon recovering from his distemper, he resolved to give up the pleasures of the grape for those of pride.

Adolphus Frederick (1751–71) was said to have eaten so many *fettisdagsbullar*, the special buns of Lent, that he burst and died. Those buns may have been irresistible, for they were plumped and sweet with sugar and raisins and whipped cream and almonds and cardamom—and served warm.

The gilded 1880's document the appearance of two more dining delights for the Scandinavian kings' tables: chinaware (dishes had previously been of pewter or wood) and veal Oscar, the understandably favorite dish of Oscar II of Sweden (1872–1907)—butter-sautéed veal cutlet overlaid with asparagus tips and Béarnaise sauce and crowned with lobster morsels.

In Scandinavia today there is no wide gap between royalty and the rest of the people. A favorite dish of Christian X (1912–47) of Denmark was lowly salt-pork gravy with boiled potatoes; and he had a passion for the popular puffed and plump pancake, *aebleskiver*. Count Folke Bernadotte often chose a simple country pea soup for his household and his guests. Currently, a Scandinavian king's cuisine might include appetizers of infinite invention built upon buttered bread; queenly soups emanating from broth and cream and egg yolks; a wealth of the freshest fish out of the nearby seas, lakes, rivers, and streams; breads and rolls of myriad nutty and tasty grains, invariably thickly spread with excellent fresh butter; local and wonderful cheeses; eggs; the finest hams and sausages; good lamb, beef, veal, mutton, and wild game birds and animals; smoked and cured and pickled and dried meats and fish; fresh garden vegetables; berries of many sorts—strawberries, blueberries, raspberries, currants, and those ethereal cloudberries; tree fruits such as apples and plums and cherries; pancakes, light or hearty; luscious and rich desserts; sweet cakes and pastries often rich in butter and almonds—and good sauces in or upon it all!

Scandinavian ladies of all ranks, including royal, practice the art of cooking. Crown Princess Margrethe of Denmark sometimes cooks at her country place; but she hesitates to adopt too much of the French cuisine, since her husband is French and might be too knowing in such matters. Her mother, the former Princess Ingrid of Sweden, on the occasion of Princess Margrethe's wedding, one night invited the royal staff and their families, who had been working feverishly to make all proper wedding preparations, to be the guests of the royal family; on that night the queen and king not only hosted the party but also served the guests.

The Low Countries

Most of the present cuisine of the Low Countries might well have been prescribed by royalty—it is so rich. Yet that Benelux cuisine probably arose out of the ranks of the industrialists and tradesmen and shippers and colonialists during their most prosperous years rather than from a popular patterning after royalty. Those 17th-century dealers in the goods of the world ate and drank with gusto and gleam. Their appreciation for fine food and understanding of the art of cooking show up in the character of the most typical Low Country dishes today: the good meat-stock soups; an abundance of fish and shellfish; the chicken- or fish-and-white-wine full-meal soup, *waterzooi;* the beef and vegetable meat stew, *hutsepot* (or *hochepot*); the beer-based beef stew, *carbonnades flamandes;* baker's bread that is honored; a doting upon vegetables including the oft-sought Belgian endive; a predilection for pancakes and waffles; fine butter in and upon all of these; the *rijsttafel* and tropical treats of the old Dutch Indies; world-renowned cheeses; a generous flow of fine locally brewed beer, Dutch gin, and French wines; cream, pudding, cake, cooky, and tart and

Baudouin of Belgium with his queen, Fabiola

pie desserts; and fine chocolate and candies, coffee, and liqueurs.

Historically, royal eating followed a sequence and style similar to those of other Western European nations. Medieval rulers had a confusion of cuisine—plenty or poverty, fine dishes or horrid ones, banqueting or banality; at best, good eating was a doubtful affair. Then followed the Renaissance attention to fine foods and dining accouterments and many a later sidelong glance to France for guidance and ideas. By the 17th century and Holland's Golden Age, food had become a highly important part of life for the common citizen; and so it was with royalty. Various rulers could dine upon whatever they wished—and that tended to be French.

In the recent days of royal democracies, the same has been mainly true: French cuisine has prevailed on most elegant and state occasions. But, considering Queen Juliana's disarming informality, King Baudouin's lack of pompousness, and Grand Duke Jean's nearness to his people, there can be little doubt that there are many times when the royal dining tables of the Netherlands and Belgium and Luxembourg present characteristic national dishes.

All eaters owe one very lovely item of classic cuisine to the 18th-century Maréchal de Luxembourg and to chance. The event was a seemingly untimely emergency call. Louis XV summoned the *maréchal* from his château just as the marshal was beginning his dinner of cream-coated chicken. With undoubted dismay, the *maréchal* left his pursuit of dining pleasures and hastened off to answer the king. When he returned, the chicken was cold, the sauce had jelled to a fine glaze, and the effect of the whole was exquisite. *Chaud-froid* (hot-cold) sauce had been created!

Royal Dane, King Oscar, and Stockholm

Royal Recipes

Royal Dane
(Danish)

1 slice white bread
  fresh butter
1 lettuce leaf
3 slices cooked ham,
  ⅛ inch thick
	3 ¼-inch wedges
	  Danish semi-soft
	  cheese
	3 asparagus tips

Butter bread generously. Place a lettuce leaf on the bread, slightly beyond the edge on one side. Fold ham, to give height, and place on the lettuce leaf overlapping. Tuck a wedge of cheese between the slices and lay one on top. Lay an asparagus tip on each piece of cheese. Serve on a small plate or wooden board. Makes 1 serving.

King Oscar
(Norwegian)

1 slice white bread
  butter
  cucumber slices
	mayonnaise
	small shrimp
	lemon garnish

Butter bread generously. Place cucumber slices on the edge of the bread in a circle. Put mayonnaise in the center and place the shrimp around. Garnish with lemon. Makes 1 serving.

Stockholm

1 slice dark bread fresh butter 5 slices salami	lettuce black olives onion rings

Butter bread generously. Fold salami and place in a fan shape on one side of the bread. Place small leaves of garden lettuce or watercress on opposite side with black olive in the center. Arrange 3 or 4 onion rings on the salami. Makes 1 serving.

Aebleskiver (Danish Raised Pancakes)

Poached Salmon

Poached Salmon

4 pounds salmon, in one piece from the middle section	4 sprigs parsley
	4 sprigs fresh dill
	12 peppercorns
6 cups water	2½ teaspoons salt
1 large onion, sliced	lemon slices
1 medium carrot, cut in 1-inch pieces	1 hard-cooked egg, sliced (optional)

For ease of handling wrap salmon in cheesecloth and tie securely. Place in a kettle just large enough to hold it, with a tight-fitting lid. Add the water, vegetables, and seasoning. Bring to a boil, cover, and simmer 30 minutes or until the fish flakes when tested with a fork. Remove from the kettle, unwrap, skin if desired, and place on a warm platter. Garnish with lemon slices and sliced egg. Serve with Pepparrotssas (Horseradish Sauce). Makes 6 to 8 servings.

Pepparrotssas (Horseradish Sauce)

2 tablespoons butter or margarine	salt
	pepper
3 tablespoons sifted all-purpose flour	freshly grated or bottled horseradish, to taste
1 cup hot fish stock	
1 cup hot milk	

Melt butter, add flour, and cook 1 minute. Add hot fish stock and blend well. Slowly add the milk and cook until thickened. Salt and pepper to taste. Stir in the horseradish just before serving. Do not heat after adding horseradish. Yields 2 cups.

Split Pea Soup

2 fresh pigs' feet, split and cut in half	3 leeks, including the tops, cut into ½-inch slices
2 fresh pigs' knuckles	
½ pound shin of beef	8 stalks celery, split and cut into 2-inch lengths
1 large onion	
8 cups water	
1 tablespoon salt	½ pound smoked sausage, cut into ¼-inch slices
½ teaspoon freshly ground pepper	
1 pound split peas, soaked overnight	

Place feet, knuckles, beef, and onion in a large kettle. Add 8 cups water, salt, and pepper. Bring to a boil and skim surface frequently during first half hour. Partially cover and simmer over low heat for 2 hours. Add the drained peas, cover, and cook for 1 hour or until the beans are very soft. Drop in the leeks, celery, and sausage and cook 15 minutes more. Correct the seasoning. Remove the meat from the bones. Place a serving of meat and vegetables in individual warm bowls and pour over the soup. Makes 6 to 8 servings.

Cabillaud à la Flamande
(Belgian Codfish)

butter or margarine
2 onions, thinly sliced
2 pounds codfish,
    cut in serving
    pieces
salt
white pepper
1 tablespoon chopped
    parsley

1 teaspoon finely
    chopped fresh
    rosemary, or
    ½ teaspoon dried
½ cup white wine
1 large clove garlic,
    crushed
½ cup stale bread
    crumbs, finely
    packed

Butter a shallow baking dish and cover bottom with half the onions. Salt and pepper the fish and lay the pieces close together on the onions. Sprinkle over the parsley and rosemary and cover with the remaining onions. Pour in the wine and dot the top with 2 tablespoons butter. Cover with foil and bake in a preheated 350°F oven for 35 to 45 minutes or until the fish flakes. Remove the foil the last 10 minutes of cooking. Sauté garlic in 1 tablespoon butter for 5 minutes. Remove garlic and sauté bread crumbs until golden and crisp. Sprinkle over the cod just before serving. Makes 4 to 6 servings.

William II of Nassau and Orange by Sir Anthony Van Dyck

Norwegian Paprika Chicken

1 frying chicken, 2 to
    3 pounds, cut into
    serving pieces
¼ cup flour
salt
pepper
½ cup butter
½ pound small mush-
    rooms, sliced
8 pitted prunes, finely
    chopped

1 medium onion,
    sliced
1 large clove garlic,
    minced
2 teaspoons paprika
1½ cups heavy cream
2½ cups chicken broth
1 cup regular
    uncooked rice
parsley

Coat chicken pieces in flour and lightly salt and pepper. Put ¼ cup butter in a heavy skillet and brown chicken on all sides. Remove to paper towel. Add the mushrooms and prunes to the skillet and stir with the pan juices until heated; remove. Add 2 more tablespoons of butter and sauté the onions and garlic until limp. Return the chicken pieces and place on top of the onions; sprinkle with paprika. Spoon over the mushrooms and prunes. Add the cream which has been mixed with ½ cup of broth. Cover and simmer for 45 minutes or until tender, basting occasionally with juices in the pan. In a saucepan heat remaining butter; stir in rice and cook until golden. Add the remaining broth; cover pan and cook rice about 14 minutes. When ready to serve turn rice onto a warm platter. Arrange chicken on top and pour over the sauce. Garnish platter with parsley and dust with paprika. Makes 4 to 6 servings.

Kohbullar
(Meat Balls)

butter
1 medium onion,
    chopped
½ cup stale bread
    crumbs, firmly
    packed
milk
1 pound ground round
    steak

1 egg, slightly beaten
1½ teaspoons salt
¼ teaspoon pepper
¼ teaspoon allspice
1 tablespoon chopped
    parsley
1½ tablespoons flour

In a large skillet sauté the onion with 1 tablespoon butter until tender. Soak bread in 1 cup milk in a medium-sized bowl; add meat and mix well. Add egg, onion, salt, pepper, allspice, and parsley and work into a smooth mixture. Take rounded tablespoons of meat mixture and form into balls. In the same skillet add 1 tablespoon butter and fry 8 to 10 meat balls at a time. Cook quickly, shaking pan to keep the balls well rounded. If necessary add more butter. Do not overcook. Remove to a serving dish and keep warm. When all are cooked, stir in flour and cook for 1 minute with the pan juices. Add 1 cup milk and cook until thickened. Strain and pour over the meat balls. Makes 6 servings.

Lapereau à la L'Aigre-Doux (Sweet and Sour Rabbit)

1 cup wine	3 tablespoons clarified
1 tablespoon vinegar	butter
1 medium onion, sliced	1¼ cups Espagnole sauce,
2 bay leaves	or beef gravy with
2 whole cloves	1½ teaspoons
4 cloves garlic, crushed	tomato purée
½ teaspoon salt	1 ounce grated semi-
3½-pound dressed	sweet chocolate
rabbit, cut in	salt and pepper
serving pieces	

Combine the first 7 ingredients and pour the marinade over the rabbit; cover and refrigerate for 24 hours. Remove rabbit from the marinade, wipe the pieces dry with a paper towel, and fry in the butter until brown. Place rabbit in a heavy kettle, pour in the marinade, add ½ cup water; cover and simmer over low heat for 45 minutes or until tender. Remove rabbit to a warm platter. Strain the liquid and stir in the Espagnole sauce and grated chocolate; cook for 1 minute. Salt and pepper to taste and pour over the rabbit. Makes 4 to 6 servings.

Brown Beans

1 pound kidney beans,	1 tablespoon chopped
soaked overnight	fresh dill or 1½
1 large onion	teaspoons dried
4 tablespoons dark	2 teaspoons salt
corn syrup	¼ teaspoon pepper
4 tablespoons white	
wine vinegar	

Place drained beans in a large kettle and pour over fresh cold water to cover. Add the remaining ingredients. Bring to a boil, cover, and simmer over low heat for 2½ to 3 hours, until the beans are very tender but not mushy. Correct the seasoning. Serve with meat. Makes 6 servings.

Saffransbröd (Saffron Bread)

¾ cup milk	¼ cup lukewarm water
½ cup butter	2 eggs, slightly beaten
¼ cup sugar	4 cups sifted
¼ teaspoon salt	all-purpose flour
1 teaspoon saffron	½ cup golden raisins
powder, dissolved	1 egg white, slightly
in 1 teaspoon water	beaten
1 package dry yeast	sesame seeds

Scald milk, add butter, sugar, salt, and saffron powder and cool to lukewarm. Dissolve the yeast in

Faience salad bowl of Chinese style decoration, with the arms of Duc de Montmorency-Luxembourg

water and add the milk mixture and eggs. Stir in 2 cups flour and beat well. Toss raisins with ¼ cup flour and add to the dough. Work in the remaining flour to make a soft dough. Turn out on a lightly floured cloth and knead for 10 minutes. Place in a greased bowl and let rise until double in bulk. Punch dough down and divide in half. Shape each half by hand into a roll about 20 inches long. Twist the two rolls together. Let rise about 30 minutes. Brush with egg white and sprinkle with sesame seeds. Bake in a preheated 375°F oven for 20 to 30 minutes or until golden brown.

Aebleskiver (Danish Raised Pancakes)

4 cups flour	3 cups milk
1 tablespoon sugar	4 eggs, separated
1 teaspoon salt	⅓ cup beer
1 teaspoon ground	juice of ½ lemon
cardamon	grated rind of 1
3 tablespoons double-	lemon
acting baking	shortening
powder	

Combine the first 5 ingredients in a large bowl. Mix together the milk and egg yolks and beat into the dry ingredients. Add the beer, lemon juice, and rind. Beat the egg whites until stiff but not dry and fold into the batter. Heat the aebleskiver pan and put 1 teaspoon of shortening into each well. Test heat by dropping in a little batter; if it forms a shape immediately the shortening is ready. The pan should not be so hot that the pancakes brown too quickly and remain uncooked in the middle. Put only about 1 rounded tablespoon of batter in each well. When batter becomes golden, turn with a fork and cook on the other side. Cook at least 5 to 6 minutes. Drain on a paper towel. Refill well each time with more shortening. Makes about 4 dozen pancakes.

RUSSIA and POLAND

Imperial Family Thanking the Tsar, Alexander II
by Michael Zichy

USSIA, A VAST country with borders in Europe, the Near East, and the Far East, has as varied and colorful a background in cookery as in every other aspect of its culture.

Rurik (862–879), a Scandinavian prince who founded a dynasty in Novgorod, brought many Scandinavian retainers with him and also the Scandinavian love for snacks with drinks before a meal; it is probable that the custom of *zakuski* began with Rurik's regime. Smoked, salted, and marinated fish of all types are essential to *zakuski*. Caviar was beloved by Russians even earlier, and was a favorite appetizer, along with sausages, pâtés, olives, and pickles, as part of the *zakuski* spread.

During the period when Kiev was the capital of Russia, beginning in the 10th century, food was plentiful at Court, but simply prepared. One banquet is recorded at which 500 dishes were presented to the tsar, most of which were probably not even touched by him or his courtiers. Table service was of silver and gold.

Bread and meat were the mainstay of both the Court and the populace. Meat was usually boiled or broiled; beef, mutton, pork, fowl, duck, and goose were common. Game was plentiful; there were cranes, deer, wild boar, hare, bear, grouse, and hazel hen (*riabchiki*). Some meats were preserved—there were cured hams and corned beef. An exceptional dish presented to the tsar might be roast meat or a ham garnished with gold leaf.

History does not record when each regional specialty reached the tables of the tsars. Chinese influences brought noodles, tea, and *pelmeni*, perhaps the earliest example of frozen food, to the easternmost provinces and Siberia. *Pelmeni*, as the Russians called the Chinese *dim sim* of filled noodle dough, were made in large quantities by the Siberians, wrapped in cloths, and placed outside to freeze; at dinner time, boiling water or broth was prepared and the required amount of *pelmeni* were taken in and boiled. These were popular for trips, because they could be carried easily.

The Mongols brought the ever-bubbling samovar as a vessel for boiling the water for tea. Soured and fermented milks such as yoghurt and koumyss, some cheeses, and sauerkraut were also brought from the East.

Poland was a part of Russia for many years, and it is believed that such dishes as borscht and fruit soups originated there. The Baltic states of Latvia, Lithuania, and Estonia were intermittently part of Russia. Cottage cheese and the use of large amounts of sour cream and butter distinguish Lithuanian cooking.

When Ivan the Terrible (1533–84) brought Italians to work on the Kremlin, they introduced the mastery of ice creams, sherbets, and pastries. Ivan was also famous for huge banquets.

At the time of the Kievan dynasty, the only fish served were locally caught or salt fish. Years later, with greater call for delicacies for the tsar's table, live fish were transported great distances in tanks.

Vegetables, boiled or raw, were popular in season, including peas, beans, and cucumbers. In order to utilize summer foods throughout the long, cold winter, cucumbers, plums, and even lemons were salted.

Desserts were simple; fruit and honey were served, and there were apples, pears, raisins, currants, figs, and prunes.

Kvas (a fermented drink made from rye bread), mead, and perry, made from pears, were probably drunk by tsar and commoner alike. The brewing process was known, and beer was mentioned in early reports; it was considered part of the meal.

Russia was converted to Christianity in 988, during the reign of Vladimir I (980–1015). Vladimir is said to have leaned toward Islam but to have rejected it when he learned that alcoholic beverages were prohibited. Christianity caused great changes in the eating habits at Court and throughout the land. The Old Testament taboos on meat with blood and birds strangled with snares were enforced; the meat of wild animals was declared unclean.

The Church declared Wednesday and Friday meatless days and encouraged the consumption of fish. The long Lenten fast was preceded by the "butter fast" of one week, during which it became the custom to consume tremendous amounts of *blini*. These were often eaten twice a day during that week with butter, sour cream, caviar, and all manner of other spreads. During Lent itself and during the other fasts of the Church, greater use was made of grains such as millet and oatmeal, and flaxseed and hempseed oils were substituted for other fats, which were prohibited. Both wheat and rye were used for bread. The wealthy had breads prepared with honey, poppyseed, oils, and spices.

The early tsars lived in accordance with the strictures of the Church. Their meals were sparse, often in the midst of huge banquets consumed by those around them. The dining halls were not enlivened by the presence of their wives. After the invasion of the Tatars in the 13th century, the *terem* was established, in which dwelled the tsar's wife and children, particularly the daughters. Even the kitchen of the *terem* was separated from that of the tsar.

Michael (1613–45), founder of the Romanov dynasty, was so poor that rich merchants, particularly the Stroganovs, had to help out with money and food. He was abstemious in eating and drinking but enjoyed providing lavishly for guests.

Alexis (1645–76), his son, left the *terem* at the age of five as a prince with his own palace; there, amid lavish furnishings, his fare remained that of any child of the day. His two daily meals consisted of porridge, stews, boiled meat or fish, rye bread, oatmeal beer, sweet turnips, nuts, and apples. No spiced foods were allowed. When Alexis ascended to the throne his frugal meals changed little. He rose at 4 A.M., spent much of the morning in prayer and work, and usually broke his fast at noon, alone in his private suite.

During Lent and other fasts he dined only three times a week. At 10 P.M. he had a frugal supper. He did not share his meals with companions, but he was not strictly alone, for each dish and cup was tasted by three different persons before it reached him. The fear of poisoning led many of the tsars to continue this practice.

There were frequent banquets for diplomats, which the tsar attended but rarely shared. The tables were set with cloths, napkins, and a cruet for each four guests, but no plates, knives, or forks were set out. Spoons were provided with sauces, and filled goblets were brought out. Meat was carved in adjoining pantries and placed on silver plates, to be shared by the guests. Table manners were crude; the nobles rarely could leave the table unassisted after eating and drinking to excess.

A love of things foreign and new led Alexis to travel, and he imported gooseberries, mulberries, vines, and herbs; he even brought cattle from the lowlands, with men to tend them. These lowlanders brought spice cakes and a variety of vegetables.

Peter the Great (1689–1725) did not emulate his father's simple ways. He ate only two meals a day, but, to quote the Duc de Saint-Simon, "what he ate and drank at his meals is inconceivable, without reckoning the beer, lemonade, and other drinks he swallowed between these repasts, his suite following his example: a bottle or two of beer, as many of wine, and, occasionally, liquors afterward; at the end of a meal strong

Sèvres plate from a service of Catherine the Great

drinks, such as brandy, as much sometimes as a quart."

Peter shared Alexis' love of travel and new ideas. He brought back Dutch boatbuilders and seamen; he even learned how to make Dutch bread and cheese. English, French and Italian architects and artisans were brought to Russia to ply their trades and use their skills. Peter popularized the employment of highly trained Turkish and Hungarian chefs and the use of French table wines. To the imported recipes the Russians made typical additions, such as sour cream, dill, mushrooms, and salted cucumbers.

The ladies of the Court emerged unveiled from the *terem*, and gave intimate dinner parties. Peter built his new capital at St. Petersburg and ordered the nobility to follow. He insisted that the women emulate Parisians in dress and manner.

Catherine I (1725–27) ate the simplest of food, but drank about six bottles of wine daily. Anna (1730–40) lived a miserable, penurious existence outside Russia until she acceded to the throne. After her long diet of dull meals of boiled beef and pickled cabbage, she soon became a spendthrift and glutton; in 1740 she died of a stroke while seated at dinner. Her cousin Elizabeth (1741–62) was a gourmand who doted on fine foods but also demanded more common fare from time to time.

Catherine the Great (1762–96) felt that she must remain abstemious at table and follow all the Church mandates about food. But her personal habits did not inhibit the great feasts at Court. The Orlov brothers, her court favorites, were known for their devotion to fine food and drink. Potemkin, another powerful adviser, supposedly spent over $200 daily for his own tables, which included service of the rarest of fruits. Banquets featured pyramids of meats and fountains of wine. Sterlet, a popular fish, would be displayed swimming in tanks before being served as soup. Catherine also brought some German influences—the *forshmak*, or warm appetizer, probably dates from her time—and French chefs whose sauces were soon the rage of the nobility.

Paul (1796–1801) ate and drank nothing that came from the palace kitchens; all his food was prepared by trustworthy German cooks and was guarded from kitchen to table.

The Russians did not merely adopt customs from others; they also had an influence on European cuisine. Alexander I (1801–25) appointed Prince Kurakin, a noted gastronome, as Ambassador to Paris about 1811; by 1816 all French society was dining "à la Russe," a style that ended the tradition of placing all food on the table at once. The Russian style allowed only flowers and desserts to be constantly present; meals were served in courses.

In 1814 Alexander returned with Prince Kur-

Easter Cake

akin to Paris; he was so impressed with the food that he requested a French chef for his table. Talleyrand soon obliged by sending Carême; it is believed that this great chef was also a spy who used his position at Court to get news for Talleyrand. Among the dishes he introduced in Russia were *charlottka*, better known under its French name, *charlotte russe*.

By the time of Alexander III (1881–94) the rich Russian cuisine, a composite of so many foreign influences, had evolved. Alexander, however, decried luxurious living. To overcome the extravagances of his wife, the tsar tried to be frugal, and ate three austere meals daily. His favorite dishes were cabbage soup (*schii*) and millet gruel (*gretcha*). He exhorted his cooks to use butter and eggs sparingly. Alexander loved ice cream, however, and even when ill and forbidden many rich foods, he begged his daughter Olga to get some for him.

Most wealthy Russians of that time customarily ate four meals daily. The *zakuski* table was covered with many delicacies; often a separate room was used for this spread. It must have hurt the tsar's frugal soul to attend a typical ball for 3,000 guests, at which a midnight supper might include lobster salad, chicken cutlets, and whipped cream and pastry tarts.

Nicholas II (1894–1917), the last of the tsars, shared his love of things Russian with his countrymen. Among the special attentions to Princess Alix while Nicholas was courting her was an occasion when he served her a supper of *blinis* and fresh caviar.

Nicholas' days ended as his distant forebears' had begun. Just before his execution he languished in prison, where he and the tsarina, lacking plates and forks, were forced to share their meals with their captors from a common bowl.

Poland

Poland, at the crossroads between East and West, was long a loosely coordinated land of pagan tribes of hunters and tillers of the soil. Its written history began about a century before England's Battle of Hastings (1066). Along with Christianity and the status of a kingdom, Poland acquired culinary sophistication.

Poland was a kind of way-station between civilizations. The Teutonic Knights Templars,

homeward bound from the Crusades, stopped to harass the relatively peaceful land of the *Lachs*, as the Poles were then called. The Jews, driven out of Britain and France in the 13th century by the Inquisition, were allowed to settle in Poland. The traders of the Hanseatic League made regular stops in Polish ports to peddle their wares. All this left an imprint on the country's eating habits.

The first written account of a royal Polish feast dates to the year 1000, when King Boleslav I (992–1025) entertained Otto III, the young German head of the Holy Roman Empire. It was unheard of for the Emperor to travel so far east, his quarters being in Rome, where he had installed a cousin as Pope Gregory V and where the rest of the world generally came to him. The reason for the trip was that famous horse-trading session known in history as the Congress of Gniezno. Otto started out expecting to go among savages; instead, he was met at the border by high dignitaries of the Polish state, ceremoniously escorted to the Court where Boleslav waited, and overwhelmed by *Lach* hospitality. The feasting lasted a week. King Boleslav, an inveterate giver of banquets, and intent on impressing the distinguished foreigners, had had a special service of gold and silver minted for the occasion; during the final and grandest feast, he gave all the gold plate away.

What had been served on those golden plates? The chronicles do not say, but other mention of contemporary foods indicates that royal banquets consisted of hot and hearty foods simply prepared: soups were made with meat and meatbones, beets or cabbage, or with barley and the delectable mushrooms that grow wild in Poland's forests. The forests also yielded boar, deer, hare, and a variety of game birds, all of which were spit-roasted in the kitchen courtyard. There was also *bigos*, a stew such as never appeared on any poor man's table.

A favorite seasoning was saffron. Wild strawberries and currants might be served, with honey instead of the still unknown sugar. Honey was also the basis of mead, the traditional national drink made with malt and hops and aged in kegs for a year or a hundred years, the longer the better. The golden liquor could fell warriors, leaving the head clear but turning the knees to putty. To this day, if a man cannot walk a straight line, the Poles say that he is (translated literally) "hopped up."

In the next five centuries Poland grew in power and political prestige. The capital was moved to

Cracow, and Polish hospitality became proverbial. Nevertheless the royal feasts, as well as the banquets given with royal magnificence by the great magnates—the Potockis, the Lubomirskis, the Czartoryskis, the Lithuanian Radziwills, all of whom became famous gourmets in Poland's age of decadence—continued to be distinguished for largesse rather than refinement of cooking. By comparison with their West European counterparts, the warrior kings and their nobles lived simply, almost in a tradition of austerity. It is significant that at the turn of the 14th century, upon the death of the devout and learned young Queen Jadwiga, her brokenhearted consort King Jagiello honored her memory by donating the gold plate and jewels in the royal treasury to the University of Cracow. This gesture on the part of the former pagan, untutored Duke of Lithuania changed the university from a third-rate seminary into a true seat of learning, where 75 years later a burgher's son named Copernicus was able to study astronomy. But the gesture could never have been made had King Jagiello cared more for gastronomic excellence than for philosophy.

In 1518 another royal marriage brought from Milan a Sforza princess to provide an heir to the aging King Sigismund I (1506–48). Queen Bona had a curious influence on the culture of her new country. Beautiful, young, incredibly wealthy, this granddaughter of French kings and Italian *condottieri* came with a train of courtiers, sycophants, gardeners, and cooks. She began by charming her elderly husband and civilizing his court. She ended as the most hated woman in Poland's history, corrupting everything she touched, including the church. In the meantime she changed Polish eating habits, introducing the tomato, the beet, savoy and brussels cabbage, cucumbers, and eggplant, first to the royal table and later to the country at large. This the Polish language acknowledged by coining a new word, *wloszczyzna,* or "things Italian," to mean vegetables. When news of her death in Milan at the age of 64 reached Poland's Court, her son did not mourn; but his chef, Balcer Plata—one of the greats in the history of Polish cooking—took it hard.

A slightly later foreign "kitchen" influence was that of Catherine de' Medici's younger son, Henry of Valois. The complicated chain of events that put that indolent young man on Poland's throne in 1573 is part of another story. His reign was brief. He stole out of his bed in Wawel Castle late at night upon hearing that his brother Charles was dead in Paris and the French throne was vacant. He left behind his chef, Dominik Alemani. Henry's successor, the good King Stephen Báthory (1576–86), a lover of fine food, appreciated the legacy. So it was that French cooking, which by then had outdistanced the Italian for elegance and refinement, became the fashion in Poland.

Even so, the old Polish dishes remained strongly in favor. During the reign of the next king, Sigismund III (1587–1632), a feast given in honor of the papal nuncio Cardinal Caetini so impressed the scribes that they chronicled it at length in *Poland's Great Courts and Manor Houses.* They were careful to give credit to the king's talented chef, a native Pole named Piotr Żeroński. They gave special mention to braised goose as the pièce de résistance. The actual recipe for this same goose turned up 100 years later in the memoirs of a priest, Father Kitowicz, who wrote that goose was "boiled and served in a sauce made with sour cream and wild mushrooms, or in a sauce made with a spoonful of honey, vinegar to taste, pepper, ginger, and, to add color and an extra fillip, a little ground charred straw" —foreshadowing the modern charcoal powder that so successfully adds an outdoorsy flavor to kitchen-broiled steaks!

It was not until after Ladislas IV (1632–48) inherited the crown that elegance finally flourished in Poland's ancient capital. Ladislas was a man of great courage and personal charm as well as a diplomat of genius, and he successfully used all these attributes in the service of his country. At one time, when it was important to impress various foreign dignitaries with Poland's wealth and self-sufficiency, he and his chancellor Ossoliński decided to give a banquet for all the ambassadors accredited to the Polish Court. The menu was to be composed solely of traditional Polish dishes, in order to impress on the rest of Europe that the kingdom had such an abundance of native products and was so advanced in animal husbandry and the cultivation of its fields, orchards, and gardens that it could feed itself entirely without foreign help. The banquet lasted for hours, was an unqualified success, and had the desired effect.

With the 18th century came the decline of Poland as a great power, but, as often happens during an age of decadence, luxury became the order of the day. The great magnates, whose fortunes rivaled those of the crown, sent their sons to be educated abroad, and the golden youth would come home with new fashions in dress, in speech,

Silver gilt chocolate pot of Maria Leszczynska, daughter of Stanislas I who became wife of Louis XV of France

in manners, and in matters of the palate. Suddenly anything that was not French did not count. An extravagant table ruined as many noblemen as did the gaming tables. And a new culinary art was created, that of desserts.

This art flourished toward the end of Poland's age of glory, the late 18th century. At that time the pastry chef had to be painter, sculptor, and poet, and an expert in heraldry as well. A well-conceived dessert for a banquet might, for instance, represent a landscape complete with bucolic village, and be decorated in addition with the coat of arms of either the master of the house or an honored guest. Nor was this the end of the creative process. Made of ice creams and ices melting at different temperatures, the landscape that represented a spring scene when it was first served proceeded to change, before the eyes of the delighted guests, to summer, then to fall, and finally to winter. This particular sleight-of-hand was mentioned by one of the nation's great poets, Adam Mickiewicz. And though the bard neglected to give the recipe, it can doubtless be found in one of the three or four vast encyclopedias of cooking, each in about eight volumes, that appeared between 1790 and 1808. But then again, it may be omitted, either because by then the word "economy" had begun to creep into the titles, or because the truly great chefs preferred to keep their secrets.

During the reign of the Saxon Elector Augustus III (1734–63), who cared nothing for the country he ruled, there came a temporary age of gluttony, as though the nobles sought through self-indulgence to lull themselves into a false sense of security. As the popular saying had it, "Under the Saxon king you ate, drank, let out your belt— and didn't feel a thing." In the last decades before the partition of Poland, the French influence returned; it continued through the Napoleonic Wars and even after the loss of independence.

But gradually the native customs also returned, on the wave of that fierce undercurrent of patriotism that finally led to liberation. The Poles, notoriously nationalistic, continue to cherish everything Polish—including Polish cooking. In the republic that calls itself People's Poland, although the splendor has long since vanished, the tradition remains. It is a good tradition of foods lovingly prepared and generously shared. The recipes are simple, for there is no time for elegance, there are no servants to provide the fancy touches; yet the open-handed hospitality remains.

Royal Recipes

Barszcz (Beet Soup)

12 medium beets, scalded and peeled	2 carrots, sliced in 1-inch pieces
13 cups water	½ parsnip, sliced
1 pound beef soup meat	1 leek, sliced
1 marrow bone, cracked	2 stalks celery, sliced
2 tablespoons rendered fat	6 sprigs parsley
1 onion, sliced	1 tablespoon salt
	12 peppercorns
	2 tablespoons lemon juice

Cut beets in quarters, add 3 cups of the water, and simmer until tender. Put remaining water, soup meat, and marrow bone in a large kettle and bring to a boil. Simmer for 1 hour, skimming the surface frequently. In the rendered fat sauté the onion, carrots, parsnip, and leek until slightly colored. Add all the vegetables, parsley, salt, and peppercorns to the kettle; partially cover and cook for another hour. Remove the beets and reduce the beet water to 1 cup. Strain the soup through a colander, reserve meat for another meal, and add the beet water to the strained broth and the lemon juice. This soup may also be served cold, garnished with slivers of hard-cooked eggs, diced cucumbers, julienne beets, and sour cream. Makes 6 cups.

Schtschi (Cabbage Soup)

½ pound each beef and pork bones	3 medium onions, coarsely chopped
4 quarts cold water	3 medium carrots, split and cut in 1-inch pieces
1½ tablespoons salt	
1 carrot	
1 medium onion	1 medium celery root, cubed
3 sprigs parsley	
1 bay leaf	1 small white cabbage, shredded
2 pounds fresh brisket of beef, all fat removed	2 tablespoons flour
	4 tablespoons minced parsley
2 tablespoons rendered meat fat	sour cream

Place the bones in a large heavy kettle, add the water and salt, and bring to a boil. Skim surface frequently during the first half hour. Add the carrot, onion, parsley, bay leaf, and brisket of beef. Cover partially and simmer over low heat for 2½ hours. Meanwhile in a large frying pan braise carrots and onions in the fat for about 15 minutes. Remove and braise the celery root and cabbage for 15 minutes, adding more fat if necessary. Stir in the flour and cook 2 minutes more. When the soup has cooked for a total of 3 hours strain into a colander, discarding bones and vegetables. Return the soup and meat to the kettle and add the carrots, onions, celery root, and cabbage. Cover and simmer for another hour. When ready to serve, remove any fat that has risen to the top and correct the seasoning. Slice the meat and put into a heated tureen, pour over the soup, and sprinkle with parsley. Serve with a bowl of sour cream. Makes 6 to 8 servings.

Rossolnik (Chicken Soup)

1 chicken, 3 to 4 pounds, cut into quarters	2 cups chopped onion
	2 tablespoons butter
giblets	2 tablespoons flour
3 quarts cold water	2 egg yolks, slightly beaten
3½ teaspoons salt	
1 large celery root, washed and trimmed	1 large dill pickle, peeled
	½ cup sour cream
6 sprigs parsley, tied together	3 tablespoons minced parsley

Place the chicken and giblets in a large kettle, add the water and salt, and bring to a boil. Skim surface frequently, and after the first half hour add the celery root and parsley. Meanwhile braise the onions in the butter, covered, for about 10 minutes. Stir in the flour and cook 2 minutes longer; add to the soup. Partially cover and simmer the soup over low heat for 1 hour or until chicken is tender. Remove the chicken and celery root and discard the parsley. Thicken the soup with egg yolks. Sliver 1 cup of chicken, chop the giblets and celery root, and put into a heated tureen. Squeeze the juice from the dill pickle into the soup and chop the pickle. Put the sour cream and pickle in the tureen and pour over the soup. Sprinkle with minced parsley. Makes 6 servings.

Rakovyye Shyeiki v Tomatnom Sousye
(Crayfish or Shrimp in Tomato Sauce)

1 quart water	½ pound mushroom
½ onion	caps, sliced
½ carrot	½ cup tomato sauce
1 slice lemon	1 cup Béchamel
½ stalk celery	sauce
3 peppercorns	¼ cup dry white wine
1 bay leaf	2 teaspoons chopped
2 teaspoons salt	dill
1 pound crayfish or	1 tablespoon chopped
shrimp	parsley

Bring the water to a boil with the next 7 ingredients; cover and cook 15 minutes. Remove the shell and black vein from the shrimp or crayfish; drop into the rapidly boiling water. When the water returns to a boil cook for 2 minutes; drain. Put the shrimp in a low casserole and cover with the mushrooms. Stir tomato sauce into hot Béchamel sauce and add the wine. Do not cook. Pour the sauce over the mushrooms, completely covering them. Put into a 350° F oven and cook until well heated, about 25 minutes. Mix the dill and parsley together and sprinkle over just before serving. Serve with kasha and rice. Makes 4 servings.

Pirog
(Fish Turnover)

8 shallots, chopped	⅛ teaspoon nutmeg
1½ teaspoons minced	2 pounds fresh
garlic	salmon, haddock,
⅓ cup butter or	or pike, cooked
margarine	and forked into
½ pound mushrooms,	large pieces
sliced	raised dough
1 tablespoon chopped	4 cups cooked cold
fresh dill	rice
2 tablespoons flour	6 hard-cooked eggs,
1 cup fish stock	chopped
½ teaspoon salt	1 egg yolk, slightly
¼ teaspoon pepper	beaten

In a large skillet, sauté shallots and garlic in butter until tender; add the mushrooms and dill and cook 3 minutes longer. Stir in the flour, add fish stock and seasoning, and cook 2 minutes more. Mix in the fish and let cool. On a floured pastry cloth, roll out the dough into a rectangle about 18 by 14 inches. Place half the rice in the middle of the dough and spread to within 4 inches of the edge on all sides. Spread half of the fish mixture on top and cover with the chopped

egg. Salt and pepper lightly. Place the remaining fish on top of the eggs and then the remaining rice. Fold over the long edges of the dough and seal. Fold ends, first cutting off a triangle from the corners. Place a greased baking sheet on top of the sealed roll and flip over, holding the cloth securely. Brush the entire smooth surface with the beaten egg. Make 4 or 5 holes on the top to let steam escape. Bake in a 375° F oven for about 30 minutes or until golden brown. Makes 12 to 14 servings.

Raised Dough for Pirog

1 envelope active dry	1 teaspoon salt
yeast	2 teaspoons sugar
¼ cup lukewarm water	4½ to 5 cups flour
1 cup milk, scalded	3 eggs, slightly beaten
½ cup butter	

Dissolve yeast in lukewarm water. To scalded milk, add butter, salt, and sugar; cool to lukewarm and add to yeast mixture. Stir in 1 cup of the flour and then add the eggs. Gradually beat in the remaining flour, adding enough to make a soft but not sticky dough. Knead about 10 minutes or until smooth and satiny. Place in a greased bowl. Cover with a cloth and let rise in a warm place until double in bulk, about 2 hours. This is now ready to be used for Pirog.

Mayonnaise de Poulets

2 whole chicken	1 clove garlic, crushed
breasts	½ teaspoon salt
1 cup white wine	water
½ carrot, sliced	½ cup heavy cream
1 small onion, cut in	½ cup mayonnaise
quarters	lettuce
1 stalk celery	4 hard-cooked eggs

Split chicken breasts into 4 pieces and put in a large heavy saucepan with wine, carrot, onion, celery, garlic, and salt. Add enough water just to cover. Simmer, covered, until tender. Cool in the stock. Remove skin, cover chicken with plastic wrap, and refrigerate for an hour or more for easier slicing. Mix the cream and mayonnaise together and add a few tablespoons of stock to make the dressing just pourable. Refrigerate. When ready to serve, slice the chicken in as large slices as possible. Put the smaller pieces in the middle of a platter and arrange the larger slices around and overlapping, piling them high in the center. Surround the base with heart of young lettuce cut in quarters and quartered hard-cooked eggs. Pour over the dressing. Makes 4 to 6 servings.

Dragomir Forshmak
(Ham and Potatoes in Sour Cream)

1 cup chopped onion	¾ pound cooked ham,
5 tablespoons butter	cut in pieces ½ x
or margarine	½ x 2 inches
1 tablespoon flour	1 medium dill pickle,
1¼ cups beef stock	peeled and thinly
1 cup sour cream	sliced
⅛ teaspoon cayenne	½ cup grated cheddar
pepper	cheese
6 small potatoes (1	
pound), cooked	
and sliced ¼-inch	
thick	

Cook onion in 2 tablespoons butter until tender. Add the flour and cook 2 minutes more. Stir in the stock, sour cream, and cayenne pepper. Cook over low heat for 5 minutes. In a large skillet, sauté the potato slices, without browning. Combine the sauce, ham, potatoes, and pickle. Put in a shallow casserole and top with cheese. Bake in a 375° F oven for ½ hour, until cheese is melted and bubbly. Makes 4 servings for a meal or 10 to 12 for Zakooskas (snack with cocktails).

Golubtsi
(Stuffed Cabbage Leaves)

boiling water	2 eggs, slightly
2 large cabbages	beaten
2 tablespoons butter	2 teaspoons salt
or margarine	½ teaspoon freshly
1 cup diced onion	ground pepper
1½ tablespoons flour	1 cup tomato sauce
1 pound ground beef	1½ cups water
1 pound ground pork	½ cup sour cream
1 cup cooked rice	

Plunge the cabbages into boiling water long enough to wilt the leaves. Separate the leaves and select and remove 20 of the largest ones. Scald the leaves in salted water and drain and dry on a paper towel. With a sharp knife cut out heavy rib at the base of each leaf. Sauté onion in butter until tender, add flour, and cook 2 minutes longer. Mix together in a bowl the meat, rice, onion, egg, salt, and pepper. Lay the cabbage leaves flat and place about ¼ cup of the filling in the middle of each leaf. Fold the leaf over, tuck in the sides and tie with a thread. Place cabbage rolls, seam side down, in a wide-bottomed pan. Combine the tomato sauce and water and pour over the cab-

bage rolls. Cover and cook over low heat for 50 minutes. Remove cabbage rolls to a warm serving dish. Correct the seasoning of the sauce. Sour cream may be stirred into the sauce or served separately. Makes 8 to 10 servings.

Bitok po Russki
(Flat Meat Dumplings)

2 tablespoons butter	1 egg, slightly beaten
or margarine	¼ cup fine dried bread
½ cup minced onions	crumbs
1 cup soft bread	3 tablespoons clarified
crumbs	butter or
¼ cup beef stock or	margarine
water	4 large potatoes, cut
1½ pounds ground	in ½-inch slices
round steak	and boiled in
2 tablespoons	salted water
chopped parsley	1½ cups sour cream
2 teaspoons salt	¼ cup grated
¼ teaspoon freshly	Parmesan cheese
ground pepper	

Sauté onions in butter until tender. Moisten soft bread crumbs with the stock. Mix together thoroughly the meat, onion, bread crumbs, parsley, salt, pepper, and egg. Form into 16 balls and flatten to 2 inches across. Dust each cake on both sides with the fine dried bread crumbs. Cook in clarified butter about 4 minutes on each side depending on desired rareness. Remove to a warm low casserole. Lay the little cakes one against the other in 2 rows down the length of the casserole. Surround with sliced potatoes. Spoon the sour cream over the cakes and potatoes. Mix the Parmesan cheese with the remainder, if any, of the dried bread crumbs and sprinkle on top of the sour cream. Place under the broiler to brown. Makes 6 servings.

Wedgwood plate from a dinner service of Catherine the Great

Cotelettes de Veau à la Provençale

Cotelettes de Veau à la Provençale

4 veal chops	¼ teaspoon nutmeg
3 tablespoons butter	salt and pepper
1 tablespoon cooking oil	Parmesan cheese, grated
4 tomatoes	½ cup white wine
2 shallots, chopped	1 cup tomato sauce
½ medium onion, chopped	1 clove garlic, crushed
½ pound mushrooms, minced	parsley

In a large skillet sauté chops in 1 tablespoon butter and oil until well browned and tender. Cut off the tops of the tomatoes and scoop out the pulp and seeds. Turn upside down to drain. Sauté the shallots and onions in remaining butter until lightly colored. Add the mushrooms, nutmeg, salt, and pepper and cook 5 minutes longer. Fill the tomatoes with the mushroom mixture and sprinkle cheese on top. Broil until brown. Dilute pan juices with wine and add tomato sauce and garlic. Simmer 5 minutes and adjust the seasoning. Strain into a sauce boat. Arrange chops on a platter, surround with stuffed tomatoes, and garnish with parsley. Makes 4 servings.

Bitki w Smietanie (Meat Balls)

1 medium onion, minced	1½ teaspoons salt
3 tablespoons clarified butter	½ teaspoon freshly ground pepper
1 pound lean ground beef	¼ teaspoon each thyme and oregano
½ pound ground pork	½ teaspoon marjoram
½ pound ground veal	3 to 4 tablespoons flour
2 eggs, slightly beaten	1 pint dairy sour cream
¼ cup milk	1 tablespoon flour
1 cup fine bread crumbs	1 cup beef bouillon

Sauté onion in 1 tablespoon clarified butter until golden. Mix the onion and the meats together. Stir the eggs, milk, bread crumbs, and seasoning together, and mix very thoroughly with the meat. Form into balls about 2 inches in diameter. Roll in flour; heat the remainder of the butter in a skillet and brown the meat balls. Remove them to a casserole, arranged in two or more layers.

To make the sauce, drain off any fat from the skillet and add the sour cream. Stir in flour thoroughly and slowly add the bouillon. Cook on the stove over very low heat for 2 minutes. Pour the sauce over the meat balls, cover, and cook gently for 45 minutes. Serve with kasha. Makes 8 servings.

Chikhirtma (Mutton Stew)

¼ teaspoon saffron	2 cups water
¼ cup water	1 pound mutton or lamb, cut into 1-inch cubes
1½ cups chopped onions	
2 tablespoons butter	2 tablespoons chopped parsley
¼ cup flour	
1½ teaspoons salt	2 teaspoons chopped dill
¼ teaspoon freshly ground pepper	
1 cup beef stock	

Soak saffron in ¼ cup water. In a large kettle cook the onions in the butter until they are tender and browned. Add the flour, salt, and pepper and cook 2 minutes longer. Stir in the stock and water and cook until thickened. Add meat, seasoning and strained saffron water, discarding the saffron. Cover and simmer for 1½ hours or until meat is tender. Adjust seasoning. Makes 4 servings.

Bigos (Hunter's Stew)

3 ounces dried mushrooms	1 pound boneless lamb
water	1 pound venison or hare or rabbit (optional)
3 medium carrots, chopped	½ pound Polish sausage
3 stalks celery, chopped	1½ pounds smoked pork loin or baked ham
half a celery root (optional)	half a game bird, duck, or chicken
6 sprigs parsley	¼ pound salt pork or bacon, diced
2 bay leaves	
6 juniper berries (optional)	2 medium onions, diced
2 teaspoons salt	2 tablespoons flour
¼ teaspoon pepper	6 pounds sauerkraut and juice
1 pound fresh pork	1 cup Madeira wine
1 pound boneless beef	

Cover and simmer mushrooms in a saucepan with 2 cups water for 1 hour or until tender. If necessary add more water as the mushrooms swell. In a large kettle put the carrots, celery, celery root, parsley, bay leaves, juniper berries, and seasoning. Add 4 cups water with the pork, beef, lamb, venison, and sausage. There should be enough water to keep the meat and vegetables from sticking. Bring to a boil, cover and braise for 30 minutes. Add the ham and game and cook 30 minutes more or until tender. Pour into a colander; reserve the liquid, discard the vegetables and herbs, and let the meat cool. Cut the mushrooms in narrow strips and reserve the liquid. Render the salt pork or bacon in the same large kettle the meat was cooked in. Sauté the onions until tender. Add the flour and cook 1 minute. Mix the liquid from the mushrooms and the meat stock into the flour with the onions, and cook until thickened. Add the sauerkraut and juice and mix well. Remove any bones, chop the meat and fowl, and add to the sauerkraut with the mushrooms. Cover and heat thoroughly. Remove from the stove, add the Madeira wine, and correct the seasoning. Arrange the meat and sauerkraut on a very large warm platter. Makes 18 to 20 servings.

Note: During the Middle Ages in Poland, Bigos was served for the hunt breakfast. The more varieties of meat used, the more delicious. Each meat or fowl was cooked in a separate cauldron with a little water and a few vegetables and herbs. This method was believed to impart a more distinct flavor, but Bigos may be cooked in one kettle. Not all the meats need be used, but the variety makes a unique flavor. This dish is better if made the day before and reheated.

Bigos (Hunter's Stew)

Fried Cheese Cakes

1 pound pot cheese
  (large dry curds)
2 eggs, slightly
  beaten
½ cup flour
½ teaspoon salt

2 tablespoons clarified
  butter or
  margarine
sour cream
fresh chopped dill

Put cheese in a strainer lined with cheese cloth; place a heavy weight on top and let drain into a bowl for several hours. Press the dried cheese through a strainer with a wooden spoon, or through a food mill. Mix the eggs into the cheese and add the flour and salt. With floured fingers form cheese mixture into twelve 2-inch cakes. Fry in butter 10 minutes on each side to a delicate brown. Serve with sour cream and chopped dill. Makes 12 cakes.

Salade Russe

1 cup each of the
  following cut in
  ¼-inch cubes:
  carrots, beets,
  turnips, peas,
  string beans, po-
  tatoes, beef or
  tongue

4 tablespoons French
  dressing
  mayonnaise
4 hard-cooked eggs,
  cut in wedges
  truffles (optional)

Boil vegetables separately in salted water until just fork tender. Drain and cool. Add the meat and toss with French dressing. Refrigerate for an hour or more. When ready to serve, drain off the dressing and form the salad in a pyramid shape in a low bowl. Spread mayonnaise over all and garnish with eggs and sliced truffles. Makes 8 servings.

Bizcocho
(Sponge Cake)

3 eggs, separated	½ teaspoon baking
2 tablespoons potato	powder
flour	⅛ teaspoon salt
1 tablespoon regular	½ cup sugar
flour	3 tablespoons water

Beat the egg yolks until lemon colored and thick. Sift the flour, baking powder, and salt together; fold into the egg yolks with a rubber spatula, and reserve. Mix the sugar and water together in a saucepan. Bring to a boil and stir until sugar is dissolved; cook over high heat until syrup spins a thread when dropped from a spoon. Remove from heat and immediately beat egg whites until stiff but not dry. Pour in the syrup in a thin stream while continuing to beat. Carefully fold meringue into egg yolk mixture. Pour into a 6½ x 3-inch spring-form pan, which has been greased and floured. Bake in a 325°F oven for about 30 minutes. It is done when a tester comes out dry. Remove from oven and cool before taking out of the pan. The top indents slightly in the middle. This cake may be used with sauces or as a base for other desserts, such as Monte Blanco.

Baklazhannaye Ikra
(Eggplant Caviar)

1 large eggplant	1½ teaspoons salt
¼ cup olive oil	¼ teaspoon freshly
1 medium onion,	ground pepper
diced	2 teaspoons lemon
1 clove garlic, minced	juice
½ cup thick tomato	dark bread
sauce	

Cut off stem end of eggplant and put in a pot of boiling water. Cover and cook until just soft when tested with the point of a knife. Sauté onion and garlic in 2 tablespoons of the olive oil but do not brown. Peel and chop eggplant and add to the onion with the tomato sauce, salt, and pepper. Cook, uncovered, over low heat for about an hour or until moisture has been absorbed. Add the remainder of the oil a tablespoon at a time during the cooking. Stir often. Add the lemon juice, correct the seasoning, and refrigerate. Serve with thin slices of any dark bread. Makes about 3 cups.

Rhubarb Kissel

1½ pounds rhubarb,	1 cup sugar
trimmed and cut	2 tablespoons corn-
into 1-inch	starch dissolved
lengths	in 2 tablespoons
2 cups water	cold water
	heavy cream

Simmer rhubarb in water for 10 minutes, uncovered. Put into a blender and purée or rub through a sieve. Add the sugar; return to saucepan and add the cornstarch. Cook over low heat until thickened. Cool. Pour into dessert dishes and refrigerate several hours. Serve with heavy cream or milk. Makes 6 to 8 servings.

Note: Kissel may be made from cranberries, apples, strawberries, etc., adjusting amounts of sugar and water.

Carrot Pastry

2 egg yolks	2 tablespoons
Béchamel sauce	chopped chives
using only 1 cup	2 tablespoons
of milk	chopped parsley
3 cups minced carrots,	½ recipe of puff pastry
cooked in salted	1 egg, slightly beaten
water	
2 hard-cooked eggs,	
chopped	

Beat egg yolks into hot thick Béchamel sauce. Add well-drained carrots, eggs, chives, and parsley. Refrigerate until cold. Roll out dough paper-thin on a lightly floured cloth. Cut out 4-inch circles with a cookie cutter. Place 1½ tablespoons of filling in center of circle. Fold two sides of the dough in and fold the near side over and roll, pressing to seal the seam and ends. Brush with beaten egg. Place on a greased baking sheet, seam side down. Bake in a 375° F oven for 30 to 40 minutes or until golden. Makes about 24 pastries.

Easter Cake

½ teaspoon saffron	3 eggs, beaten
1 tablespoon vodka	¾ cup toasted slivered
½ cup milk, scalded	almonds
¾ cup granulated	½ cup golden raisins
sugar	½ cup chopped mixed
¾ cup butter or	candied fruit
margarine	flour
grated rind of 1	1 cup sifted confec-
lemon	tioners' sugar
1 teaspoon salt	4 teaspoons lemon
2 packages dry yeast	juice
½ cup lukewarm water	glacéed cherries

Soak saffron in vodka. In a large bowl combine scalded milk, sugar, butter, grated lemon rind, and salt. Let cool to lukewarm. Sprinkle yeast over warm water to dissolve thoroughly. Add yeast and eggs to milk mixture, stirring until well blended. Add almonds, reserving 2 tablespoons for later use, raisins and candied fruit. Strain vodka into the batter, discarding the saffron. Gradually beat in flour enough to make a medium dough and knead about 10 minutes, until smooth and satiny. Place in a greased bowl, cover with a towel, and let rise in a warm place until double in bulk, about 2 hours. Punch down, divide in thirds, and place in 3 well-greased coffee tins, the bottoms lined with greased wax paper, or in 1 three-pound shortening can. Cover and let rise until double in bulk. Bake in a 350° F oven for 30 to 40 minutes. Let cool 15 minutes before

removing from cans. Combine sugar and lemon juice. Spoon over tops of cooled Kulitch, sprinkle with reserved almonds, and decorate with glacéed cherries. Kulitch is always sliced in rounds across the cake. The top is taken off and used as a lid on the remaining cake.

Chrust, chyli Faworki
(Cookies)

3 egg yolks	2 cups all-purpose
1 whole egg	unsifted flour
3 tablespoons granu-	1 tablespoon rum
lated sugar	fat for frying
6 tablespoons medium	confectioners' sugar
cream	

Beat eggs until pale yellow and slightly thick. Add sugar gradually and continue to beat until very thick, about 5 minutes. Pour in cream slowly while continuing to beat. Fold in the flour with a spoon and add the rum. The dough should be soft, but firm enough to roll out. Divide the dough into half, covering the remaining dough to keep from drying out. Roll out on a lightly floured cloth to about ⅛ inch thick. Cut into strips 4 inches long by 1 inch wide. Cut one end on a slant. Make a slit about 1 inch long lengthwise in the center of each strip and put the slant end through the slit. Drop into 375° F fat and fry until golden brown. Drain on paper towel and sprinkle with confectioners' sugar. Repeat with the remaining dough. Serve hot or cold. Makes about 6 dozen cookies.

Fruit Bars

1 cup dried apricots,	2 cups flour
finely chopped	3 eggs, slightly
1 cup currants	beaten
1 cup golden raisins	1 cup strawberry jam
1 cup almonds,	½ cup sugar
chopped	¼ teaspoon salt
1 cup walnuts,	
chopped	

In a large bowl mix the first 5 ingredients together. Toss the flour with the fruit and nuts and mix well. Beat the eggs into the strawberry jam; add the sugar and salt and beat well. Pour over the fruit-nut mixture and stir together. Grease a jellyroll pan, 11 by 15 inches, and spread the mixture evenly over the pan. Bake in a 300° F oven for 30 minutes. Remove from oven and cut in diamond shapes. Return pan to the oven for 6 minutes to dry the edges. Cool before removing from the pan. Makes about 46 pieces.

Babka Yablochnaya (Apple Charlotte)

Babka Yablochnaya (Apple Charlotte)

8 medium apples,
    peeled, cored, and
    chopped in ½-
    inch cubes
½ cup sugar
½ cup water
¼ cup butter
    grated rind of 1
    small lemon

grated rind of 1
    small orange
½ cup ground almonds
½ cup golden raisins
1-pound loaf pum-
    pernickel, crusts
    removed
3 eggs, separated
½ cup sweet white
    wine

Cook the apples, sugar, and water together until apples are soft but hold their shape. Add the butter, grated peels, nuts, and raisins; mix gently. In a large bowl crumb the bread and add the apple mixture; toss lightly. Beat the egg yolks until thick and lemon colored; beat in the wine. Mix into the apples and bread crumbs. Beat the eggs whites until stiff but not dry and fold in. Grease a 2-quart Charlotte mold, lining the bottom with wax paper, and spoon in the pudding. Bake in a 350° F oven for about 1 hour 15 minutes. Serve warm with Apricot Sauce.

Apricot Sauce

1 cup dried apricots
2½ cups water

½ cup sugar
⅛ teaspoon salt

Combine all the ingredients in a saucepan. Simmer over low heat until the apricots are very soft. Put liquid and apricots into a blender or press through a strainer. Makes about 2 cups.

GREECE

Constantine II of Greece, Ingrid of Denmark, Anne-Marie of Greece holding her daughter Alexia, Queen Mother Frederika of Greece, and Frederick IX of Denmark

N GREECE THE *kafeneion* or sidewalk café is the modern counterpart to the ancient agora. Every main thoroughfare and square is lined with cafés where Greeks talk, eat, and sip coffee. It is a place to conduct all sorts of transactions and business matters, to play dominoes and read the newspapers, but mostly to talk politics under large expanses of awning and to nibble at *mezedakia* (assorted hors d'oeuvres). Inside the café, eating and talking combine into a single, inseparable ritual. The fare is abundant and varied—Feta cheese, Kalamata olives, salads with cucumbers, tomatoes, and onions, bits of smoked herring, fried squid, *lakerda* fillets (a tuna-like delicacy from the Black Sea), slices of *kokoretsi* (lamb organs grilled on a spit). *Retsina* (resinated wine) and *ouzo* (a liqueur) refresh the tongue and permit pauses between the polemics.

The tradition has ancient roots, for *symposium* literally means "drinking together." As for eating, the Greeks seem always to have been serious about it, but not excessively so. There has never been a great Greek gourmand; even in the most extravagant excesses of the Byzantine court there was no one to approach Vitellius, the affable 1st-century Roman emperor remembered chiefly as one of the greatest eaters and drinkers of all time. The word for the science of food, gastronomy, is of Greek origin, but those for extravagant eating—gourmet, gourmand, and glutton—derive from French and Latin.

Greek royalty in modern times, like the Greek *kouzina* (cuisine), has been borrowed. There has not been a native Greek on the throne since May 29, 1453, when the Ottoman Turks ended 1,000 years of Byzantine civilization.

On one occasion, about half a century earlier, when food and royalty were tightly bound in tradition and ritual, the fate of an empire hung on a meal. For on Christmas day in the year 1400 a banquet was given by King Henry IV of England, at his palace of Eltham, to celebrate the holy day and to honor an exotic and distinguished guest, the Byzantine Emperor Manuel II Palaeologus.

Byzantine emperors were no mere mortals.

Although they could be of humble birth—peasants, butchers, shepherds—a supernatural mystery surrounded them once they were crowned. The emperor or *basileus* was lawful heir of Augustus and Constantine, Viceroy of God, in fact Christ himself—*Christos Basileus*. And he played the role with spectacular drama and ritual. Meals were full of allusions to the Last Supper. There were twelve places at each table and twelve tables faced his own. When the *basileus* entered the dining hall, dressed in purple and wearing a white tiara on his head, guests shielded their faces as if dazzled by the splendor of his presence. Food was abundant but never excessive. Dishes were passed by means of moving trays, beginning with hors d'oeuvres of caviar, olives, ginger, and salad served with *garos* sauce, a fish sauce famous in antiquity. Hot dishes consisted of game and poultry. Wines from the island of Chios (which still produces a popular Greek wine) were served with the sweets and cakes. The meal was completed by fruit, which was lowered theatrically from the ceiling in large bowls. Following dessert, the *basileus* broke and blessed the bread, completing the symbolism by raising a cup of wine to his lips.

Each course was accompanied by entertainment or instruction: music, miming, and dancing for the first; fiery readings from St. John Chrysostom for the second; Hindu jugglers and Chinese acrobats with dessert. The meal was a solemn religious ritual, so serious that anyone dropping a plate and marring the rite was subject to decapitation.

When the emperor traveled or went to war, rations were not stinted. One hundred horses were required to haul the silverware, cooking implements, and food. Some 50 cows, 200 foals, 100 geese, and 100 goats and sheep were herded along until needed for the pot.

But on Christmas day in 1400, when Manuel II was feted by King Henry, he could not have had much of an appetite for food. He had made the long journey from Constantinople in a desperate appeal for aid against the Turks, who had progressively chipped away his far-reaching empire until only Constantinople and a few outposts remained. Manuel had already failed to elicit much help from Paris. England was sympathetic, but not about to dispatch troops to help the Greeks. In 1402 Manuel had to hurry home on news that the Sultan was marching against Constantinople. A fortuitous attack on the eastern domains of Turkey by Timur the Tatar diverted the Sultan's attention, and Byzantium gained a brief respite; the final fall came some 50 years later, in 1453.

The Revolution of 1821 brought independence to Greece with the aid of the Great Powers, who imposed a monarchy on the new nation. Otto (1832–62), the second son of King Louis of Bavaria, was proclaimed king. He ruled the country so badly that he was eventually sent packing; the Powers then brought in a Danish dynasty. It was a sorry business and very un-Greek; the transplant never quite took. The history of the next 150 years was a dizzying chronicle of depositions, changes of government, coups, war, and exiled rulers. Any investigation into the royal family and its habits, tastes, and idiosyncrasies at the table produces only an ordinary *giouvetchi*, an undistinguished stew of indifferent origin, filling but unmemorable.

A French journalist, Edmond About, traveled through Greece in the 1850's and left a scathing account of life under King Otto, including some caustic observations of court life. Young Prince Otto, before he became King of Greece, had eaten black bread along with the other royal children. When Otto married Amelia, daughter of the Grand Duke of Oldenburg, in 1847 and set up a royal household, there was little local tradition of great cuisine to adopt. About found little to ap-

Red-figured vase

prove in the Greek Court. He ridiculed the palace, which he described as having the appearance of a barracks from one side and a bastardized version of the Parthenon from the other. He disdained the pomp and ceremony, and mentioned food in connection with the royal household only three times. The first was in an anecdote concerning the captain of a frigate, a fellow Frenchman who was admitted to "the ceremony of kissing hands"—those of the queen. The captain fancied that Amelia's eye lingered a moment too long on him and subsequently, during a stop-over at the island of Poros, he dispatched several bushels of the largest, most beautiful apples, along with a saccharine love note alluding to the Trojan War legend of Paris, Aphrodite, and the golden apple. (The queen complained to the French ambassador, and the captain was relieved of his command.) The second reference to the royal palate also concerned the queen. Whereas Otto was feeble and sickly, Amelia apparently had the constitution of a dirndled milkmaid. She is described as a woman of "remarkable appetite," who was never hungrier than when observing the palace staff at their work, consuming four meals a day "not to speak of sundry intermediate collations." What they consisted of, About leaves unrecorded. The third story is found in a description of a court ball. The decor is described as resplendent, if overdone, the lighting in the ballroom brilliant; but the refreshments that close the occasion are less than brilliant, the disappointing little cakes "handed around are almost all gingerbread in disguise. As a finale there is some fighting to get at the soup."

The fervor of Greek nationalism soon banished gingerbread from the royal table. In 1862 Otto returned from a cruise to find that a bloodless revolution had deposed him. While factionalism was spreading into civil war, the Great Powers quickly settled on a Danish prince to rule Greece; he became King George I (1863–1913). One of his sons, Prince Nicholas, who lived until 1938, left a long memoir in which there is nothing memorable concerning the royal table.

George I reigned for half a century, until his assassination in Salonika in 1913, but no king after him was to hold the throne for long. Politics has continued to dominate the talk in Greek cafés during the 20th century, just as survival has preoccupied the monarchy to the exclusion of such amenities as royal dining.

Royal Recipes

Moussaka
(Beef and Eggplant Casserole)

butter	½ cup tomato purée
2 pounds ground round steak	3 medium eggplants
1 large onion	4 tablespoons flour
salt	white pepper
pepper	2 cups hot milk
2 teaspoons oregano	3 eggs
1 large clove garlic, finely minced	2 cups grated Parmesan cheese
1 1-pound can whole tomatoes, cut into quarters	

In a large skillet brown the meat in ¼ cup butter, and remove. Sauté the onion until tender. Add 1½ teaspoons salt, ½ teaspoon pepper, oregano, garlic, tomatoes, and tomato purée. Return the meat, cover, and cook over low heat for 1 hour, stirring frequently. Peel eggplants and cut lengthwise into ½-inch slices. Arrange on broiler rack and brush with ¼ cup melted butter. Sprinkle lightly with salt and pepper and broil until golden on both sides. In a small saucepan melt 2 tablespoons butter, add flour, ½ teaspoon salt, and ¼ teaspoon white pepper, and cook 1 minute. Stir in hot milk and cook until thickened. Beat eggs slightly and add about 1 cup of the hot sauce to the eggs, beating constantly. Return egg mixture to the sauce and remove from stove. Line a baking dish with a layer of eggplant, a layer of meat, and a sprinkling of cheese; repeat, ending with a layer of eggplant. Pour over the sauce, sprinkle with cheese, and bake in a preheated 375°F oven for 1 hour. Makes 6 to 8 servings.

Dolmadakia Yialandji
(Stuffed Grape Leaves)

2 cups chopped onions	½ cup chopped parsley, reserve stems
¾ cup olive oil	2 teaspoons chopped fresh dill or
1 cup uncooked rice	1 teaspoon dried
1¼ teaspoons salt	2 teaspoons chopped fresh mint
¼ teaspoon freshly ground pepper	½ cup lemon juice
½ cup chopped scallions (including green tops)	water
	30 grape leaves in brine

Sauté onions in ½ cup olive oil until almost tender, and add the rice. Cook for 10 minutes. Add the salt, pepper, scallions, chopped parsley, dill, mint, ¼ cup lemon juice, and ½ cup water. Cover and cook for 15 minutes. Separate grape leaves and wash to remove brine. Lay out leaves with the underside of the leaf up. Put 2 heaping teaspoons of the stuffing on each leaf. Roll up the base and fold in the sides, rolling tightly to the end of the leaf. Place some of the parsley stems on the bottom of a large skillet and fit in a layer of rolls. Place stems between the next layer. Add remaining olive oil, lemon juice, and 1 cup water. Weight with a heavy plate. Cover and simmer for 20 minutes. Add ½ cup more water if necessary and cook 20 minutes more. Makes 30 rolls.

Kourabiedes
(Shortbread)

1 cup butter	2¼ cups sifted
6 tablespoons	all-purpose flour
confectioners'	whole cloves
sugar	confectioners' sugar
1 egg, separated	for topping
1 ounce brandy	(optional)

Cream butter and sugar thoroughly. Gradually beat together until very light and creamy. Add egg yolk and brandy and continue to beat until thick and a light lemon color. Gradually add flour and knead slightly. Shape dough, with floured hands, into 1½-inch balls. Stick each ball with a whole clove and brush with slightly beaten egg white. Place on an ungreased baking sheet and bake in a preheated 350°F oven for about 20 to 25 minutes or until golden. Yields 4 dozen.

Fenikia
(Honey-Dipped Cookies)

3½ cups flour	1 tablespoon brandy
2¼ teaspoons baking	½ cup chopped nuts,
powder	walnuts or
½ cup vegetable oil	pistachios
¼ cup melted butter	syrup
¼ cup orange juice	

Sift flour and baking powder. Mix the oil, butter, orange juice, brandy, and ¼ cup nuts together. Gradually stir in the flour and knead into a firm dough. Form into a ball and cut into sixteenths. Form each piece into an oval, patting it into shape, slightly pointed at each end and about 4½ x 2½ inches. Slide onto an ungreased baking sheet. Bake in a preheated 350°F oven for 20 to 25 minutes or until golden. Cool thoroughly before dipping into syrup.

Syrup

3 ounces honey	½ cup water
½ cup sugar	1 teaspoon lemon juice

Combine all ingredients in a small saucepan and boil for 3 minutes. Pour into a 9-inch cake pan and cool. Immerse cookies in the syrup and baste several times. Remove to a baking sheet. Sprinkle with the remaining chopped nuts. Store in an air-tight tin. These cookies may be baked and stored and put into the syrup when needed. Yields 16 cookies.

Karidopeta
(Nut Cake)

1 cup butter	2 teaspoons baking
1½ cups sugar	powder
5 eggs	1 teaspoon cinnamon
2½ cups sifted	1 cup walnuts, chopped
all-purpose flour	

Cream butter and sugar together. Add eggs, one at a time, beating after each addition. Beat until thick and a light lemon color. Shake in, little by little, the flour, baking powder, and cinnamon that have been sifted together. Stir in walnuts. Turn into a greased 12 x 8 x 2-inch pan and bake in a preheated 350°F oven for 30 to 35 minutes or until golden. Remove from oven and while hot pour cool syrup over the cake. Cut in diamond shapes after cake has absorbed the syrup.

Syrup

2¾ cups water	1¾ cups sugar

Combine water and sugar and boil over high heat for 10 minutes. Cool before using.

Moussaka (Beef and Eggplant Casserole)

ASIA and the MIDDLE EAST

Shah Jahan on Horseback

ENTURIES BEFORE EATING in Europe rose from being a mere act of survival to one of social grace, cooking in Asia had long been established as an art. In fact, Asia is where cooking began, according to current archaeological findings. About 9,000 years ago agriculture and the domestication of animals came into being in Mesopotamia (roughly corresponding to modern Iraq). Not long thereafter unnamed innovators founded a cuisine that evolved over the centuries into the fabled royal banquets of ancient Babylonia and Sumeria and has persisted, often little changed, down to modern times.

Persia—now Iran—had a sophisticated kitchen long before the Middle Ages in Europe had even begun. About a thousand years ago the Persians began to develop a cuisine based on rice, which is still central to their cooking. Starting with two basic dishes, *chelo,* rice topped with a variety of meats and sauces, and *polo,* a pilaf in which the other ingredients are mixed in with the rice, Iranian cooks developed a whole series of dishes of great subtlety and charm.

Persia's greatest poet, Firdausi, who lived about A.D. 1000, wrote a long epic poem, the *Shah Namah,* about his country's kings, going back to the beginning. The first Persian king of all is credited with the invention of cooking, and one may wonder whether it was not this invention that made him king.

The Persian Court liked to celebrate birthdays with special dinner parties at which a whole animal—ox, horse, or camel—would be roasted. Since Persia is the home of the peach, and noted for the magnificence of its fruits, including the famed Persian melons, these royal birthday dinners must have been more than memorable.

In India, cooking was regarded as one of the 64 arts, and princes as well as princesses used to learn to cook. Since it was considered improper to take food without sharing it with guests and relatives, entertaining was an everyday affair, with a marriage an excuse for a banquet.

Wars, which raged intermittently, did not take the mind of the Court off food. On the contrary, there were moments when war, food, and peace were so inextricably linked that they have come down to us in art form. There is a 17th-century miniature depicting the Mogul Emperor of India, Jahangir (1605–27), imagining a peace parley with his enemy, Shah Abbas I of Persia. The two rulers are shown seated on a beautifully decorated small sofa flanked by two male attendants, one of whom holds a white dove in one hand and a small gilded stag on wheels in the other.

The stag, a drinking vessel of German design, was inspired by the Automata of al-Jazari, an Arab inventor who delighted in mechanical conceits. First the stag was filled with wine, and the mechanism was set in motion. As soon as it had run down, it was handed to the nearest king, who emptied it. But just what it did, no one bothers to say.

On the footed table in front of the monarchs is an Italian ewer and wine glasses together with what appear to be two elaborate wine decanters. There are two narghiles (water pipes) and two trays of assorted fruits including a melon, grapes, peaches, apricots, and mangoes. Scattered around are small dishes of nuts, including pistachios. It is known that Abbas was fond of wines (especially those from Shiraz), sweetmeats, and fruits, and often used to wander through the Maidan, the market of his capital, then considered to be one of the finest markets in the world, pleasantly redolent of the mingled odors of fruits, flowers, and roasting coffee. How clever of Jahangir, who wanted peace with Abbas after Abbas had retaken Kandahar from him in 1622, to dream of a peace settlement in the sort of ambience he knew would appeal to his enemy instead of planning a vast banquet of the rich foods for which his cooks were famous!

Both Persians and Indians loved picnics and both countries enjoy good picnic weather, warm and sunny, with rain very predictable. Shady groves and gardens were preferred spots, since the noon sun can be disagreeably hot in these regions. Sometimes the picnic would be that most delightful of all, the indoor-outdoor picnic, taking place in a palace courtyard full of trees and flowers but with all conveniences within reach.

The picnics were elaborate. Cooks and cookpots and servants and foods of all kinds were considered essential. Meats, fowl, and fish threaded on skewers and grilled over charcoal were particularly esteemed. Whole pigeons or doves, on individual skewers, or whole small fish, were popular. Cauldrons, which were set over wood fires

and used for stews, were remarkably similar to the soup kettles of today. Fruit, sweetmeats, cakes, and wine were included as a matter of course.

It is very likely that Jahangir served turkey at palace banquets, though it may well have been considered a bit tricky for a picnic. There is, in the Victoria and Albert Museum in London, a painting of a turkey in Persian miniature style that Jahangir commissioned in 1612. Since the bird, the *huexolotl* of the Aztecs, was not known until after Cortes conquered Mexico in 1521, one has some measure of the extreme sophistication of both the Mogul and Persian courts.

A favorite court dish at the time of Akbar (1556–1605), father of Jahangir and the greatest of the Mogul emperors, was a whole sheep stuffed with a series of smaller animals and finally with a hard-cooked egg, the whole assemblage roasted in front of a fire. (The technique of stuffing a large animal with smaller ones is still popular in parts of northern India and Pakistan, although the kings and courts have disappeared.)

Cooks had a wide selection of both domesticated animals and wild game to choose from. At that time there were boars and pigs (prohibited to Moslems), cows (prohibited to Hindus), goats, sheep, deer, water buffalo, rabbits, hares, domestic chickens, pigeons, doves, partridges, pea fowls, and other wild fowl. Lamb was probably the favorite meat, with venison a close second.

Akbar, who is said to have been fond of palm wine laced with opium and spices, extended his original kingdom in north-central India to include Afghanistan, Baluchistan, and nearly all of India north of the Godivari River, about halfway down the peninsula. He had courts at Delhi and Agra and later at Fatehpur Sikri that were centers of the arts, letters, and learning, and because he was so impressed with Persian culture the later Mogul Empire bears an indelible Persian stamp.

The Mogul cuisine, rich and lavish in its imperial days, is still the finest in the subcontinent. Before 1948, when the independent Indian Government was established, Hyderabad was the largest of the Indian princely states ruled over by His Exalted Highness, the Nizam, with a Moslem aristocracy of *nawabs* under him. As in the past, the wedding of a son or daughter was the occasion for a feast as lavish as the wealth of the *nawab* permitted, with a guest list running into the hundreds. The description of one such wedding party in prewar India has all the glamour of *The Arabian Nights,* with the trees in the palace gardens decked with colored lights, women guests in brilliantly colored full-length silk skirts with gold and sequin embroidered jackets and filmy white scarves, and the turbaned men in the Moslem court dress of high-collared, long, black jacket and narrow trousers, the jackets often fastened with jeweled buttons.

The menu could have been chosen by Akbar himself but for the whisky and champagne. The fruit drinks were the same as his Court must often have enjoyed, sherbets made of pomegranate, melon, and mango juices, sweetened, mixed with water, and chilled, reflecting the influence of the Persia he so greatly admired.

The chief glory of the Mogul kitchen is its lamb dishes; *muzbi,* a special appetizer traditionally served at feasts, is a splendid example. This is an ancient dish and is cooked outdoors on a grill over a charcoal fire built in a pit. Lamb breasts are marinated for several hours in a mixture including garlic, onion, spices, and curds, then are drained, cut into squares, rolled in a paste of ground nuts, and broiled on skewers, and eaten with an accompaniment of sliced onion, fresh chutney, and wedges of lime.

Although in modern India the Western dining table and chairs are commonplace, the older tradition has persisted. At the wedding feast, guests sat on the floor, grouped around low tables decorated with flower petals and containing various desserts like the *halvahs* (made with various kinds of flour, and flavored with nuts, fruits, or spices). For the main dish there were whole sheep, highly seasoned, stuffed with a rice pilaf, roasted chickens, and hard-cooked eggs, then cooked in *ghee* (clarified butter) in enormous covered pots. In addition there were other traditional Mogul dishes such as rice and lamb *biryani,* lamb curry, *kebabs* (skewered lamb morsels) of many types, and the usual accompaniments such as *dhal* (lentil purée), and finally, of course *paan* (betel nut, spices, and lime paste, wrapped in a betel leaf), which is chewed as a digestive and ceremonially ends the meal. On festive occasions the *paan* is covered with silver leaf.

In 1882, Valentine George Littleton Holt, who was secretary to one of the Moslem *nawabs,* wrote to his wife Charlotte Elizabeth in England of his pleasure in the subtly different *kebabs,* and his appreciation of the *murg masalam,* a Mogul chicken dish; but it was the lamb curry that stirred him most, and he promised her a recipe. The original is lost, but his grandchildren still have a recipe for a lamb curry that evokes the glory of the Mogul kitchen.

Food patterns were laid down early in much of Asia, and although new foods were introduced and waves of puritanism from time to time curtailed the drinking of alcohol either as wine or spirits, many of the foods of the remote past are still popular. *Loochi,* thin cakes made of wheat flour and fried in *ghee,* were long popular at palace banquets and are still a favorite of guests at the sumptuous feasts that mark marriages in high Hindu society.

Just as in the past, Hindus do not eat beef. Many are vegetarian, and, according to one Bengali writer, some orthodox Brahmans and pious widows of Hindu society still avoid exciting vegetables such as onions and garlic, a prohibition laid down in early days.

A description of a typical wedding feast at the time of King Madanapala (A.D. 1130) of the Pala Dynasty of Bengal reveals that the marriages of the sons and daughters of Hindu princes were magnificent and extremely elaborate affairs with quite formal rules for the type of food to be served.

The dinner, it was emphasized, must consist of every conceivable type of food and drink. There should be food that must be chewed, like cakes; some to be eaten, like rice; some to be sucked (sic), like soup; some to be licked, like honey; and some to be drunk. It was also considered vital to balance the six basic tastes; thus the menu had to have one dish in which the flavor was predominantly pungent, another bitter, another sour, another astringent, another salt, and another sweet. There was some controversy over the order in which the dishes should be served, some authorities beginning with sweet and going on to salt, sour, astringent, pungent, and bitter, and others reversing this, beginning with bitter and ending with sweet. Today in high Hindu society the penultimate dish would probably have a sour flavor predominating, with the last dish sweet. The skill of the cook was demonstrated by the degree of subtlety in which spices and herbs were blended to produce a dish in which the dominant flavor suggested itself rather than being overwhelming.

The Bengalis of the medieval period had plenty of foods to choose from. The climate was good, neither too hot nor too cold, and there was ample water for agriculture. Bengal was a large state, including most of what is now Orissa, Bihar, and part of Pakistan. It was indeed a land of plenty, as well as a land of good cooks, each with his own specialty—one skilled in vegetable cooking while another cooked only fish, and so on. The cooking equipment, which included fry-

Portrait of His Excellency Shaikh Hasan Christi

ing pans and pots of various sizes made of iron or copper, added up to a considerable *batterie de cuisine*.

The menu for one wedding feast, which must have taxed the capacity of even the most resolute diner, included dishes of fish, boiled, fried, grilled, and spitted. There was lamb curry and venison curry; meats fried in *ghee* and others boiled with rice; vegetables and spices to make a pilaf; both pork and lamb cooked with curds and salt; meats cooked with vinegar, salt, and white mustard; soups; partridges, ducks, fowls, and pigeons cooked in various ways; *dhals;* rice and barley;

fresh chutneys; breads of many kinds; sherbets and sweets (including a rice pudding); and fresh fruits including coconuts, bananas, mangoes, jackfruit, pomegranates, and oranges. In addition the cooks had all the spices that Europe imported at great cost and trouble. In common use were cinnamon, cloves, cardamom, pepper, turmeric, nutmeg, ginger, asafoetida, fenugreek, saffron, coriander, fennel, mustard and poppy seeds, cumin, tamarind pulp, and rose water, as well as such basic seasonings as onion and garlic. The cooks also had honey, refined sugar, brown sugar, and sugarcane juice. In addition to the sherbets they had wine made from both black and green grapes, as well as imported wines and distilled liquors made from rice, honey, and date palm juice.

The Bengalis were particularly discriminating about varieties of rice, which was first cultivated in India. A Sanskrit work talks about a strain of rice whose grains are large and scented and of an exquisite taste. It was said to be specially remarkable for its shining color and was called "the rice for the use of the great." Undoubtedly it was rice of this high quality that appeared on the *thalis* of the maharajas and other, lesser princes.

Because of the undivided family, households in India have tended to be large, and this is nowhere truer than in the palaces of the princes. When guests are invited to celebrate a wedding, a birth, or a religious festival, the numbers become impressive. And perhaps the most memorable occasion is the 10-day festival of Dasehra, which celebrates Rama's victory over the army of the demon Ravana and the rescue of his wife Sita, and pays tribute to the goddess Durga, who aided him. In Mysore the nobles of the region chose this festival to pay their annual tribute, a sack of gold coins, to the maharaja. After India became a republic, the maharaja was no longer a powerful ruler, but the festival is still celebrated, with nine days devoted to the worship of Durga and the final day to the celebration of Rama's victory.

The ceremonial aspect of Dasehra is breathtaking. The turbaned maharaja, in gold brocade and necklaces of precious stones, sits on a gold and silver throne under a canopy decorated with a golden, bejeweled peacock, surrounded by nobles and retainers almost as grandly dressed, and with all sorts of entertainers adding color to an already brilliant scene. In the final torchlight procession, the maharaja rides in a golden *howdah* atop an elaborately decorated elephant.

The foods traditionally served at the festival are as grand as the royal pageantry. Certain dishes, among them *payasam*, a semiliquid sweet with a rice base, are cooked on the first day. Other dishes are added on subsequent days, but all the accumulated dishes are cooked each day, and by the tenth day the menu has swelled to dozens of dishes: curries and chutneys, rice dishes both sweet and savory, stuffed dumplings, soups, yoghurt dishes, many kinds of small rich cakes, *dhals*, and rice-flour pancakes, not to mention all manner of savory snacks made from bananas, eggplant, and potatoes.

Traditional Indian service of food differs from that of other countries. Each diner has his or her *thali*, a round metal tray of silver, brass, or nowadays often stainless steel. The whole meal is presented at one time, except of course in the case of feasts such as Dasehra, at which no individual *thali* could possibly hold all the dishes available, and large straw mats are placed on the floor to serve as giant *thalis*. Rice or bread is served on the *thali*, and the other dishes are in *katories*, small metal bowls. A typical meal might consist of a curry or two, bread and/or rice, *dhal*, *raita* (a raw vegetable and yoghurt dish), a vegetable dish, one or more of the fresh chutneys as relishes, and a dessert of fresh fruit or a pudding. It is traditional to eat with one's fingers, using the right hand. *Chapatis* or other types of bread are used as both spoon and fork.

The ebb and flow of conquest in western Asia has somewhat blurred the lines of culinary distinction. Arabia, conquered by Persians and Turks among others, was itself a conqueror with a glittering civilization, but its center moved from Asia, and to appreciate the Arabian kitchen today one must dine with a Bedouin sheikh. Bedouin means "desert dweller" in Arabic, and these are the nomad people of Arabia, Syria, Jordan, and Iraq. The tribe is said to be a community of equals headed by a sheikh, but since the women of the ruler's entourage are excluded from almost everything but hard work and get only the leftovers to eat, it is a dubious sort of equality.

The *mansaf* or formal Bedouin dinner of today still takes place in the sheikh's desert tent and differs little from dinners described a hundred or more years ago. How long the institution can survive the march of progress is dubious, but it is hard to envisage the hot dog taking over from the traditional *mansaf* dish, which consists of rice rich with butter, sautéed pine nuts, almonds and topped with pieces of boiled lamb; it is served on huge trays lined with *shrak*, a type of flat wholewheat bread, and the lot is served with a sour-milk sauce. And, of course, coffee to drink, for the Bedouins are strict Moslems.

The meal begins with a traditional washing of the hands, and grace. There are no table implements, and only the right hand may be used, a convention requiring considerable dexterity and a nice sense of how hot the food is. There are no tables or chairs. Diners sit in a circle on the carpeted and cushioned tent floor around the commonly shared platter. Rice pudding may be served as a dessert and, after a second hand-washing, more coffee, made from the pulverized bean and served thick and sweet in tiny cups. Not as lavish as a Mogul feast, perhaps, but certainly a close relative and a testimony to the culinary cohesiveness of the region.

When the Turks first embarked on the path of conquest that led to the founding of the Ottoman Empire, they had considerable military genius but no cuisine. They picked up their first cooking lessons in the 11th century, when they conquered Persia with its sophisticated and elegant food. By the end of the 13th century much of the Byzantine Empire had been conquered, the Arab states were vassals, and a rich, diversified kitchen had come into being. Naturally enough, there were regional differences; but with the emphasis on lamb as a favorite meat, the prohibition of pork, the talent for *mazza* (appetizers), and the love of sweetmeats, it was genuinely one kitchen.

It is sad that no menus or recipes are available from the archives of the imperial kitchens in the great palace complex of Topkapi in Istanbul, seat of the Ottoman sultans. Nevertheless, some idea of how the Court ate in the 17th century can be gathered from the fact that there were 10 kitchens, each with its own specialty—soup, fish, meat, bread, pastries, and so on. There were 200 cooks who fed 3,000 to 5,000 people daily, and the list of kitchen stores purchased over a year indicates what types of food were most popular. Meat heads the list, but vegetables and salads are well represented, with spinach, cabbage, and lettuce popular. Rice was a favorite food, as was *kaymak*, a kind of clotted cream. Some of the table appointments used by the sultans, the ladies of the harem, and the courtiers are on display in the museum areas of the palace, and if the food was as extravagant as the plates it was served on, the imagination falters. One coffee service is set with diamonds, and there are spoons of solid gold. World War I saw the end of it all.

There is, however, a record of a dinner party given in 1835 at the harem of the Egyptian chargé d'affaires, Mustafa Effendi, and attended by a Miss Pardoe of England, then on a visit to Constantinople. She describes both the menu and the ambience. Women were, of course, strictly segregated and were seated in order of importance, the first wife and her guest taking precedence. Nine slaves served the ladies, who ate without benefit of knives and forks, using their fingers, or when this was impractical, eating with spoons from a common dish. Hand-washing in tepid rose water poured by slave girls signaled the end of the meal, after which the ladies retired to another apartment for the same sort of thick, sweet coffee served in small cups with which the segregated Bedouin sheikh and his company finished their meal.

Miss Pardoe records the menu as composed of anchovy cakes, *Imam Bayaldi* (The Imam Fainted, an eggplant dish that is said to have caused a Turkish priest to swoon with delight), *dolmates* (vine leaves stuffed with rice and meat), cinnamon-wine soup, pilaf-stuffed chickens, cucumber and yoghurt salad, *bourma* (syrup and nut pastry), *sharbatee gulab* (rose-petal sherbet), and lemonade. A modest and pleasant meal, suitable for ladies.

Thailand, influenced by both India and China, nevertheless has a kitchen entirely its own. Traditionally diners recline against cushions on the floor in front of low, inlaid lacquer tables. Each diner is presented with a tray on which are a series of footed china dishes, some covered, some not, and a larger, covered bowl of rice. The smaller dishes contain individual servings of soup, various curries, fish, vegetables, sauces—usually one very hot sauce made of fresh, hot chili peppers —and salad, to be followed by dessert and fruit. The number of dishes depends on the occasion and the circumstances of the diners.

King Rama I, who founded the city of Bangkok and the present ruling dynasty in 1783, was in the habit of taking two meals a day of this type, one roughly at noon and one in the early evening. This pattern of eating is true for palace and people down to the present day, although many Thai

people have adopted the Western table and chairs. Table implements are decorative spoons and forks, often of bronze, carved and with buffalo-horn or ivory handles. Knives are not necessary, as meat never is served in large chunks but is cut up, as in Chinese cooking.

When King Rama dedicated the Emerald Buddha in 1809, he invited members of the royal family and gentlemen of the Court to take part in providing a meal, in the Thai tradition, for the monks of the Wat (temple)—2,000 of them.

It was a sumptuous meal, consisting of rice accompanied by sausages, duck eggs, *kai p'anaeng* (deviled capon), fried prawns and pork, fried eggplant, omelettes, quenelles, prawn broth, bam-

Mohammed Reza Pahlavi, Shah of Iran

boo shoots, *namprik* (a sauce made of dried shrimps and hot chili peppers), *plahaengphad* (salt fish in coconut milk), watermelon and *khanom foy* (mung bean cakes), crystallized rice, *khanom phing* (bean-flour and coconut cakes), "chicken entrails" (fried batter dipped in sugar syrup), banana chips, *sankhya* (custard cooked in a green coconut shell), golden shreds (eggs cooked in syrup), and *khanom talai* (steamed rice-flour cakes).

A meal given today for monks would not differ basically from this one of 160 years ago, although different dishes might be chosen from the Thai repertory.

Thai curries are hot but, unlike Indian curries, rely far more on herbs than on spices. Many other dishes fall into the category of stir-fry, re-

Mahendra Bir Bikram Shah Deva of Nepal

flecting a Chinese influence even though they are different from Chinese dishes. Foods are always beautifully presented, each dish a work of art. Thai fruit, especially durian, mangosteen, pineapple, papaya, and pomelo, are uniquely good and always form part of the dessert.

Since Rama's day the habit of taking a meal called *krunag wang* (refreshments) at about 3 o'clock has developed, and breakfast has been adopted. Five-o'clock tea is now supplanting the 3-o'clock refreshments, and Western alcoholic drinks are served in the upper social echelons, a development of the last 40 years or so.

Bhumibol Adulyadej of Thailand

Thai royalty has always taken an interest in cooking. The queen of King Rama I made her own special soup, *kaengron*, from shrimps, pork, chicken, and the small round apple cucumbers that grow in tropical regions. King Chulalongkorn, who reigned from 1868 to 1908 and who fancied himself as a maker of *namprik* (hot sauce) and *kaeng phed* (curry), had a novel system for organizing a New Year's party and encouraging good cooking at the same time. Back in the days when Thai kings had many wives, King Chulalongkorn had 32, each with her own quarters in the palace. It was the custom for each wife to submit a dish for the party, with the king judging and dispensing prizes.

The best Thai cookbook available today is the work of a princess, Sibpan Sonakul, and the reigning monarch, King Bhumibol Adulyadej, himself took the photographs that appear in the book. It is not an exaggeration to say that it was the Court which refined and enlarged the cuisine that is now common to all the people.

Little is left on record concerning the foods of the Khmer civilizations, the builders of Angkor Wat in Cambodia. The empire collapsed in the 15th century, and people who have dined with Prince Sihanouk in Phnompenh, the capital, seem to have had French food and wines, reflecting the French conquest of Indochina.

This is also true of the royal cuisine of the Annamese kings, whose palaces and royals tombs in Hué, South Vietnam, were recently destroyed in war.

About 100 B.C. the Chinese invaded the kingdom that existed in what is now North and South Vietnam, and remained—despite the efforts of the Vietnamese to dislodge them—for about 1,000 years. Chinese influence can be seen in the fact that the Vietnamese use chopsticks and the Chinese stir-fry method of cooking. Their kitchen has remained Vietnamese, however, and they have many delightful culinary habits, such as wrapping morsels of shrimp, pork, mushrooms, and scallions in rice paper, frying the package, wrapping it in a lettuce leaf, and dipping it in hot sauce. The Court may well have relished such delicacies, but unfortunately much information has been lost through wars and time. It may well be that in libraries and private collections scattered round the world great treasures are awaiting the gifted and perceptive translator who must be linguist, cook, botanist, and historian, with the intuition of an angel and the patience of Job.

Royal Recipes

Baba Ghannuj
(Eggplant Appetizer)

½ cup sesame seeds
(tahina)
1 medium eggplant
2 cloves garlic, finely
minced
2 tablespoons lemon
juice

salt and pepper
1 to 2 tablespoons olive
oil (optional)
1 medium onion,
minced
1 tablespoon chopped
flat-leaf parsley

Put sesame seeds into a blender and process until they become pasty in texture. Place whole unpeeled eggplant in a pan or on a piece of foil and bake in a preheated 400°F oven for 45 minutes. Cool, scrape out the pulp with a spoon, and mash with a fork. Drain off any excess liquid. Add the tahina, garlic, and lemon juice and whip together with a fork. Correct the seasoning. Turn into a serving bowl and spoon over the olive oil. Sprinkle with onion and parsley and serve with Arab bread. Makes 6 to 8 servings.

Cinnamon Wine Soup

4 cups dry red wine
1 2-inch piece cinnamon
stick
1 strip lemon peel
2 cups chicken stock
3 tablespoons sugar or
to taste

2 tablespoons
cornstarch
2 tablespoons cold
water
2 egg yolks, well beaten

Simmer wine in an enamel or stainless steel saucepan, partially covered, with the cinnamon and lemon peel for 10 minutes. Add the chicken stock, sugar, and the cornstarch dissolved in cold water. Cook over low heat, stirring constantly until thickened. Correct the seasoning. Slowly pour ½ cup of the hot soup into the egg yolks, beating constantly. Pour the mixture back into the soup and cook 2 to 3 minutes longer. Do not boil after adding the yolks. Serve hot or cold. Makes 6 servings.

Tabouleh
(Burghul, Tomato, Parsley Appetizer)

½ cup burghul or kasha
(cracked wheat)
cold water
3 medium tomatoes,
peeled and finely
chopped
¾ cup finely chopped
flat-leaf parsley
2 tablespoons finely
chopped mint
leaves

2 scallions, finely
chopped, using
both the white and
green
4 tablespoons olive oil
4 tablespoons lemon
juice
salt and freshly
ground pepper

Grind burghul or kasha in a blender and soak for 1 hour in cold water to cover. Pour the wheat into a sieve and press out all the water. Add all the ingredients and salt and pepper to taste. Put into a serving bowl and chill. Serve as an appetizer with Arab bread. Makes about 12 servings.

Fesenjan (Persian Duck)

Namprik
(Shrimp Hot Pepper Sauce)

2 tablespoons dried salted Oriental shrimp, soaked for 1 hour or more	2 tablespoons tamarind pulp, broken into small pieces
4 cloves garlic, finely minced	½ to 1 teaspoon seeded and finely minced hot fresh pepper
2 teaspoons brown sugar	3 tablespoons nam pla (fish soy)
3 anchovy filets	2 teaspoons lime or lemon juice

Drain shrimp and process in a blender with the remaining ingredients to make a paste, or pound in a mortar and pestle. Salt to taste. This is a heavy, rather sticky mixture, to be served with rice, fish, or cooked vegetables. Yields about ½ cup.

Fesenjan
(Persian Duck)

1 5-pound duck, cut into 8 pieces	3 cups pomegranate juice or cranberry juice
2 medium onions, chopped	1½ teaspoons salt freshly ground black pepper
½ teaspoon turmeric	
1 cup chopped walnuts juice of 1 lemon	

In a large skillet brown the pieces of duck on all sides. Remove the duck to a paper towel and drain. Pour off all but 2 tablespoons of fat, and cook the onions and turmeric until the onions are transparent. Add the remaining ingredients, cover, and cook 15 minutes over low heat. Place the pieces of duck in the skillet, cover, and simmer for 1½ hours. Turn the pieces once or twice during the cooking. Arrange the duck on a heated platter. Remove any fat that has risen to the top and serve the sauce in a bowl. Rice may be served in a separate dish or around the duck platter. Makes 4 servings.

Alo-Balo Polo
(Chicken and Cherries with Rice)

1 3½-pound chicken, cut into serving pieces	1 pound sour cherries, pitted
salt and freshly ground pepper	⅓ cup sugar
	2 cups long-grain rice
2 tablespoons olive oil	6 tablespoons clarified sweet butter
1 medium onion water	⅛ teaspoon ground saffron

Salt and pepper chicken lightly. Heat oil in a large heavy kettle and sauté chicken. Remove to a paper towel and sauté the onion. Return chicken to

the kettle, add 1 cup water, cover, and simmer over very low heat for 45 minutes. Put cherries in a saucepan with the sugar and 1 cup water. Cover and cook over very low heat for 5 to 8 minutes. The cherries must retain their shape and not be mushy. Shake rice into 4 cups of rapidly boiling salted water and boil for 5 minutes. Drain. Remove the chicken from the kettle and discard the onion. Add 4 tablespoons

of the butter to the hot liquid in the kettle and put half the rice in. Lay the chicken pieces on top with half the cherries. Add the remaining rice and cherries and ½ cup of the cherry liquid. Cover and cook for 20 minutes over low heat. Mix the saffron with 1 tablespoon water. Melt the remaining 2 tablespoons butter in a small saucepan and stir in the saffron. Remove 1 cup of rice from the top of the kettle and toss with the saffron until it is completely mixed and becomes a bright yellow color. To serve, place the rice and cherries on a warm platter. Arrange the chicken on top, with the remaining rice and cherries put on at random. Scatter over the saffron rice. Lift out the brown crust from the bottom of the kettle and arrange around the edges of the platter. This is a very colorful dish. Makes 6 servings.

Alo-Balo Polo (Chicken and Cherries with Rice)

Mughlai Biryani
(Spiced Lamb)

1 pound yoghurt	½ teaspoon ground
¾ cup clarified butter	cinnamon
3 large onions, thinly	1 teaspoon ground
sliced	cumin
1 cup blanched ground	2 tablespoons seeded
almonds; reserve 2	and chopped fresh
tablespoons for	hot green pepper
garnish	3 tablespoons chopped
1 tablespoon chopped	coriander leaves or
fresh ginger root	1 teaspoon
6 cloves garlic, minced	powdered coriander
½ teaspoon cayenne	1 tablespoon chopped
pepper	mint
salt and pepper	½ cup fresh lemon juice
3 pounds boneless lamb,	1 cup milk
cut in 1-inch cubes	¼ teaspoon ground
water or stock	saffron
2 cups uncooked rice	¼ cup golden raisins
½ teaspoon ground clove	(optional)
¼ teaspoon ground	1 hard-cooked egg,
cardamon	sliced (optional)

Put yoghurt in a cheesecloth and let drain while preparing dish. In a large kettle sauté onion in 4 tablespoons of the butter until golden; remove and reserve. Add 2 more tablespoons of butter and sauté almonds, ginger, garlic, and cayenne pepper until the almonds are lightly colored. Salt and pepper the lamb and add to the kettle. Cover with water and simmer uncovered for 1½ hours. Cook the rice and reserve. Mix together the clove, cardamon, cinnamon, cumin, hot pepper, coriander leaves, mint, and lemon juice and stir into the drained yoghurt. Remove the cooked lamb to a casserole and toss with the spiced yoghurt and half the onions. Spread half the rice on top. There should be about 1 cup of liquid left in the kettle; reduce if necessary, stir, and pour over the rice. Add the remaining onion and rice. Heat the remaining butter, milk, and saffron and pour over the top. Cover and cook in preheated 325°F oven for 1 hour. Garnish with reserved almonds and if desired with raisins and hard-cooked egg slices. Makes 8 servings.

Kibbi Nayya
(Uncooked Wheat and Meat)

1 cup burghul	1 medium onion,
1 pound lean uncooked	minced
ground lamb	salt and pepper

Soak the burghul in cold water for 30 to 60 minutes. Drain through a sieve and squeeze out all the water. Mix the burghul, lamb, and onion together with salt and pepper to taste. Garnish with chopped scallions and serve with Arab bread. Yields 3 cups. Kibbi may also be formed into 6 flat 4-inch cakes or 1 large cake, seasoned with a little allspice, nutmeg, and cayenne pepper, and fried or broiled.

Kebab

3 pounds lamb, cut in	½ cup lemon juice
slices 2 x 4 x ⅜	1 large onion, grated
inches	olive oil

Marinate kebab overnight or for several hours in lemon juice and onion. When ready to cook, drain and pat dry with a paper towel. Thread meat on skewers, brush with oil, and cook over charcoal or broil in oven. Serve with chelo. Makes 6 servings.

Bhutuwa
(Fried Mutton)

½ cup mustard oil or	1 tablespoon finely
cooking oil	minced garlic
¼ cup ghee	(lasun)
1 pound mutton or	½ teaspoon turmeric
lamb cut in ¼-inch	(cesar)
cubes	¾ teaspoon salt
¼ teaspoon coriander	1 tablespoon chili
⅛ teaspoon jimbu or	powder (khursani)
saffron	1 tablespoon cumin
½ to 1 tablespoon finely	powder
chopped hot	⅛ teaspoon freshly
pepper (khursani)	ground pepper
3 1-inch pieces dried	(timur)
ginger root	1 teaspoon fresh
(adhuwa)	ginger root,
	chopped (adhuwa)
	1½ cups water

Heat oil and ghee together. Add meat and brown well. Add all the remaining ingredients, cover, and cook 1 hour over very low heat. Remove dried ginger root. Serve with rice or cracked wheat. Makes 3 to 4 servings.

Ghee
(Indian Butter Oil)

Cut 1 pound of unsalted butter into several pieces. Melt completely over low heat. Increase heat and bring to a boil. Immediately reduce heat as low as possible and simmer uncovered for 45 minutes. Carefully pour the golden ghee through a dampened flannel cloth. Store ghee in a covered crock or jar in the refrigerator. This clear oil gives a delicious nutlike flavor to food.

Chelo
(Buttered Rice)

2 cups Iranian rice or regular long-grain rice	butter
salt	6 egg yolks
water	pepper
	sumac (optional)

Wash Iranian rice and soak overnight with 2 tablespoons salt. If regular rice is used, soak 2 hours or more. Drain and rinse. Drop rice slowly into 4 cups rapidly boiling water with 2 teaspoons salt added. Do not let the water stop boiling while adding the rice. Stir and boil for 5 minutes uncovered. Drain thoroughly. Melt 4 tablespoons butter in a heavy pan and add the rice and 1 cup water. Mound the rice slightly in the center. Cover with wax paper or foil and a tight-fitting lid and cook over medium heat for 20 minutes. The water should be absorbed and a golden crust formed on the bottom. Place pan on a wet towel for 5 minutes to help loosen the crust. To serve, place a mound of rice on each of 6 warm plates and top with 1 tablespoon butter. Make a little well in the rice and drop in an egg yolk. Sprinkle with salt, freshly ground pepper, and a lit-tle sumac, if desired. Divide the crust equally on each plate. Serve with kebab. Makes 6 servings.

Iman Bayildi
(Stuffed Eggplant)

3 medium eggplants	2¼ teaspoons salt
½ cup olive oil	½ teaspoon freshly ground pepper
3 cloves garlic, finely minced	1 teaspoon sugar
6 medium onions, chopped	2 tablespoons finely chopped flat-leaf parsley
6 medium tomatoes, peeled, seeded, and chopped	

Simmer eggplants in water for 10 minutes. Re-move and cool. Cut in half and carefully scoop out the pulp, leaving enough around the edge to make a firm shell. Heat the oil in a large skillet and sauté the garlic and onions. Add the eggplant pulp, toma-toes, salt, pepper, and sugar. Cook for 15 minutes or until eggplant is tender, stirring often. Correct the seasoning. Spoon the mixture into the eggplant shells. Place in a greased baking dish. Cover with foil and bake for 30 minutes in a 375°F oven. Sprinkle with parsley and serve at room tempera-ture. Makes 6 servings.

Baba Ghannuj (Eggplant Appetizer)

Raita
(Cold Spiced Tomato and Yoghurt)

1 pound yoghurt	½ to 1 teaspoon seeded
1 large tomato, peel and	and finely minced
seeds removed and	hot pepper
coarsely chopped	1 tablespoon coriander
1 teaspoon caraway	leaves, chopped
seeds	salt and pepper
	to taste

Stir the yoghurt until smooth. Drain the chopped tomato and add with the remaining ingredients. Chill. Makes about 2 cups. Serve with curry or as an appetizer.

Variations: (1) Cucumber Raita: Omit tomato and add seeded, grated, and drained cucumber. (2) Onion Raita: Omit tomato and add 2 medium chopped onions and 3 tablespoons of chopped fresh mint.

Pooris
(Fried Unleavened Bread)

2 cups whole-wheat	1 teaspoon salt
flour	4 tablespoons ghee
2 cups all-purpose flour	oil for deep frying

Mix the flours and salt together and work in the ghee or butter. Add enough water to make a stiff dough. Knead about 10 minutes or until smooth and elastic. Cover with a damp cloth and let rest for an hour or more. Divide dough in half and keep a damp towel over it until ready to use. Divide each half into 6 equal portions, form each into a ball, and roll out into a circle about 5 inches in diameter. Fry in 375°F fat one at a time. Press any flat areas down under the fat with the back of a spoon for even puffing. Turn the pooris and cook on the other side until a golden brown. Drain on paper towels. Serve warm. Makes 12 pooris.

Chapatis
(Griddle-Fried Bread)

3 cups whole-wheat	1 teaspoon salt
flour	1½ cups water
1 cup all-purpose flour	ghee

Mix the flours and the salt together in a bowl.

Add about 1½ cups of water to make a stiff dough. Knead for 10 minutes or until dough is smooth and elastic. Cover with a damp cloth and let rest for 2 or 3 hours. Knead again for 5 minutes. Divide dough in half and form into 2 balls. Flatten each slightly and cut into 8 equal portions. Form each into a small ball and roll out into a 5-inch circle. Cook in a hot ungreased small skillet. Shake pan while cooking to keep from burning. The flat bread will blister slightly and start to turn brown. Cook for 1 to 2 minutes on each side. Spread with ghee and serve warm. Makes 16 chapatis.

Naan
(North Indian White Bread)

4 cups all-purpose flour	1 tablespoon sugar
1 tablespoon baking	2 eggs
powder	1 cup milk
¼ teaspoon baking soda	2 teaspoons ghee
½ teaspoon salt	

Mix the dry ingredients together in a bowl. Break the eggs into the mixture and work them in with the milk to form a firm dough. Turn out onto a lightly floured cloth and knead for about 10 minutes or until smooth and glossy. Grease top of dough and the bowl with a little ghee. Cover bowl and let the dough rest in a warm place for 3 hours. Divide the dough in half and form into two balls. Cut each ball into fourths. Roll out each triangle into a tear-drop shape about 6 or 7 inches long and ⅜ inch thick. Place loaves in a preheated 450°F oven for 10 minutes. The tops will be golden brown and the loaves will be puffed and partially hollowed. Makes 8 loaves.

Dessert Raita
(Fruit Yoghurt)

1 pound yoghurt	2 tablespoons lemon
3 tablespoons confec-	juice
tioners' sugar	4 bananas, thinly sliced

Stir the yoghurt until smooth and mix in the sugar. Sprinkle lemon juice over the sliced bananas, drain, and add to the yoghurt. Chill. Makes 4 to 6 servings.

Any fresh fruit in season may be used. For a variation, called Sultana Raita, substitute ½ cup golden raisins for the fruit.

Kibbi Nayya (Uncooked Wheat and Meat) and **Raita** (Cold Spiced Tomato and Yoghurt)

JAPAN

Hirohito

INGERING MISTS OF spirituality regarding food and of divinity surrounding the emperor have effectively veiled the eating habits of the imperial family of Japan. Only here and there in Japanese history appears a glimpse of a celadon plate imported from 12th-century China and reserved in Japan for imperial use, or a blue-and-white rice bowl on the emperor's tray. Over the gap of centuries occasionally echo the sounds of silks and laughter as a party from the imperial Court sallies forth from the capital early on a spring morning to search in the nearby hills for fresh greens to take home to the palace kitchen.

A reticence remains in discussing the present emperor, too, but those who know him say that while enjoying with foreign guests the various delights of French cuisine prepared by the palace chefs, in the closeness of his family he also enjoys the simplicity and directness, the combination of bland and salt, the relation of field, sea, and woodland, that are the essence of Japanese cuisine: the quality of being *assari*—plain, simple, straightforward, even spartan, but with delicacy.

In the fertile though narrow fields of Japan, with a range of climate from south to north like that of the east coast of the United States from Georgia to Maine, farmers for more than 12 centuries have produced numerous grains, vegetables, and fruits: rice, wheat, and millet, soy beans and red beans, the long white *daikon* turnip, yams and sweet potatoes, taro, leafy vegetables, melons, cucumbers, small eggplants, mustard, and persimmons, plums, peaches, mandarin oranges, and grapes. The coastal waters abound in fish, shellfish, and edible seaweed; trout are found in the fast-flowing streams, and ducks in quiet bays and ponds; salt has been dried from the sea. The woodlands and mountains shelter ferns, mushrooms, and other succulent leaves and stalks as well as bear, deer, wild boar, rabbits, and pheasants. Although the farmers and fishermen themselves have often had meager, restricted diets, a varied and abundant supply of foodstuffs has usually been available to the rulers of the land.

The core of the Japanese diet for farmer and emperor alike, however, since even before Nara became the first official capital of Japan in the

180

8th century, has been short, plump, glutinous grains of rice grown in wet fields and steamed or boiled without salt. The word for boiled rice, *gohan,* has come to mean a meal itself. Rice is the center of any complete meal, and all other dishes are thought of as accessories, although sometimes, as when men are drinking together, or in the extremely refined cuisine of the tea cult, the accessories so overshadow the staple that little or no rice is eaten at all.

The early indigenous cuisine of Japan was influenced by China in the 8th and 9th centuries (when soy sauce and chopsticks were introduced, together with a Buddhist-inspired squeamishness about eating four-footed creatures), by China again in the 13th century (when with Zen Buddhism strictly vegetarian meals became the fashion), by the Portuguese of the late 16th century (who introduced *tempura* and sponge cake), and by the world at large, but especially France, in the 19th and 20th centuries. The Japanese have been eager to learn, and the ruling families have been able to sample and adapt as exciting foreign dishes came to their attention. Preparation of Japanese meals, however, has remained relatively unchanged since ancient times and includes delicate washing and cutting followed by steeping, simmering, boiling and grilling—traditionally over charcoal—for those foods not eaten raw. Ovens, and the baking made possible by them, are not a part of Japanese tradition.

As the cult of preparing and drinking tea flourished especially in the 16th century, the presentation of food came to be a highly developed art in court and upper-class circles, with a fascination (to be found in other aspects of Japanese culture as well) by form to at least as great a degree as by content. With emphasis on delicacy and sensitivity of appearance, every care came to be taken in the selection of plates, cups, and bowls to suit the season, the time of day, the shape, color, texture, and flavor of the particular morsel being served, and whether it was first, or middle, or last in the order of service. The morsel itself might be only a tiny shred of vegetable or fish, prepared to enhance its intrinsic flavor and not obscure its natural form.

But together with willingness to try the new and elaborate attention to the presentation of food, there is in Japan an attitude of reserve about the consumption of food, rooted in the relationship of the gods of the Shinto faith to crops and other foods, strengthened by meticulous rules of etiquette formulated in the imperial courts of Nara and Kyoto and by the practitioners of the tea cult, and further articulated from time to time by such disciplinarians as the 13th-century military dictators of Kamakura.

A rare record of dishes prepared for Emperor Hirohito and the Empress Nagako, and a good illustration of Japanese cuisine at its best, however, appears in Oliver Statler's *Japanese Inn*—the Minaguchi-ya visited by the monarchs in October, 1957. There, dining in seclusion, the emperor and his consort were presented with the products of woodlands, fields, and sea arranged in a pattern of hors d'oeuvres, a soup, and an odd number of main dishes accessory to boiled rice, followed by fruit.

Chestnuts, mushrooms, quail, shellfish, trout caviar, sea bream, and lobsters were broiled or grilled or left raw save for delicate salting, flavored with rich, dark Japanese soy sauce, or chives, or ginger, or *katsuobushi* (stone-hard dried bonito, flaked by a sharp blade): a few delicate morsels, each retaining insofar as possible its intrinsic flavor and shape. Sea-turtle meat and eggs were simmered in a *katsuobushi* broth, flavored by chives and ginger, and served as soup.

The central portion of the meal consisted of dishes of chicken, of sea bream again (this time broiled instead of raw), and of simmered pork, the flavors clarified or gently modified by the tender green tops of white radish or slivers of crisp radish meat, by a touch of mustard for the pork, and by the broth—so widely used in Japan for steeping, or simmering—of diluted soy sauce fortified by the sweet rice wine known as *mirin* and sharpened by lemon juice. Boiled, unsalted white rice followed, sticky enough to hold together when picked up by chopsticks, accompanied by slices of tiny salt-pickled eggplant, vinegared ginger shoots, and "Nara pickles"—sliced small melon, sweet-pickled to a reddish brown in *sake* lees. Fruit was the only dessert. Hirohito is a teetotaler, but with such a meal there might be *sake* to drink as well as tea.

The menu resulted from weeks of deliberation and reflected the preferences of the imperial couple, the caution of the imperial household office whose approval it had to meet, the desire of the Minaguchi-ya to provide the best of the seaside locale and autumn season, and Japanese traditions of 1,200 years.

Royal Recipes

Suimono
(Clam Soup)

12 large or 24 small cherrystone clams	1 teaspoon shoyu (soy)
5 cups water	2 teaspoons sake
	salt

Wash and scrub the clam shells thoroughly. Place the clams in a bowl of fresh water for an hour. Bring the 5 cups of water to a boil and drop in the clams. Boil until the clams open. Remove from the heat. Add the shoyu and sake and salt to taste. Pour broth into soup bowls and place 2 or 3 clams in each, depending on size of the clams. Makes 4 servings.

Agemono
(Tempura)

shrimp	ginkgo nuts
green peppers, cut in strips	sweet potatoes
	onions
dried mushrooms, soaked 30 minutes or more	lotus root
	eggplant

Shell and devein the shrimp, leaving the tails attached. Cut the green pepper into slices. Drain and dry the mushrooms. Thread the ginkgo nuts on skewers. Peel and thinly slice sweet potatoes, onions, lotus root, and eggplant. Cook in Tempura batter (below), and arrange attractively on a tray or plate.

15th-Century Tempura Batter

1 egg	3 half eggshells of sifted flour
2 half eggshells of ice-cold water	oil

Break the egg into a small bowl. Fill ½ of the shell twice with ice-cold water and pour over the egg. Stir slightly with chopsticks with a back-and-forth motion; do not beat or stir in a circle. Sprinkle the flour over the top of the egg mixture and stir in, disregarding small lumps. Dip the shrimps and vegetables in the batter and drop into 2 inches of boiling oil (375° F). Do not cover more than half of the oil surface with the tempura at one time. Cook until a delicate brown and drain on a paper towel. Serve with Dipping Sauce.

Dipping Sauce

2 cups dashi (available in Japanese grocery stores)	½ cup shoyu (soy sauce)
	½ cup mirin (sweet wine)

Combine ingredients in a saucepan and bring to a boil. Yields 3 cups.

Tempura (uncooked) and, *facing page,* Tempura (cooked)

Yakimono
(Broiled Salmon)

4 slices salmon, 1 inch thick	2 tablespoons vinegar
salt	1 teaspoon sugar
4 tablespoons shoyu	4 small cucumbers
mirin	

Salt salmon slices lightly on both sides. Put skewers through each piece and place on a rack over a pan about 3 inches from the heat. As soon as the surface is seared, turn and sear the other side. Combine shoyu and 4 tablespoons mirin and dip the slices in the mixture. Return to the broiler and broil about 2 minutes on each side. Dip again and broil. Cook no longer than 6 minutes on each side.

Mix vinegar, 1 tablespoon mirin, and sugar together. Make a fan shape of each cucumber to serve with the salmon. To make the fan, slice ends off the cucumbers and cut to form a rectangular shape. Cut thin slices almost to the end. Pour over the vinegar mixture and serve a fan on each plate with the salmon. Makes 4 servings.

Nimono
(Eggs, Chicken, and Vegetables)

½ pound uncooked chicken, skin and bones removed	2 tablespoons oil
6 dried mushrooms, soaked 30 minutes or more	4 tablespoons dashi
	3 tablespoons mirin (sweet wine) or sherry
1 medium onion	3 tablespoons shoyu (soy sauce)
2 dozen snow peas or 1 ounce cooked fresh spinach	3 tablespoons sugar
	1 teaspoon salt
	3 eggs, slightly beaten

Cut chicken and mushrooms in short, thin strips. Cut the onion in half and slice. Simmer peas 5 minutes and drain. In a skillet fry onions and mushrooms in the oil until almost tender. Combine dashi, mirin, shoyu, sugar, and salt and pour over mushrooms and onions. Place chicken on top. Cover and simmer over medium heat for about 12 minutes. Spread snow peas on top of chicken and pour over the beaten eggs. Cover and cook until the eggs have set. Turn out on a warm dish and cut in pie-shaped pieces. Serve in small bowls and pour over any remaining juices. Makes 6 servings.

Note: Dashi is a soup made from powered katsuobushi and kombu; it is available in Japanese grocery stores.

Tsukemono
(Pickled Cucumbers)

4-inch piece of daikon (Japanese radish), or 1 medium turnip	3 thin slices ginger root, cut into thin strips
2 cabbage leaves (optional)	1 tablespoon salt
2 cucumbers	2 tablespoons shoyu (soy sauce)
5 red radishes	2 tablespoons vinegar
	sesame seeds
	grated rind of 1 lemon

Cut daikon and cabbage into short, thin strips. Cut the cucumbers and radishes in thin slices. Combine vegetables and ginger in a bowl and sprinkle with salt; toss and mix well. Cover the vegetables with a plate and press the mixture down with a heavy weight. Leave undisturbed for 4 or 5 hours. Drain and press all water out. Add the shoyu and vinegar and toss lightly. Serve with sesame seeds and grated lemon or orange rind. Makes 8 servings.

Meshimono
(Red Rice)

¼ cup azuki (red Indian beans), soaked overnight	1¼ cups mochigome (glutinous rice), washed and soaked 2 hours
water	
salt	3 tablespoons black sesame seeds

Cook the soaked beans uncovered with 2 cups of water and 1 teaspoon of salt until tender. If necessary add more water during the cooking. Drain rice and put in a 2½-quart saucepan; add salt, 1¾ cups water, and the beans and liquid. Bring to a boil over high heat and immediately turn down to medium; cook 10 minutes uncovered. Turn the heat lower and cook 10 minutes more. Remove from heat, cover, and let stand for another 10 minutes. Parch the sesame seeds in a small dry skillet, shaking the pan to have them evenly toasted. Mix with 1 teaspoon salt and sprinkle over the rice and beans. Makes 4 to 6 servings.

Clam and Onion Salad

water	3 tablespoons dashi
1 pound Welsh or green onions	3 tablespoons vinegar
6 tablespoons miso	1 cup cooked small clams or sliced large clams
3 tablespoons sugar	

Bring water to a boil and drop in the onions. Boil for 3 minutes and drain. Cut onions into 1½-inch lengths. Combine the miso, sugar, and dashi and stir in the vinegar. Stir the clams and onions together and add the miso mixture. Serve in small bowls. Makes 4 servings.

Note: Miso is a mixture of malt, salt, and mashed soybeans; dashi is a soup made from powdered katsuobushi and kombu. Both are available in Japanese grocery stores.

Spinach With Sesame

4 tablespoons sesame seeds	4 tablespoons shoyu (soy sauce)
	1 pound fresh spinach

Place sesame seeds in a small frying pan and parch over medium heat until a light brown color. Grind in a mortar, add shoyu, and grind again until it is well mixed and crushed. Drop spinach into boiling water and boil 3 minutes. Drain well and cut into 1½-inch lengths. Toss with the sesame-shoyu mixture. Serve in small bowls. Makes 3 to 4 servings.

Sunomono
(Vinegared Dishes)

30 tairagai (mussels) or bay scallops	2 teaspoons shoyu (soy sauce)
vinegar	4 tablespoons mirin (wine)
1 cucumber	1 tablespoon sugar
salt	

Slice mussels or scallops, if desired, and put in a small bowl. Pour over enough vinegar to cover. Score cucumber and slice paper-thin. Sprinkle with salt and about 2 tablespoons vinegar. Refrigerate mussels and cucumber until ready to serve. Mix shoyu, mirin, and sugar together and pour over the cucumbers. Serve mussels and cucumbers as a relish or with wine. Makes 4 servings.

Shrimp and Cucumber Salad

1 large cucumber	1½ teaspoons vinegar
salt	½ teaspoon shoyu (soy sauce)
2 to 4 tablespoons chopped shrimp or lobster	1 tablespoon mirin (wine)
4 to 6 tablespoons blanched and chopped watercress	½ teaspoon sugar
pieces of slivered red pickled ginger	1 green onion (garnish)

Score cucumber and cut off both ends. Cut almost in half lengthwise. Bend back each side slightly without breaking it. With a blunt knife remove the seeds from both sides. Sprinkle each side with salt. Press shrimp into each half of the cucumber. Lay the watercress on top of the shrimp and press firmly. Place the slivered ginger down the center. Close the cucumber, tie with string, and chill. When ready to serve, remove string and cut cucumber into ½-inch slices. Arrange on serving plate in a circle, overlapping the slices. Mix together the next 4 ingredients and pour over the salad. Garnish with a curled green onion. Makes about 14 slices.

Shrimp and Cucumber Salad

CHINA

Empress Sung Chen Tsung

 N CHINA, FOOD was considered an important phase of living even in very ancient times. More than 20 centuries B.C., the legendary Emperor Shên Nung of the Celestial Empire is said to have taught his subjects food preparation, along with agriculture and methods of fishing and hunting. Each succeeding dynasty introduced new dishes and improved the old, so that over the centuries there evolved in China a culinary art unrivaled in its perfection. Throughout the world today, people of taste and discernment appreciate the exceptional qualities of Chinese cookery.

The revered philosopher Confucius, born 551 B.C., set forth rules pertaining to food as follows:

Rice must be polished, cleaned, and washed before cooking.

It must not be harmed by heat or dampness.

Meat must be minced finely.

Fish must be fresh.

Any food that is discolored or bad must not be eaten.

Food that is not cooked properly or is not in season must be avoided.

Meat that is not properly cut or food served without its proper sauce must not be partaken of.

Though there may be a large quantity of meat, one should not exceed the proportion of the rice.

No limit is placed on drinking of wine; however, one should not become confused by overdrinking.

Wine and dried meat purchased in the market must not be eaten.

One must refrain from overeating.

Nearly every emperor of China after Confucius' time, regardless of the dynasty, seriously considered the eminent philosopher's teachings.

That "necessity is the mother of invention" is shown in the development of Chinese cuisine. Although the area of China is larger than that of the United States, only 11 per cent of its land is arable. This limitation, coupled with occasional drought, floods, and other natural catastrophes, forced the Chinese to become acutely conscious of food. Everything that could grow on land and sea—root, tree, fungus, animal, fish, and bird— was explored to determine its edibility and its food value.

In cooking, as in painting, music, writing, flower arranging, and other arts, there are principles to be followed; those who are inspired know when to break the rules to create something new and exciting. So it was with chefs of the imperial court.

Flavor, aroma, texture, size, and color are the elements needed in the creation of a gourmet meal.

Sweet, briny, sour, pungent, and bitter used in various combinations stimulate the palate.

Judiciously blended vegetable, flower, fruit, meat, fish, grain, oil, and condiment give off an aroma that delights the sense of smell.

Textures of food, especially when used in variation, give much pleasure. The Chinese enjoy a smooth dish of soybean curd, served with crisp fresh vegetables, crunchy water chestnuts or nuts, gelatinous agar agar, soft steamed bread, fine-textured braised fowl or meat, and elastic bean curd skin.

Colors that please the eye increase the appetite; therefore, any combination of colors, providing it is fresh and pleasing, will enhance a dinner.

Over the years, imperial cooks mastered these elements, as the recipes created during the different dynasties proved.

Stories abound concerning the influence of food on China's political history. Emperor Hsüan Tsung of the T'ang Dynasty (713–756) was dethroned because of the uncontrollable appetite of his voluptuous, moon-faced concubine, Yang Kuei Fei, for fresh litchis, a fruit grown in the southern provinces. To please his loved one, the emperor ordered his general in charge of cavalry to deliver a fresh supply of litchis to Yang Kuei Fei daily by couriers on horseback. Eventually the people rebelled against such flagrant misuse of their tax money and got rid of Emperor Hsüan Tsung with his family's blessing.

Several centuries before the printing press came into use in Europe, a publication called *Tung Chin Men Lu* (Dream of the Eastern Capitol) made its appearance in Hangchow. Along with reminiscences of life in the Northern Sung Court (960–1127), told by an imperial refugee who had fled from barbarian invaders, the publication mentioned two dishes of Shantung origin: *fu yung chi szu* (fried chicken with egg whites) and *liu jou p'ien* (pork slices fried and simmered in cornstarch dressing). The delicate seasoning and the ingredients of those recipes reflect the refined taste of the Sung Dynasty, which flourished in the Southern Sung Court (1127–1279) economically, intellectually, and culturally, and even-

Genghis Khan

Empress Yüan Shih Tsu, wife of Kublai Khan

Emperor Sung T'ai Tsu

tually led the rest of China. The world-famous lustrous sea-green celadon porcelain was produced during this time in China.

History relates that the army of Genghis Khan owed its early military success in part to its use of "instant" rations. After conquering China, Genghis Khan, the founder of the Mongolian Empire (1206–1698), plundered Turkestan, Russia, Persia, and the lower Volga River valley and laid the foundations of a far-flung Eurasian empire. Unlike the agricultural Chinese, who were sedentary, the Mongols had a nomadic background, enabling them to be skillful mobile warriors on horseback.

An army cook concocted a *roux* consisting of flour fried with butter and mixed with sugar, sesame, walnut meats, and shelled watermelon seeds, which the soldiers carried in their pouches. When hungry, they mixed the dry ingredients with enough water to form a paste, which sustained them against hunger and malnutrition.

Mongolians introduced the barbecue grill, still in use, on which they roasted slices of mutton and vegetables. They also invented what is known as *huo kuo* (fire pot), a copper pot with a deep circular well enclosing a charcoal brazier and its chimney. The well is filled with broth, in which slices of mutton, vegetables, bean curd, and mung bean vermicelli are cooked.

Butter, cream, and milk were introduced into the imperial cuisine by the Mongolians, as well as whipped cream and crab apple jelly, and glazed crab apples and walnuts.

In spite of the extensive domains under Mongolian control and, for the first time, the introduction into China of Europeans with vast knowledge, internal dissension among the Mongol princes broke out into civil war. This strife, coupled with debaucheries of the Court, brought the Yüan (Mongol) Dynasty to a close.

Many delectable foods, particularly chicken dishes, were produced in the imperial court during the Ming Dynasty (1368–1644). Some of the recipes recorded in the archives of the imperial family of Ming are jellied chicken; fried chicken with peppercorns; chicken and cucumber with sauce; stewed chicken; chicken, shrimp, and vegetable soup; Chinese cabbage soup with chicken broth; fried fish with wine lees and cornstarch; and jellied fish. Emperor Hung Wu (1368–99) was partial to food produced in Honan, Shantung, and Hangchow.

Emperor Ming T'ai Tsu

During this dynasty the imperial kilns produced exquisite porcelain in tremendous quantities, much of it for use on the dining table. The best known were celadon, three-color glaze known as Shansai, white made from Kao-ling clay, and white base with gold, red, and blue—the last very rare. Fine-quality silks, from satin to brocade, and cotton fabrics were manufactured and exported to Southeast Asia and even to Europe.

A complete moral degeneration, coupled with natural disasters, brought the Ming Dynasty to a sad end.

China's last imperial family, the Ch'ing, came into power in 1644. Originally Manchurian nomads who had spent most of their time on the northern steppes grazing sheep and horses, they did not attach much importance to culinary arts. After becoming rulers of China, however, they assimilated the ways of the cultured Chinese.

On July 5, 1619, when Nurhachi, a Manchu chieftain, encamped on the Manchurian bank of the River Ch'ing near the Great Wall, neighborhood farmers offered him dove, Chinese cabbage, leaves of beefsteak plant, and rice. He asked that the foods be cooked. He so thoroughly enjoyed

Glazed ceramic vase, Chung ware

Empress Ming Ying Tsung

boiled rice mixed with dove meat and wrapped in leaves that he ordered the Manchurian princes to eat this food every year on the 5th of July. The dish was later improved upon by Empress Dowager Tzu Hsi (1898–1908), and is now known as *ts'ai pao ke sung* (vegetable rolls with minced dove).

When Emperor K'ang-hsi (1662–1722) inspected the constructions on the Yellow River in Honan, he was served a dish of *wa kuai yü* (fried river fish). He enjoyed it so much that he ordered it to be entered in the list of imperial recipes.

Emperor Yung Cheng (1723–35) was fond of *ch'ing ch'ao hsia jen* (fried shrimp), especially shrimp from the lower Yangtse.

The tables of other emperors could not equal the grandeur of those of Emperor Ch'ien Lung (1736–96), whose Court was considered the epitome of Chinese culture.

Observance of traditional conventions of the Ch'ing Court was strict, and the emperor's freedom was limited. Every morning, when he lived in the imperial palace in Peking, he was awakened by a eunuch at four o'clock. After the emperor had eaten a bowl of warmed swallow's nest sweetened with crystal sugar, he proceeded from his palace on a palanquin with four guards in the front and several eunuchs in the rear to Tai Ho Tien Hall, where he held daily audience. He returned in like manner and rested. He had breakfast at nine. The following menu was recorded on May 10, 1754, the 18th year of his reign:

Main course dishes: fat chicken, pot-boiled duck, and bean curd, cooked by Chang Erh; swallows' nests and julienned smoked duck, cooked by Chang Erh; a bowl of clear soup, cooked by Jung Kuei; julienned pot-boiled chicken, cooked by Jung Kuei; smoked fat chicken and Chinese cabbage, cooked by Chang Erh, salted duck and

Porcelain covered bowl, Hsüan-te ware

pork, cooked by Jung Kuei; court-style fried chicken.

Pastries: bamboo-stuffed steamed dumplings; rice cakes; rice cakes with honey.

Pickles, served in a ceramic container patterned with hollyhock flowers: Chinese cabbage pickled in brine; cucumbers preserved in soy; pickled eggplant.

Boiled rice.

After breakfast, the emperor studied documents submitted by various ministers and promulgated instructions for the Military Plans Office. Then he interviewed both Manchurian and Chinese officials about important state affairs. Thereafter the emperor returned to his palace or to some other place to enjoy refreshments. Between

two and three in the afternoon, lunch was served, and if the emperor happened to be out in the garden, men of the refreshment division followed him with two round bamboo baskets containing refreshments, tea, a small portable stove, a heating pot, and a portable table so that food might be ready within minutes. For winter, two beautifully made silver bowls were used—an upper bowl with a cover, for food, and a lower bowl for hot water. Another type was a half-inch-thick iron bowl, in which cooked food was placed; then well-heated iron plates were placed above and under the bowl. When the emperor was served, food was transferred from the iron bowl into a porcelain bowl. The temperature of the food was tested by a eunuch, who placed his hand on the outer side of the bowls before placing them on the emperor's table.

Each emperor had preferences in food, and these were the responsibility of the cook, whose name was always written on the menus so that any food might be duplicated upon request. Also, this made it convenient for the emperor to reward a cook for certain foods that he appreciated. This custom was observed from the beginning to the end of the Ch'ing Dynasty.

Bestowal of dishes of food, especially to the emperor's favorite consort, was a custom within the Court. *Yi p'ing kuo* ("excellent casserole"), inherited from the Ming Dynasty, was often sent as a gift from the emperor to his consort or to the empress dowager. It was a casserole of chicken, water chestnut, duck, green onion, ginger, Chinese cabbage, dried shrimp, dove egg, dried sea cucumber, Chinese ham, shark's fin, and condiments.

Because some of the empress dowagers had bad teeth, they usually preferred the tender vegetarian dishes of Buddhist origin. *Ch'ing cheng shih chin tou fu* (steamed brocade-like array of vegetables with bean curd) is one such dish.

The monthly stipend of the cooks of the imperial cuisine was a nominal 5 or 6 silver liangs. One liang was enough to buy 50 eggs in those days. The cooks, however, made up for their meager income by selling left-overs.

The emperor was obliged, according to protocol, to abstain from any involvement with money. Governmental bureaus outside the Court were not authorized to delve into imperial household finances. As a result, the cooks and the servants were able to take advantage of these customs—that is, until the reign of Empress Dowager Tzu Hsi, who flouted the imperial code and one day had an account of the imperial cuisine audited. She found that an egg on her table cost her 2 silver liangs, one-third of the cook's salary.

The imperial cuisine was a subsidiary office of the imperial household and comprised 60 servants in all, in five divisions: fish and meat, vegetables, roasts, refreshments, and rice. Each division had two sections, each with its chef and five cooks. A supervisor watched over the cooks, and an accountant procured and accounted for all food supplies.

The cuisine of the Ch'ing Dynasty derived its cooking methods and styles mainly from three areas of China:

Shantung: The Ming Dynasty employed Shantung cooks for more than two centuries. They were especially skilled in preparing chicken in various ways. Many Ming dishes were retained by the Ch'ing.

Manchuria: The Manchurians preferred mutton and various game fowl and animals, probably because of their nomadic heritage. Although mutton dishes date back to pre-imperial days, they are now known and famous as Peking dishes. After the Manchus became rulers of China, the cooks of the imperial cuisine improved upon the Manchurian dishes.

South China: Emperor Ch'ien Lung made two tours to Soochow and Hangchow in southern China, whose people were most gracious to the emperor. At that time he became very fond of their duck, shrimp, and fish dishes, especially with their piquant sweet-and-sour sauces. A cook from Soochow later became an imperial cook.

The fund designated for building the Chinese navy was misappropriated by the Empress Dowager Tzu Hsi to construct the Summer Palace outside of Peking. On the lake in the palace grounds was built a marble boat on which the empress dowager entertained with delicious Chinese cuisine while the musicians played to her distinguished guests from a nearby hill.

Sir Reginald F. Johnston, in his book *Twilight in the Forbidden City*, said of the empress: "Her contribution to her country's naval forces exists to this day in the form of a Marble Boat in the Summer Palace Lake, of which the best that can be said is that while the rest of the Chinese fleet perished ingloriously at Weihaiwei, it was destined to survive both the China-Japan war and the Manchu Dynasty."

When a banquet was planned, an invitation inscribed in gold on heavy red paper, folded in four, and listing the names of all the guests, was delivered by an imperial messenger to each of them. Although this invitation had to be acknowledged, the person honored by receiving it was saved from possible embarrassment or boredom, for he was forewarned about his fellow-guests and could decline the invitation.

The cooks would select the very best to please the guests. Courses numbered up to 49. The banquet was opened by 8 to 16 cold dishes,

Glazed ceramic perfume box, K'ang-hsi ware

known as *ya tsuo ts'ai* (sitting-duck food). Yellow wine and other rice and sorghum wines were served with the dinner. The name of the dinner depended upon the name of the main dish: for example, shark's fin, swallows' nests, sea cucumber, or Peking duck dinner. The last main dish was usually a whole fish, a custom introduced for phonetic reasons. The same word means "fish" and "more"; thus, the serving of fish was another way of expressing the sentiment: "We will invite you again."

The cooking methods of the imperial cuisine were similar to those of the West. The cooks braised, boiled, basted, broiled, baked, deep-fried, shallow-fried, cured, marinated, roasted, steeped, steamed, simmered, and smoked.

The Chinese stressed the importance of the

Porcelain plate of the Ch'ing Dynasty

cutting of their food. It must be uniform in size and shape, and small enough to be picked up easily with chopsticks. The cutting was accomplished with an imposing cleaver. With it the cook was able to julienne, cube, shred, slice, rollcut, chop, and mince.

The condiments used were ginger root, green onion, garlic, orange peel, peppercorn, red pepper, licorice, sesame, star aniseed, cardamom, cinnamon, soy sauce, soy paste, shrimp sauce, oyster sauce, and the seasoning now known as monosodium glutamate.

The use of chopsticks dates back many thousands of years, and neither fork nor knife have replaced them. It is said that the original chopsticks were made of bamboo because of the smoothness and lightness of the wood. The imperial families of China for many hundreds of years used silver or a combination of silver and ivory chopsticks for self-protection. Should there be poison in the food, it was thought that the silver would tarnish and the ivory disintegrate.

The dining table had a highly polished surface of ebony, lacquer, or marble, which was never obscured with a cloth. Hot towels in the winter and cold ones in the summer were used in place of napkins. Usually these towels were perfumed with a refreshing fragrance. During the banquet, servants would change them after every few courses. Flowers were not used on the table. A silver soup spoon, silver chopsticks with their holder, a silver wine cup, delicate yellow porcelain dishes of various sizes, and a small yellow bowl for soup were placed for each guest. The primary color yellow was used throughout because it was the imperial color. Also, sets containing condiments were placed at intervals on the table. As the banquet progressed, dishes and bowls were changed by the eunuchs as the need arose. When the banquet came to a close, the guests were invited into the drawing room. Each was served tea, perhaps in a delicate eggshell teacup of pale green or white, with cover. One was surprised upon removing the cover to sense a light fragrance of orchid arising with the steam. Two preserved wild chartreuse orchids floated on the surface and came to full life in the pale liquid jade. The wild field orchid of the *Cymbidium* genus was the imperial flower of the Ch'ing Dynasty.

Although the Ch'ing period experienced the ultimate in artistic and scholarly accomplishments, the system was not flexible enough to cope with the changes of the 20th century. Only a few who enjoyed the elegance of that imperial cuisine remain to tell the story.

Royal Recipes

San Hsien T'ang
(Chicken, Shrimp, and Vegetable Soup)

2 green onions
8 snowpeas
2 dried mushrooms,
    soaked
1 teaspoon chopped
    ginger root
¼ pound chicken breast

¼ pound shrimp,
    shelled and
    deveined
4 cups chicken stock
2 tablespoons soy sauce
½ teaspoon salt

Cut vegetables, chicken, and shrimp into slivers. Bring stock to a boil and put in all ingredients. Cook 5 minutes. Correct the seasoning. Serve hot. Makes 4 servings.

Ch'ing Ch'ao Hsia Jen
(Fried Shrimp)

1 pound shrimp,
    shelled, deveined,
    and cut into slivers
cornstarch
6 tablespoons sesame
    oil

1 tablespoon chopped
    ginger root
3 green onions,
    chopped
5 tablespoons wine
1 teaspoon salt

Dust shrimp with cornstarch. Bring the oil to a boil and stir in the ginger and onion. Cook 2 minutes, add the shrimp, and cook until lightly golden. Add wine and salt and cook 3 minutes more. Serve hot. Makes 2 to 4 servings.

Ch'ing Ch'ao Hsia Jen (Fried Shrimp) and Fu Yung Chi Szu (Fried Chicken with Egg White)

Cha Pa Kuai (Fried Chicken with Peppercorns)

Wa Kuai Yü
(Fried River Fish)

sesame oil	1 tablespoon cornstarch
2 green onions,	dissolved in ½ cup
chopped	water
1 tablespoon chopped	1 1-pound trout or
ginger root	similar fish, head,
1 tablespoon soy sauce	tail and fins
1 tablespoon vinegar	removed, and cut
1 tablespoon sugar	on the slant into
1 tablespoon wine	½-inch slices
1 tablespoon water	

Heat 1 tablespoon oil over medium heat and fry onions and ginger root for 5 minutes. Stir in the next 5 ingredients and bring to a boil. Add the dissolved cornstarch and cook, stirring constantly, until the liquid thickens. Keep warm. Bring 2 cups of oil to 375°F and fry the fish until just golden. Remove to paper towel and drain. Arrange slices of fish overlapping on a small warm narrow dish and pour over the sauce. Makes 2 servings.

Cha Pa Kuai
(Fried Chicken with Peppercorns)

3 tablespoons soy sauce	2 tablespoons
1 green onion, cut in	cornstarch
slivers	½ cup water
1 inch ginger root,	1 egg
peeled and	3 cups sesame oil
quartered	10 peppercorns, parched
2 whole chicken breasts,	in frying pan over
split and cut in half	medium heat
	1 teaspoon salt

Mix the soy sauce, onions, and ginger root together. Dry chicken pieces with paper towel and moisten each piece with the soy mixture. Let stand 20 minutes. Dissolve cornstarch in water, add egg, and beat together to make a batter. Heat the oil to 375°F, dip chicken pieces into the batter, and fry until light brown. Drain on paper towel and sprinkle with crushed peppercorns mixed with the salt. Makes 2 to 4 servings.

Fu Yung Chi Szu
(Fried Chicken with Egg White)

3 egg whites
2 tablespoons water
1 tablespoon wine
1 teaspoon salt
1 tablespoon sugar
1 teaspoon chopped
　　ginger root
2 green onions, cut into
　　2-inch slivered
　　pieces
　　cornstarch
¾ pound chicken, cut
　　into 2-inch slivers
3 tablespoons sesame
　　oil

Combine the first 7 ingredients and 1 teaspoon cornstarch. Dust chicken lightly with 2 to 3 table-spoons cornstarch and fry in hot oil until chicken turns white. Turn down the heat and add the egg white mixture, stirring constantly. Cook until mixture is set. Serve hot. Makes 2 to 4 servings.

Tsui-Chi
(Drunk Chicken)

1½ cups water
　　salt
1 thin slice peeled
　　fresh ginger root
1 green onion
1 whole chicken breast,
　　cut in half
½ cup dry sherry

Bring the water to a boil and add 2 teaspoons salt, ginger root, and onion. Drop in the chicken and cook 10 minutes. Remove from heat and let cool in broth. Discard skin and bones. Sprinkle the chicken with ½ teaspoon salt and put in a small bowl. Pour the sherry over the chicken, cover, and refrigerate for 24 hours. Cut into cubes when ready to serve. Make 4 to 6 servings.

Liu Jou P'ien
(Pork Slices Fried and Simmered
in Cornstarch Dressing)

2 egg whites
½ cup water
1 tablespoon wine
3 tablespoons soy sauce
1 teaspoon sugar
½ inch peeled ginger
　　root, chopped
1 green onion, chopped
¾ pound fresh pork
　　tenderloin, cut into
　　slices 1 x ½ x ⅛
　　inches
　　cornstarch
4 tablespoons sesame
　　oil

Combine in a bowl the egg whites, water, wine, soy sauce, sugar, ginger and onion. Dust the pork lightly with 2 to 3 tablespoons cornstarch. Heat oil and fry the pork for 3 minutes over high heat. Lower heat and add egg white mixture, stirring constantly. Cook until set. Serve hot. Makes 2 to 4 servings.

Wu Hsiang Chu Kan
(Pork Liver Cooked with Five Spices)

1 pound pork liver
　　water
3 tablespoons soy sauce
1 tablespoon wine
1 teaspoon sugar
1 teaspoon Five Spices

Wash pork liver thoroughly, cover with water, and boil for 30 minutes over medium heat. Discard the water and add 1 cup of fresh water, soy sauce, wine, sugar, and Five Spices. Cover and simmer for 1 hour. Remove the liver, pat dry with paper towel, and cut into slices about 1 x 2 x ⅛ inches. Refrigerate and serve as an appetizer.

Note: Five Spices (Wu Hsiang) is available ready-mixed in powdered form; or, combine ½ teaspoon each of star aniseed, licorice root, ground cardamon, dried orange peel, and cinnamon.

Shrimp and Bean Curd Salad

½ cup dried shrimp
½ pound cooked
　　spinach, chopped
2 tablespoons sesame
　　oil
½ teaspoon M.G.
　　(monosodium
　　glutamate)
½ cake bean curd
2 to 3 ounces boiled
　　ham, chopped
3 tablespoons soy sauce
3 tablespoons salad oil
3 tablespoons vinegar

Soak shrimp in hot water for 20 minutes. Drain and chop. Toss drained spinach with oil and M.G. Drop bean curd into boiling water, squeeze dry in paper towel, and break into small pieces. Place spinach in a bowl and surround with shrimp, ham, and bean curd. Chill before serving. Mix soy sauce, salad oil, and vinegar together, and serve with the salad. Makes 2 servings.

Niu Yu Ch'ao Mien
(Flour Fried with Butter)

2 tablespoons butter
1¼ cups flour
4 tablespoons sugar
2½ tablespoons sesame
　　seeds
¼ cup chopped walnuts
1½ tablespoons dried and
　　shelled watermelon
　　seeds or chopped
　　pine nuts
¾ cup water,
　　approximately
1¼ teaspoons vanilla

Melt butter in a medium frying pan and add the next 5 ingredients. Stir constantly over medium heat until the mixture turns a light brown. Store in a covered jar in the refrigerator. When ready to use, add water and vanilla to form a paste. This may be used as a dessert or as a filling in small meringue shells. Yields 1½ cups.

AFRICA

Haile Selassie of Ethiopia

HE FOODS OF Africa are as complex and varied as its history. But the life style of North Africa has remained the same century after century, and this is reflected in the cuisine—how food has been cooked and which foods have been preferred in royal households.

A favorite food of King Hassan II of Morocco (1961–   ) is *treed*, a pastry that has long been a favorite of sultans, kings, and their subjects and is considered the oldest of the Arab dishes. It was probably introduced into Morocco at about the time of Mulai Idris, 8th-century descendant of the Prophet Mohammed, who fled into Morocco and brought with him the story that Mohammed liked only one thing more than *treed*—his wife.

In Morocco the full grace of North African hospitality and cookery is perhaps best developed, and within the country are variations in the methods of cooking. Fez, for example, has a manner of cooking dating back to the 14th-century period of the Merinid sultans.

During this era, especially during the reigns of Abu'l-Hasan (1331–51) and Abu 'Inan (1351–58), Fez became one of the great world centers of learning and religion. The royal households of that day consumed a great amount of meat, including mutton, goat, beef, chicken, pigeon, and, following the discovery of America, turkey. The recipes followed ancient tradition, partly of Andalusian origin. Mutton was stewed in a closed vessel. The head was considered a special delicacy, as it is in much of the Arab world today, particularly in Libya.

Descriptions of dining habits of the sultans of that day in Fez do not differ greatly from what is experienced elsewhere in modern Morocco. Guests squatted on cushions around a low table, serving themselves directly from the platter with their right hands. Before and after the meal, hands were washed carefully, and the mouth was rinsed at the end.

For century after century in Morocco, this has been a ritual in royal households, as in many others: A servant takes around a pitcher and basin in which each guest washes his hands. Then each receives a napkin, often the size of a towel, and bread is brought to the table, followed by the dishes. Utensils usually are not used for eating, with the occasional exception of spoons. Fingers are used to take solid foods, and bread is used to soak up liquids. After hands have been washed at the end of the meal, tea or coffee is served. An important part of the ritual of hospitality throughout North Africa is the serving of heavily sweetened, often mint-flavored or spiced tea.

The etiquette and decorum of dining in ancient Morocco, as well as its carefully prepared cuisine, have been reflected in the royal households of the 20th century. King Mohammed V (1927–61) had a reputation as a gourmet. His son, King Hassan II, lacks this personal reputation; but Hassan, who has a keen interest in food and often personally selects the menu, quickly won esteem for his hospitality and for the cuisine of his household. At the Moroccan embassy in Washington, he entertained Presidents Kennedy and Johnson, and his sister, Princess Lalla Nezha, became official hostess there in 1967 when her husband, Ahmed Osman, was named Ambassador to the United States. The Embassy became famous for dinner parties; its dress and music were modern, but the format was ancient. Through the centuries, the royal families of Morocco provided *diffas*, or festive meals, on special occasions. To the accompaniment of folk dances, guests would gather in colorful traditional tents to enjoy the national dishes of *couscous* (also spelled *kus kus*) and *biastaela*, roasted sheep, chicken, sweet almond pastries, and other dishes.

King Hassan likes to start the day with a quick cup of black coffee, followed by a substantial breakfast of meat and vegetables, fruit, and more coffee. The king has a late lunch, sometimes as late as 3 P.M., followed by a siesta, and a late dinner, sometimes about midnight. He enjoys family picnics in the country. The meal consists of chicken or *mishoui* (roast mutton), or *couscous*.

Couscous, a staple coarse grain dish to which meat, vegetables, or other foods are added, is served in much of North Africa, but not in Ethiopia, which is as different in cuisine from North Africa as it is in religion. The staple item of diet in Ethiopia, an ancient Christian kingdom enclave in a world of Islam, is *injera*, a round, limp, slightly sour bread of spongelike texture. *Injera* is to the household of Emperor Haile Selassie what *couscous* is to the household of Hassan II. The emperor also enjoys *wat*, a thick, highly

Hassan II of Morocco

spiced sauce that is eaten with or on *injera*. When meat or vegetables are added, *wat* becomes a fiery stew.

Although a man of simple dignity and taste, Emperor Selassie learned early in his reign the value of staging lavish banquets. He arranged one in 1931 when he sought the support of the feudal *rases* (dukes) for his new constitution. After enjoying the emperor's food and wine for several days, the warlords discovered that their soldiers had been paid off, and they had little choice but to pledge loyalty to the emperor. One *ras* who remained away from the banquet, Ras Hailu of the kingdom of Gojjam, was well known for his own lavish entertaining. He served great quantities of *t'alla*, a barley beer fermented with leaves of the gesho plant, and *t'aj*, a honey-based drink which is more alcoholic than *t'alla*.

As is the case in many lands, one of the best ways a guest can compliment a host in Africa is to eat heartily. There is, in fact, an Arabic proverb that suggests that the amount of food eaten is the best measure of a guest's regard for a host: *Al akl'ala kadd el mahabeh*—literally, "the food equals the affection." Even easier to remember is the simple Moslem grace before meals: *Bismillah* —"in the name of the Lord."

Couscous
(Lamb Stew with Semolina)

1 teaspoon salt
1¼ cups boiling water
1 pound semolina meal
½ cup melted butter
2 tablespoons olive oil
2 pounds lamb, cut
    into 1½-inch
    cubes
3 cups chopped onion
½ cup chopped parsley
½ cup chopped
    coriander
¼ teaspoon pepper
½ pound chick-peas,
    soaked overnight,
    or ½ pound
    drained canned

¾ pound turnips, cut
    into 1½-inch
    cubes
1 pound carrots, split
    and cut into
    2-inch lengths
1 pound zucchini, split
    into fourths and
    cut into 2-inch
    lengths
1½ pounds fresh peeled
    tomatoes or
    equivalent
    canned, cut in
    quarters
3 medium green
    peppers, cut into
    strips

Add the salt to the boiling water and pour over the semolina. Toss with a fork to moisten all the grains and mix in ¼ cup melted butter. Dampen a cloth and line a large strainer or colander. Spoon the semolina in, covering with the ends of the cloth, and reserve. In a large 8-quart kettle brown the meat in the oil and remove. Sauté the onion until lightly colored, add parsley, coriander, 1½ teaspoons salt, and ¼ teaspoon pepper. Return the meat, add drained chick-peas, and mix all together. Add water to cover. Place strainer with semolina over the meat and cover. Simmer for 1 hour. Remove the semolina to a bowl, add ¼ cup more butter, and toss together. Add turnips, carrots, and zucchini to the kettle, return the semolina to the strainer, and replace in the kettle. Simmer for 1 hour. Add tomatoes and green peppers and cook for 30 minutes more. When ready to serve, heap the semolina on a very large warm platter. Place the vegetables around the edge and the meat in the center. Pour the broth over the entire dish. Makes 10 servings.

Couscous (Lamb Stew with Semolina)

Alecha (Chicken with Sweet Sauce)

Kaab el Ghzal
(Gazelle Horns)

1⅓ cups all-purpose flour, sifted	¾ cup ground almonds
butter or margarine	1½ teaspoons cinnamon
¼ teaspoon salt	1 teaspoon orange flower water
confectioners' sugar, sifted	1 egg white, slightly beaten
3 to 4 tablespoons cold water	

In a mixing bowl combine flour, ½ cup butter, salt, and 2 tablespoons confectioners' sugar. With a pastry blender cut in the shortening until mixture looks like coarse cornmeal. Sprinkle in the water, a tablespoon at a time, until flour is moistened. Gather dough together and press into a ball. Refrigerate while making the filling. Mix the almonds, cinnamon, 1½ tablespoons melted butter, ½ cup confectioners' sugar, and orange flower water together to make a paste. Roll out dough paper-thin and cut into strips 3 inches long by 1½ inches wide. Take about ¾ teaspoon of filling and roll pencil-thin to fit on a strip of dough. Press the two long edges together, and roll to seal the seam. Slightly curve the dough, point the ends, and brush with egg white. Place on a lightly greased baking sheet and bake in a preheated 375°F oven for about 30 minutes. Serve with mint tea. Makes 32 horns.

Alecha
(Chicken with Sweet Sauce)

½ cup butter	2 cloves garlic, crushed
3 cups chopped onion	1 cup water
½ teaspoon ground ginger	1 2- to 3-pound broiler-fryer chicken, cut into serving pieces
½ teaspoon curry powder	
1 teaspoon salt	4 hard-cooked eggs, shelled and scored
¼ cup tomato paste	

Sauté onions in butter in a large skillet until tender and golden. Mix together the ginger, curry, salt, tomato paste, garlic, and water and add to the onions. Score chicken skin, for extra penetration of flavor, and place in the skillet. Cover and simmer over medium heat for 30 minutes, turning often in the sauce. Add the eggs during the last 10 minutes of cooking. Place chicken on a warm platter with the eggs and pour over the sauce. Makes 4 servings.

Zigne Watte
(Spiced Meat Sauce)

3 cups chopped onions
1 cup Niter Kebbeh
1½ teaspoons salt
1 tablespoon cayenne
   pepper
½ teaspoon allspice
2 pounds round steak,
   thinly sliced and
   chopped

Place the onions in a large dry skillet and cook over medium heat until brown, about 20 minutes. Stir the onions continuously to keep them from sticking. Add the Niter Kebbeh, cook 5 minutes, and stir in the salt, cayenne pepper, and allspice. Simmer over low heat for 15 minutes. Add the chopped steak, toss, and cook for 5 minutes or more according to taste. Serve with injera. Makes 4 servings.

Niter Kebbeh
(Garlic-Spiced Butter)

½ pound unsalted butter
½ cup chopped onion
10 cloves garlic, crushed
1 tablespoon chopped
   fresh ginger root
2 teaspoons turmeric
¼ teaspoon ground
   cardamom seed
2-inch piece cinnamon
   stick
⅛ teaspoon ground clove

Cut butter into several pieces. Melt over low heat until completely liquid. Increase the heat and bring to a boil. Add all the remaining ingredients and immediately reduce the heat as low as possible; simmer for 45 minutes. Strain through a dampened flannel cloth.

Injera
(Ethiopian Bread)

4 cups flour
4½ cups cold water
1 cup boiling water
2 teaspoons baking
   powder
½ teaspoon soda
1 teaspoon salt

Mix the flour and cold water with a whisk to make a smooth batter; strain, if necessary. Cover and set aside for 4 or 5 days to ferment slightly. When ready to cook, pour off all the water that has risen to the top. Measure and pour half the batter into a bowl. Add 1 cup boiling water. Beat with an electric beater for 10 minutes on low speed. Mix beaten batter and remaining batter with the baking powder, soda, and salt to consistency of crêpe batter. Grease lightly and heat a 10-inch non-stick skillet or a heavy omelet pan. Test a drop; if

the batter cooks immediately without browning, the pan is ready. Turn down the heat to low, remove the pan from the heat, and pour in ½ cup of the batter, swirling the pan to cover the bottom completely and evenly. Cover and cook about 1 minute, or until batter is set and bubbles cover the surface. Do not turn. Remove bread with the fingers and the help of a spatula. Place on a cold surface. Cook remaining batter. To serve, line a large round tray with injera. Fold the remaining ones into fourths and place in the center. Alecha or Zigne Watte is poured over the injera, and pieces are torn off with the fingers to scoop up the sauce. Makes 16 injeras.

Note: Injera, the bread of Ethoipia, is made from teff, a millet-like grain of Europe and Asia; no grain like it is available in the United States, and the available flours and pancake mixes are a poor substitute. Injera is usually made about 24 inches in diameter.

Zigne Watte (Spiced Meat Sauce)

PACIFIC ISLANDS

Kamehameha IV of Hawaii

HE ONLY PLACE in the vast Pacific where royal feasts still are served in an authentic setting is in the tiny Kingdom of Tonga, the one surviving monarchy in the thousands of islands and continents touching the Pacific basin. Tonga staged an impressive feast in 1970 during the South Pacific tour of the British royal family. The royal hosts and guests were seated on the ground on tapa cloth and shared the menu, picking up the morsels of food and eating with their fingers.

A similar royal feast was served in 1953 during another royal tour. Elizabeth II, newly crowned queen of England, her husband Philip, Duke of Edinburgh, and King Taufa'ahau of Tonga, then crown prince, shared the fare with the late Queen Salote.

On both occasions, the principal entrée was roast pig cooked in an underground oven. The Tongans like their pork a little on the rare side, in contrast to the crisp, well-done pigs served in other areas of Polynesia and in Fiji. Other specialties that came from the ovens included chicken

cooked in coconut milk, yams, baked breadfruit, taro, and fish. The meal was followed by singing and dancing, as are most native feasts in the South Pacific.

Polynesian and Fijian menus are similar because in both areas the people live on the fish from the sea around them, on the fruits that grow without cultivation, on the root of the taro plant (either pulverized into pasty *poi* or baked), and on the pigs and chickens originally imported by the Europeans.

It has been about 80 years since the monarchy last ruled the present state of Hawaii, but the yellowed archives preserve menus that reveal the gastronomical preferences of the Hawaiian kings and queens.

Some of the later Hawaiian monarchs toured Europe extensively and returned to the islands with European court dress, a German bandmaster, and European menus and table service. Occasionally, however, native foods were also served.

An interesting meal was served to the Duke of Edinburgh at Iolani Palace in Honolulu on

July 26, 1869, with King Kamehameha V (1830–72) as host. Dishes with an island flavor included turtle soup and boiled and fried fish, surely from Hawaiian waters; otherwise the Polynesian contribution to the menu was almost nil, and the eight wines were all imported. Entrées included roasts of beef and mutton, a fricandeau of veal, ham, roast turkey, pigeon pie, and wild duck and rice curry. There also were eight vegetables, among which boiled *kalo* (taro) was a concession to island foods. Another, on a roster of eleven desserts, was coconut pudding.

On September 25, 1872, Kamehameha V offered a less lavish dinner, for which the menu was printed in French; it included *bananes frites* and *taro frit*.

King Kalakaua (1874–91), called by his people "the Merry Monarch" because, among other reasons, he did away with an earlier missionary ban on the dancing of the hula by women, was the first sovereign to call things by their proper Polynesian names on printed menus. Thus a breakfast he served on November 19, 1877, featured boiled *kumu* (goatfish) and fried mullet for the fish course. At a dinner at Iolani Palace on February 14, 1883, the fish course included *uhu* (parrot fish), *ulua* (jack), *oio* (bonefish), and *moi* (threadfish), as well as *kumu* and mullet.

Queen Liliuokalani (1891–93), last reigning monarch of Hawaii, made "boiled *kumu* with Hollandaise sauce" the fish course at a dinner on April 8, 1892. The days of Hawaiian pomp and circumstance, with their elaborate menus, is long gone, but Iolani Palace remains and the fish with the Hawaiian names are still in the surrounding sea.

Today, as formerly on less formal occasions, the Hawaiian menu is served at a *luau*, with the roast pig, baked yams and bananas, sea spinach called *limu,* and other delicacies roasted and baked in an underground oven called an *imu.* All are served on mats along with *poi,* of the consistency of paste, bland-tasting *haupia* (coconut pudding), and *lomi* made from diced salt salmon, tomatoes, and chopped onions. Commercial *luaus* are staged at major Waikiki hotels, and church or baby *luaus* (on an infant's birthday) are held somewhere around the islands every weekend.

Another Polynesian monarchy of about the same vintage as the Hawaiian was in Tahiti. King Pomare II, whose reign began in 1803, was beset by problems, not the least of which was alcoholism. Queen Pomare reigned for fifty years, until

1877, and was followed by her weak-willed son, Pomare V, who was the last of the monarchs. During this period royalty staged feasts called *tamaaras,* which are still held on occasion. The Tahitian menu varies somewhat from that of other Polynesian centers. Tahitian *poi* is sweet, being made from bananas, pineapples, and papaya crushed and rolled into a paste, with taro powder added, and then baked. In place of the traditional *poi* made from the taro root, baked breadfruit is used more extensively in Tahiti than elsewhere. Also served are fresh raw fish marinated in lime juice with onion, sliced tomato, and coconut cream added, and yams.

When Pomare V was host at *tamaaras,* he was reported more partial to the wine list than to other elements of the menu. After having turned over his kingdom to France for 40,000 francs per year, he had pangs of remorse and took to drink-

Princess Kailulani, daughter of Princess Likelike

ing. His headstone in a cemetery near Papeete is a giant brandy bottle.

In Fiji, which is part of Melanesia rather than Polynesia, the early *ratu* or chiefs had a fondness for "long pigs" or human beings until the last cannibal king, Cakabau (pronounced Thakambau), was converted to Christianity and turned over his war club and his islands to Queen Victoria on October 10, 1874. His two grandsons, Ratu Edward and Ratu George Cakabau, are well-educated, and traveled gentlemen, equally at ease in London restaurants or at the native feasts.

The menu of Fiji varies slightly from that of the other islands. At the traditional *kava* ceremony, the powdered root of the pepper tree mixed with water is strained with hibiscus fibers and dipped from a large wooden bowl by coconut cups called *bilos*. The most honored of the guests is served first by a native who approaches in a crouch, offers the cup, and claps his hands. The guest then drains the cup, spins it toward the *kava* bowl, and claps his hands. *Kava* tastes bland but the pepper stimulates and cools the taste buds.

A typical menu includes stone-roasted pig, *dalo* (taro), *lolo* (coconut milk), *ilka lolo* (chopped and marinated raw fish), turtle, yams, baked bananas, and—a special delicacy—baked sugarcane tips. Sometimes a heart of palm salad is served on royal Pacific menus. However, in areas where coconuts are raised for copra, palm is seldom featured, for when the heart of a palm tree is removed, the tree dies.

In the Samoan culture, the chiefs and their spokesmen, the High Talking Chiefs, are still paramount in village and family life. The feasts in American and Western Samoa rival those of other areas.

The same is true in such areas as Micronesia and New Caledonia, where the chiefs and their villages often give reciprocal feasts, or special feasts planned for visiting dignitaries. Because of the common environment and the migration of peoples between islands, all of these fares are similar. Some foods are eaten more frequently than others because they are more available. Taro, either baked or in the form of *poi*, is a staple of the diet in the South Pacific, but is currently grown in Hawaii only in a few places because of the lack of land for farming. Few turtles are found in the heavily fished waters off Hawaii, whereas they are plentiful in Fiji.

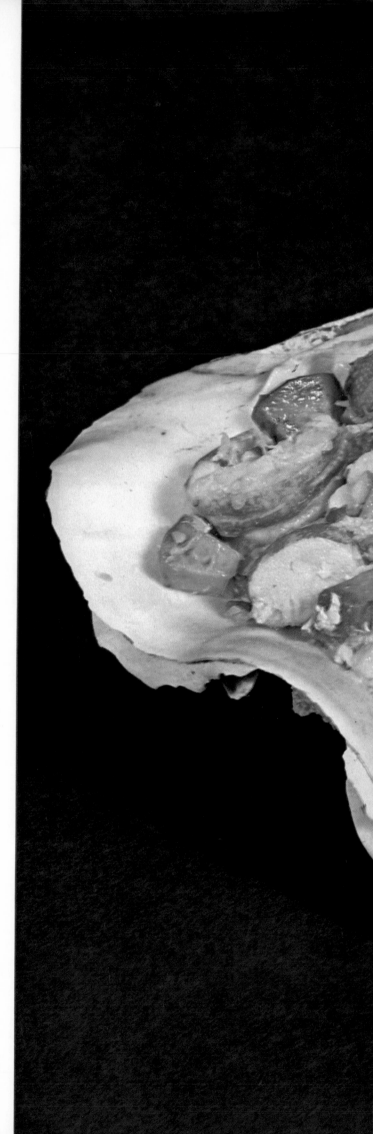

Pacific Salad

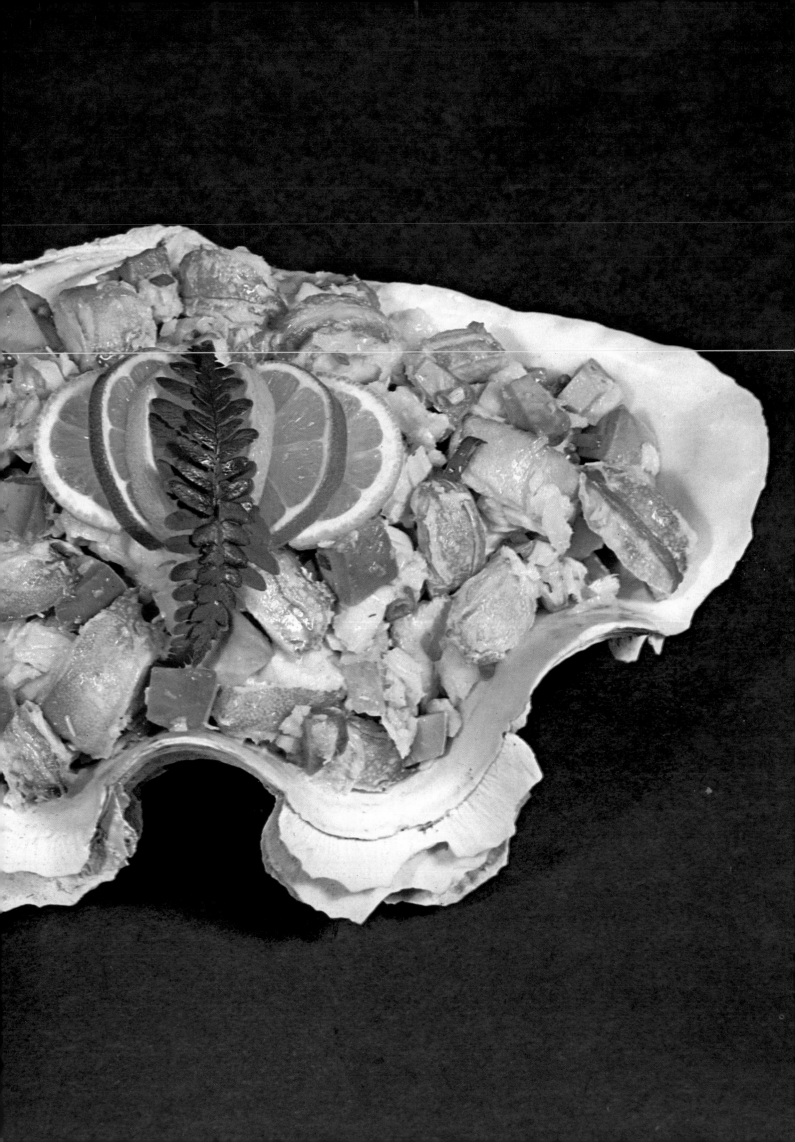

Baked Fish with Banana-Onion Stuffing

2 pounds whole cleaned fish, bluefish or bass	1 large green banana, cut into ¼-inch slices
juice of 2 limes	½ cup grated fresh coconut
salt	
1 medium onion, thinly sliced	

Slit stomach opening to the back of the fish and remove backbone and as many small bones as possible. Rub flesh with lime juice and sprinkle with salt. Place sliced onion in the cavity. Toss bananas with lime juice and arrange on top of the onion. Do not skewer or sew the fish together. Place the fish on a baking sheet covered with well-greased foil. Rub the skin with lime juice and press on grated coconut. Cover the fish loosely with foil. Bake in a preheated 375°F oven for 30 minutes. Remove the foil during the last 5 minutes of cooking to brown the coconut lightly. Serve on a board covered with fresh leaves or on a warm platter. Makes 4 to 5 servings.

Curried Fruit and Chicken

2 cups rice	1 to 2 bananas, cut into ¼-inch slices
chicken broth	1 cup cubed fresh papaya
2 cups Coconut Milk	1 cup cubed fresh mango
¼ cup cornstarch	1 cup cubed fresh pineapple
1 teaspoon salt	3 cups cubed cooked chicken
1½ teaspoons curry powder	3 coconut shells, halved
¼ cup cold water	
juice of 1 lime	
1 medium avocado, cubed	

Cook rice in chicken broth. Bring Coconut Milk and 1½ cups broth to a boil and add cornstarch, salt, and curry powder that has first been mixed with the cold water. Stir constantly until thickened. Sprinkle lime juice over the avocado and banana. Toss with the other fruits and the chicken. Line 6 half coconut shells with rice and place a serving of the fruit mixture on top. Spoon over some of the curry sauce and serve the remainder in a bowl. The fruit mixture should be at room temperature and the rice and sauce hot. This may also be served in a large serving dish. Makes 6 servings.

Curried Fruit and Chicken

Pork and Cowpeas

½ pound dried cowpeas, soaked overnight	2 large onions, chopped
salt	1 large clove garlic, chopped
1 pound boneless pork, cut into strips	2 large tomatoes, chopped
1½ x ½ x ½ inches	pepper

Drain peas, cover with water, add 1 teaspoon salt, and simmer covered for 1½ to 2 hours or until tender. Trim pork and render fat to make 2 tablespoons. In a large skillet brown the meat in the pork fat, remove, and fry the onions and garlic until tender and brown. Add tomatoes, replace the meat, and stir in 1 teaspoon salt and ½ teaspoon pepper. Cover and cook for 30 minutes. Combine the beans and meat and cook 15 minutes more. Correct the seasoning. Makes 6 servings.

Pacific Salad

4 tablespoons salad oil	½ cup Coconut Milk
lime juice	1 avocado
2 tablespoons Coconut Cream	½ pound cooked lobster meat, cut into pieces
salt	
1 pound cod or halibut, bones and skin removed	½ cup chopped scallions lemon and lime slices (garnish)

Combine oil, 1½ tablespoons lime juice, Coconut Cream, and salt in a bottle. Shake well and reserve. In a small saucepan simmer fish with ½ cup Coconut Milk and ¼ teaspoon salt for 5 or 6 minutes. Let cool and flake in large pieces. Peel and cut avocado into cubes and sprinkle with lime juice. In a glass bowl mix the fish, avocado, lobster meat, and scallions. Pour over the dressing and toss lightly. Garnish with lime and lemon slices. Makes 4 to 6 servings.

Coconut Cream and Coconut Milk

Puncture eyes in the end of the coconut with an icepick. Drain the liquid and strain to remove particles. Crack the nut with a hammer, breaking it into several small pieces. Peel off the brown skin and grate the white meat, or process in a blender. Heat ¼ cup of the strained liquid and pour over the grated coconut. Let stand for 15 minutes or more and then squeeze through a dampened cloth. This will make a rich coconut cream.

To make coconut milk for cooking fish, veg-

etables, and desserts, add 1 or 2 cups of coconut liquid or water to the same grated coconut, let stand 15 minutes or more and squeeze through a dampened cloth. Discard the grated coconut meat after being used for extracting cream and milk.

Note: Packaged or canned coconut may be substituted, but because it is sweeter, the recipe must be adjusted. Pour one or two cups of hot cow's milk over the package of coconut, allow it to stand 15 minutes, and boil over low heat for 10 minutes. Strain and squeeze through cloth as above.

Island Pudding

1½ pounds sweet potatoes	6 tablespoons ground kukui (Macadamia) nuts
2 green bananas	
2 tablespoons brown sugar	3 coconut shells, halved
1 to 2 tablespoons Coconut Cream	grated fresh coconut

Boil unpeeled sweet potatoes and bananas until soft, about 15 minutes. Peel, and mash together with the sugar. Add Coconut Cream to make a moist consistency. Stir in the nuts. Pile the pudding into 6 half coconut shells and sprinkle grated coconut on top. Cover with foil and bake in a preheated 375°F oven for 30 minutes. Remove the foil during the last 5 minutes of cooking to toast the grated coconut. If coconut shells are not available, use a small casserole. Makes 6 servings.

Avocado Whip

3 avocados	1 cup grated fresh coconut
¾ cup sugar	
2 tablespoons lime juice	

Cut avocados in half and remove pulp, being careful to keep the skins intact. Put half of the pulp, sugar, and lime juice in a blender. Process just until thick and creamy. Repeat. Stir in ½ cup grated coconut. Refill shells and sprinkle remaining coconut on top. Makes 6 servings.

Baked Bananas

4 green bananas	¼ cup light brown sugar
butter or margarine	ground kukui nuts (Macadamia)
½ cup pineapple juice	

Wipe bananas with a damp paper towel. Cut in half lengthwise, but do not peel. Spread the cut surfaces with butter. Mix the pineapple juice and shell and sprinkle with nuts. Place clusters of small leaves between the shells and a flower in the center. Makes 8 servings.

Broiled Pineapple

1 large pineapple	juice of 1 lime
½ cup rum	guava jelly
butter	ground kukui nuts
1 large banana	(Macadamia)

Peel pineapple and remove eyes and core. Cut 6 slices about ¾ inch thick. Soak slices in rum for 1 hour or more, turning often. Spread butter on both sides and edges of the pineapple slices and place on a rack over a broiler pan. Cut banana in ½-inch slices and toss in lime juice. Arrange on rack with pineapple. Spread guava jelly on both the pineapple and banana slices. Place under broiler and broil 5 minutes, turn, spread with jelly again, and broil 5 minutes more. Remove to warm individual serving plates and sprinkle ground nuts on top. Makes 6 servings.

Queen Emma, wife of Kamehameha IV

sugar together and pour into a baking pan just large enough to hold the bananas. Place them cut side down in the syrup. Bake in a preheated 375°F oven for 20 minutes. Remove to warm individual dessert plates, spoon over some of the syrup, and sprinkle with nuts. Makes 4 servings.

Coconut Pudding in Guava Shells

⅓ cup sugar	2 cups Coconut Milk
¼ teaspoon salt	16 guava shells
4 tablespoons cornstarch	(2 1-pound cans)
4 tablespoons cold water	ground kukui nuts (Macadamia)

Mix the sugar, salt, cornstarch, and water together. Heat the Coconut Milk and add the cornstarch mixture. Cook until thick, stirring constantly. Pour into a bowl, cool, and refrigerate. When set, put into a blender and process just until it is thick and creamy. Pour back into the bowl and refrigerate for several hours. Arrange the guava shells in a circle on a large platter. Spoon pudding into each

The royal china in a buffet at Iolani Palace, Honolulu

Illustrations

Index to Recipes

Page numbers shown in italic type refer to illustrations of the food.

General Index

The recipes listed in this index are discussed in the history sections on the various countries. In many cases these dishes or similar ones are included in the recipe sections and can be found in the Index to Recipes.